# ALPINE SKIING

## Steps to Success

John Yacenda, PhD
Alpine and Technical Director
Alpine Sports
Reno, Nevada

**Leisure Press**
Champaign, Illinois

## Library of Congress Cataloging-in-Publication Data

Yacenda, John, 1947-
   Alpine skiing : steps to success / John Yacenda.
     p.  cm. -- (Steps to success activity series)
   ISBN 0-88011-455-X
   1.  Downhill skiing.  I. Title.  II. Series.
GV854.Y32  1992
796.93'5--dc20
                                             91-31380
                                               CIP

ISBN 0-88011-455-X

Acquisitions Editor: Brian Holding
Developmental Editor: Judy Patterson Wright, PhD
Assistant Editors: Moyra Knight and Kari Nelson
Copyeditor: Wendy Nelson
Proofreader: Dawn Levy
Production Director: Ernie Noa
Typesetters: Yvonne Winsor and Kathy Boudreau-Fuoss
Text Design: Keith Blomberg
Text Layout: Denise Lowry and Tara Welsch
Cover Design: Jack Davis
Cover Photo: Wilmer Zehr
Line Drawings: Sharon Barner
Path Diagrams: Gretchen Walters
Printer: United Graphics

Instructional Designer for the Steps to Success Activity Series: Joan N. Vickers, EdD, University of Calgary, Calgary, Alberta, Canada

Leisure Press books are available at special discounts for bulk purchase for sales promotions, premiums, fundraising, or educational use. Special editions or book excerpts can also be created to specification. For details, contact the Special Sales Manager at Leisure Press.

Printed in the United States of America

10  9  8  7  6  5  4  3  2

**Leisure Press**
A Division of Human Kinetics Publishers, Inc.
Box 5076, Champaign, IL 61825-5076
1-800-747-4457

*Canada Office:*
**Human Kinetics Publishers, Inc.**
P.O. Box 2503, Windsor, ON N8Y 4S2
1-800-465-7301 (in Canada only)

*Europe Office:*
**Human Kinetics Publishers (Europe) Ltd.**
P.O. Box IW14
Leeds LS16 6TR
England
(0532) 781708

# Contents

# Series Preface

The Steps to Success Activity Series is a breakthrough in skill instruction through the development of complete learning progressions—the *steps to success*. These *steps* help individuals quickly perform basic skills successfully and prepare them to acquire more advanced skills readily. At each step, you are encouraged to learn at your own pace and to integrate your new skills into the total action of the activity.

The unique features of the Steps to Success Activity Series are the result of comprehensive development—through analyzing existing activity books, incorporating the latest research from the sport sciences and consulting with students, instructors, teacher educators, and administrators. This ground work pointed up the need for three different types of books—for participants, instructors, and teacher educators—which we have created and together comprise the Steps to Success Activity Series.

This participant's book, *Alpine Skiing: Steps to Success*, is a self-paced, step-by-step guide that you can use as an instructional tool.

The unique features of this participant's book include

- sequential illustrations that clearly show proper technique for all basic skills,
- helpful suggestions for detecting and correcting errors,
- excellent drill progressions with accompanying *Success Goals* for measuring performance, and
- a complete checklist for each basic skill for a trained observer to rate your technique.

Many of the activities in the Steps to Success Activity Series also have a comprehensive instructor's guide. However, one has not been developed for alpine skiing.

The series textbook, *Instructional Design for Teaching Physical Activities* (Vickers, 1990), explains the *steps to success* model, which is the basis for the Steps to Success Activity Series. Teacher educators can use the series textbook in their professional preparation classes to help future teachers and coaches learn how to design effective physical activity programs in school, recreation, or community teaching and coaching settings.

After identifying the need for various texts, we refined the *steps to success* instructional design model and developed prototypes. Once these prototypes were fine-tuned, we carefully selected authors for the activities who were not only thoroughly familiar with their sports but also had years of experience in teaching them. Each author had to be known as a gifted instructor who understands the teaching of sport so thoroughly that he or she could readily apply the *steps to success* model.

Next, all of the manuscripts were carefully developed to meet the guidelines of the *steps to success* model. Then our production team, along with outstanding artists, created a highly visual, user-friendly series of books.

*The result:* The Steps to Success Activity Series is the premier sports instructional series available today.

This series would not have been possible without the contributions of the following:

- Dr. Rainer Martens, Publisher,
- Dr. Joan Vickers, instructional design expert,
- the staff of Human Kinetics Publishers, and
- the *many* students, teachers, coaches, consultants, teacher educators, specialists, and administrators who shared their ideas—and dreams.

Judy Patterson Wright
Series Editor

# Preface

Welcome to the world of alpine skiing, a most wonderfully exhilarating and emotionally liberating sport. Nice balance: physical exertion along with emotional relaxation and the inimitable skier's high. Some call the skier's high "the rush," owing to the speeds they choose to travel at; I call it "the moment," owing to the episodes of personal and spiritual insight so plentiful to skiers whose skiing is a dance with the mountain instead of a contest of strength and power.

Anyway, here we are together with what I hope is a common goal: learning to ski in a way that is safe, fun, and adventurous and that prepares you to continue to develop as a skier for as long as you choose to pair up with the mountain. If you get at all hooked on alpine skiing, you'll be like countless millions of other skiers who plan a fair portion of their winters around the sport.

It's not only active skiers who are touched by the "moments" in skiing. It's not unusual to meet skiers who have been away from the sport for as many as 20 years and have been lured back to the mountain to discover, frequently to their surprise, that the body just doesn't forget a good thing, and they're quickly back to their old form—even if styles have changed.

So, what about your reasons for picking up this book? You want to learn to ski from scratch? The book's step-by-step approach to developing skiing fundamentals that are the basis of all skiing skills, beginner through expert, is ideally suited to you. Maybe you already ski, but doubt the strength of your fundamentals; again, the book's step-by-step approach to all facets of beginning and early intermediate skiing allows you to visit whichever area of skill development you choose for a brushup course.

Perhaps you're a ski instructor at a local resort or an activities director at a nearby school or college, and you want to expand your repertoire for working with beginning and early intermediate skiers. Welcome aboard; borrow at will from the book for use in your teaching. More skilled skiers mean a safer skiing environment for all on the mountain.

Over many years of teaching and writing about alpine skiing, and watching novice skiers both succeed and fail at becoming accomplished on the slopes, I identified what I feel are the essential ingredients and steps to learning to ski in a fashion that promotes success at every juncture in the learning. With my method, the acquisition of each skill builds confidence in your ability to balance and maneuver yourself on the snow. My method also encourages you to combine different skills to achieve a sense of control over the various skiing challenges you face as a new and early intermediate skier.

Consider this three-part concept of the basic fundamentals of alpine skiing with the intention of using this concept as an important step to a higher level of performance.

1. *Technical skills*: This includes being balanced over your skis, having a muscularly relaxed stance, being versatile in the use of different kinds of turns and the connecting of these turns, having control of your skis in varied conditions, controlling speed, using ski poles appropriately, maneuvering efficiently on flat and sloped terrain, and being versatile in using your skis.

2. *Physical attitude*: This includes being relaxed while reacting to assorted on-the-mountain surprises, thereby avoiding inappropriate movements or muscle contractions. At times, your attitude is one of playfulness and adventurousness.

3. *Mental and spiritual focus*: This includes confidence, followed by a sense of pride in one's accomplishment; goal setting and determination; self-acceptance and inner direction; a desire to learn and willingness to accept a measure of self-defined "failure"; embracing the process of personal growth through sport; acknowledgment of the factors that trigger fear; and kindness to oneself and others on the learning path.

By following the steps in order, you can proceed from beginner to intermediate skier level with this book. Depending on how much time you have for skiing, you may accomplish this process in a single season, or over several seasons. When you consider the time investment in completing each step, it's important that you think in terms not of how long a calendar period it will take to "graduate" from one step to the next, but of how many minutes and hours it might take to attain proficiency in the skills learned in each of the steps. By estimating the time investment in hours, you can more accurately plot your course of learning, given the amount of time you choose to work on specific skill development. A sample time estimation is shown in Figure 1.

The essential consideration is how much time you choose to spend practicing. Skiing, even beginning skiing, is no fun if it's all work and no cutting loose and giving it a try unbridled by precision and form. Nevertheless, too much cutting loose and not enough practice leads to poor fundamentals and a future of stagnation as a skier. When you make your choice, err to the side of practice in your early skiing, and you'll be ready to take on increasingly more adventurous challenges.

In the short of it, though, it takes only that first time they complete a run down a beginning trail without a hint of a tumble to convince people this sport is for them.

I must say with pride, appreciation, and love that without the photographic help of my daughter, Tayesa, illustrating this book would have been most difficult. As well, I must thank my thousands of students and other athletes for helping me develop a teaching style of sport skills that is progressive and cumulative, and that fully embraces mental and spiritual dimensions throughout, albeit subtly expressed. And my deep appreciation to Brian Holding and Judy Patterson Wright for bringing this project to me, and most especially to Judy for helping me discover the excitement and value of the Steps to Success series format. I just hope my interpretation of a most complex and challenging sport is one you will find exciting and valuable.

John Yacenda

| Step number | Skill or concept | Learning time | Skill category |
|:---:|:---|:---|:---:|
| 1 | Safety | 1-3 hr | |
| 2 | Maneuver on flat terrain | 1-3 hr | |
| 3 | Get up after falling | 30-60 min | |
| 4 | Basic skiing stance | 30-90 min | Beginning |
| 5 | Stopping | 15-90 min | |
| 6 | Simple turns | 1-3 hr | |
| 7 | Inside-ski steering and side slipping | 3-12 hr | |
| 8 | Ski the fall line | 6-18 hr | Early intermediate |
| 9 | Controlled skidding | 15-30 hr | |
| 10 | Parallel turns | 10-50 hr | |
| 11 | Pole use | 5-10 hr | Intermediate |
| 12 | Adapt to variable terrain and snow quality | 100+ hr | |

Figure 1.  Time estimation chart.

# The Steps to Success Staircase

Get ready to climb a staircase—one that will lead you to be a balanced intermediate skier with good skiing sense and good mountain sense. You cannot leap to the top of the staircase in one exposure to alpine skiing; you get there by climbing one step at a time.

Each of the 12 steps you will take is an easy transition from the one before. The first few steps of the staircase provide a foundation—a solid foundation of basic skills and concepts to help you ski safely, develop mental resolve, and act courteously on the slopes. As you progress further, you will learn how to connect groups of those seemingly isolated skills. Skiing is perpetual motion until you stop . . . or fall. You can be certain that as one skill appears ''done,'' another is called into action. The more you ''automatize'' skiing, assuming your practice is ''perfect practice,'' the more secure you can feel about your new association with the mountain. All skills work together while you, the skier, are moving at variable speeds down a snow-covered trail. As you near the top of the staircase, the climb will ease, and you will find that you have learned the skills necessary to take yourself out on the mountain, alone or with friends, to ski and enjoy the wonders and personal rewards of alpine skiing.

To prepare to become a good climber, familiarize yourself with this section, as well as with ''The Sport of Alpine Skiing,'' ''Learning to Ski Is Not a Muscular Feat,'' ''Equipment and Clothing,'' and ''Preparing Your Body for Success'' sections for an orientation and to understand how to set up your practice sessions around the steps.

Whenever you feel the need to take a closer look at any fears you may have about learning to ski, or learning to ski better, read the appendix. The appendix offers an important discussion of the common fears associated with beginning skiing and how to control these in order to proceed with learning with confidence and resolve. This understanding is more personal than any of the other steps you will take.

Follow the same sequence each step of the way:

1. Read the explanation of what is covered in the step, why the step is important, and how to execute or perform the step's focus, which may be on basic skills, specific concepts, tactics, or some combination of the three.

2. Follow the numbered illustrations (Keys to Success) showing exactly how to position your body to execute each basic skill successfully. Because skiing is a sport that links a series of movements to create symmetry, there are four general parts to each skill: preparation phase (getting into a starting position), execution phase (performing the skill that is the focus of the step), transition phase (a period of perpetual motion that leads to completion of the task), and completion phase (either pausing or halting that often triggers a return to the preparation phase).

Review the Focus Key within each of the Keys to Success sections to get additional information as follows:

  a. the intended path of travel (shown in black),

  b. the portion of the intended path illustrated (shown in red),

  c. either the fall line or no slope,

  d. either the direction of movement or no movement, and

  e. the angle of descent relative to the fall line (indicated by a Fall Line Exercise Position or FLEP number), as appropriate.

Study the symbols located at the end of this section.

3. Look over the common errors that may occur and the recommendations for how to correct them. As skills develop, error correction becomes more a problem of skills coordination than of making adjustments in basic mechanics. Any error in the early stages of skiing needs to be corrected before moving on to later stages of skiing, or it will impede your progress.

4. Read the directions and the Success Goals for each drill. Practice accordingly and record your scores. Compare your score with the Success Goal for the drill. You need to meet the Success Goal for each drill before moving on to practice the next one, because the drills are

arranged in an easy-to-difficult progression. This sequence is designed specifically to help you achieve continual success. The drills help you improve your skills through repetition and purposeful practice. All drills are designed to teach your skiing body how to move within a range of error dictated, in part, by your balance, flexibility, and general level of physical fitness.

5. As soon as you can reach all the Success Goals for one step, you are ready for a friend who understands the skill—such as your teacher, a pro, or a trained partner—to evaluate your basic skill technique against the items listed in the Keys to Success. This checklist is a qualitative or subjective evaluation of your basic technique or form. Using correct form can enhance your performance. Cut corners and you cheat yourself!

6. Repeat these procedures for each of the 12 Steps to Success. Then rate yourself according to the directions in the "Rating Your Total Progress" section at the end of the book.

Foremost, pay attention to your attitude about learning to ski; it has much to do with your success, as well as how safely you ski. Generally, don't expect to be perfect; likewise don't expect to fail. Do, however, accept frustration, because it will come, though I hope only in fleeting doses. After all, you'll be wearing unusual coverings on your feet and standing on an uncommonly slippery surface that can change at a moment's notice, regardless of how stable you'd like it to be. Beneath your "shoes" will be extra long "soles" that are securely attached by a spring-loaded binding device that releases on its own when you fall, and isn't always the easiest to put back on if too much snow gets on the "soles" of your boots or in the bindings. Yes indeed, not at all complicated, this skiing, and you've yet to make a turn. Fascinating, yes, and you'll love it!

Good luck on your step-by-step journey to developing your skiing skills, building confidence, experiencing success, and having fun!

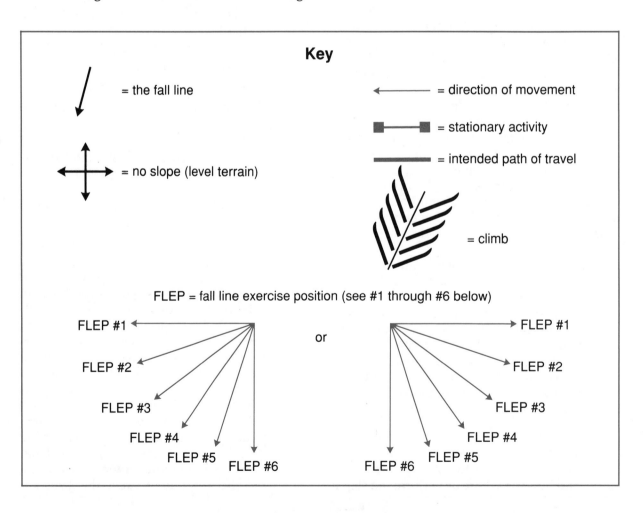

**Key**

= the fall line

= no slope (level terrain)

= direction of movement

= stationary activity

= intended path of travel

= climb

FLEP = fall line exercise position (see #1 through #6 below)

FLEP #1

FLEP #2

FLEP #3

FLEP #4

FLEP #5

FLEP #6

or

FLEP #1

FLEP #2

FLEP #3

FLEP #4

FLEP #5

FLEP #6

# The Sport of Alpine Skiing

Travel across snow-covered earth or ice on "planks" made of large animal bones may have been the first form of skiing. Early skis have been unearthed throughout the Scandinavian countries. The Hoting Ski is considered to be the oldest, at 4,500 years, and is on display in Stockholm, Sweden. Other skis dated 2,500 and 1,500 years old have also been discovered.

The skis of old are not at all like what we ski on today, although the basic idea is the same: gliding across snow and ice. Early skis (and poles) made of pine, birch, or ash were fashioned such that skiers could propel themselves over varied terrain inaccessible on foot. These were functional Nordic skis. Today's Nordic (i.e., cross-country) skis are finely styled and engineered for track, skating, backcountry, and telemark skiing. Today's alpine (i.e., downhill) skis have also undergone an evolution since the first time skiers tried skiing as sport.

Written historical references to skiing and skiing competition date back to the early centuries A.D. (500 to 1200). Colorful accounts of skiing were recorded in books over the next 500 years. Skis of many shapes and sizes were described, even sets of skis with one ski longer than the other (e.g., in Lapland, where the left ski was long and grooved, and the right ski was shorter and covered with fur for traction).

The strategic use of skiers as military scouts by the Norwegians dates back to A.D. 1200. Three centuries later, Sweden used ski troops against Denmark, and in another 4 centuries, ski troops were used to fight in the Alps in World Wars I and II—the United States used ski troops in World War II.

As a sport activity on the broader scale, skiing is considered to have begun in the early 1800s, with scheduled advertised races and jumping competitions coming into fashion in the second half of the 1800s. Early on, ski competition was focused primarily on cross-country races and ski jumping. Skiing was introduced to the United States in the mid-1800s by Norwegian immigrants, and America's first ski club was formed in 1887 (in Ishpeming, Michigan).

Many consider Austrian skier Mathias Zdarsky to be the pioneer of alpine ski technique. His book *The Lilienfelder Skilauf Technik* was the first of its kind to analyze ski technique, and although Zdarsky's technique is nowhere to be found today, his ski school was the first to successfully teach hundreds of persons to ski down mountains.

Early skis and skis of the first half of the 1900s were made of wood and laminated. Lengths in the 1800s tended to be longer. In the early 1900s skis took on more radical shapes and shorter lengths. Bindings and boots were primitive in the early years of skiing, but as technology advanced and skier interest increased, boots, bindings, and skis continued to evolve.

In the early 1930s, Austrian skier and metal worker Rudolph Lettner devised metal edges for his wooden skis, and once you add an edge to a ski, ski performance changes, as do demands for better and safer equipment. Ski-binding, boot, and ski technology evolved. By the 1940s alpine skis took on their characteristic shape—in most respects the same overall shape they bear today, with variations in sidecut, flex, weight, and other technical aspects of the skis.

As technology advanced and skiing became more and more accessible, the ski instruction industry took on new meaning, because many new techniques were being developed in different areas of the skiing world. By the late 1930s, ski schools were operating in many parts of the United States, and ski schools are a major part of host ski resorts.

In 1950, Howard Head produced the Head Standard Ski, which was made of aluminum strips with metal edges and a plastic-coated base. This rugged ski would change the construction and durability of skis around the world. Head's innovation led thousands of skiers to discard their old wooden skis, a pair of which my father bought me in 1957. I was 10 at the time and a non-skier, and "old-fashioned" hickory and ash laminated skis were a bargain at the Salvation Army store. Today, I ski on Head's top-of-the-line racing skis.

The first Winter Olympics were held in Chamonix, France in 1924, and they were held three more times at 4-year intervals through 1936. No Olympic Games were contested again until 1948, when the Winter Games resumed in St. Moritz, Switzerland. In the history of the Olympics, the Winter Games have been held in the United States three times, twice in Lake Placid, New York (1932 and 1980), and once in Squaw Valley, California (1960).

Skiing grew by leaps in the 1950s because it was newly accessible to broader ranges of participants.

Chair lifts, surface tows, and aerial trams were on the scene, and ski areas were in full operation in many places in the United States by then. New thinking on technique and the introduction of new, more durable, flexible, and comfortable boots, refined ski designs, and highly efficient and safe bindings continued in the 1960s through the 1980s.

## ALPINE SKIING TODAY

Today in the '90s and into the next century, alpine skiing offers an expanding diversity of opportunities for persons of all ages and athletic abilities. In alpine skiing's infancy, the thrill of the hill was "schussing" straight down snow-covered mountains. Thus, the name *downhill* skiing, to distinguish it from Nordic telemark skiing, was hatched and in many ways still lingers in the public lexicon. Although the expressions alpine skiing and downhill skiing are used interchangably, there's good reason to make a distinction between these terms and Nordic skiing.

Alpine skiing encompasses the disciplines of racing (e.g., slalom, giant slalom, super-G, and downhill), powder skiing, ballet, free skiing, mogul skiing, freestyle aerial jumps, learning to ski, family and social/recreational skiing, ski teaching, skiwear fashion, ski equipment fashion, and the ambiance of the ski resort in the daytime and after hours.

Some might argue that alpine skiing includes Nordic telemark skiing and snowboarding, and to the extent that trails intersect alpine hills, that Nordic track and cross-country skiing should be included under the "alpine" umbrella. However, I don't agree in the least: Alpine skiing is as stated; snowboarding is snowboarding with alpine and freestyle disciplines. Although alpine skiing and alpine snowboarding are technically related, on those days when I "ride" (snowboard) in the morning and hop onto my skis in the afternoon, I am keenly aware of each one's distinctiveness. With track, skating, alpine telemark, racing, and backcountry disciplines, Nordic skiing is Nordic skiing.

Alpine skiing is as friendly a sport as anyone could wish, in terms of equipment, clothing styles, comfort, ease of terrain, variety of terrain challenges, and instructional help. Lift-ticket prices and holiday crowds? Okay, well, almost as friendly as anyone could wish.

# Learning to Ski Is Not a Muscular Feat

When people learn any new sport in which maintaining balance while in motion is a paramount concern, they often find they have sore, aching muscles and joints 24 to 48 hours afterward. Aside from the physiological reason for this, muscles and joints are overused while learning a new sport like skiing, because a lack of balance-promoting skills must be compensated for by using muscular strength to stay upright, and muscular strength and bone leverage on the joints to maintain balance. Both approaches to balance are unusually fatiguing, and this is why many persons think you need a lot of muscular strength to ski.

Such a mind-set prompts many unfortunate but common experiences in learning to ski. Well-meaning friends teach others using an accelerated "follow me" method. Some of their "students" do very well; others plug away at getting down the hill. Most beginning skiers under the coaching of friends or instructor get down the hill with a fall here and there. Lacking instruction, however, skiers learn to employ an unnerving variety of mechanical and muscular manipulations to brace themselves against the "slippery" terrain. They rely on instincts to survive the beginning challenges they face, and often develop a survival-oriented, defensive approach to skiing.

## BUILDING ADVENTURE INTO BEGINNING SKIING

The most effective way to learn to ski, as I see the process, is to make three connections among your body, mind, and spirit. First, you must be able to see yourself as a skier—to at least create a mental picture of the possibility of your skiing and wearing strange-looking boots and whatever other attire you select. Second, you must test the validity of your image, and be ready to experience the feel, literally, of boots on your feet and skis attached beneath as you are challenged to maneuver on them. Third, after facing your first challenges on skis, you must allow your mind, and the spirit with which you pursue the learning of skiing, to readjust the original "image" of you as a skier and your potential to learn. You are wise to spend your first attempts just maneuvering

around on skis and seeing yourself balanced and in control on the snow.

So, take that "before" picture of you as a skier—it is an important first step. What does your picture reveal? If your picture shows a confident skier, you've got a head start on the process, and your learning can proceed with vigor. If, however, your picture reveals a timid or fearful skier, your learning may have to be paced down, and you are best advised to take it a little at a time.

If your picture shows an ambivalent, suspicious skier, it's likely that your spirit isn't at the helm of your learning, and that someone else (e.g., a spouse, friend, or social club member) has pushed you into learning to ski. This kind of motivation warrants your very careful evaluation before going any further.

If you can take a picture—any of the kind noted above—you can learn to ski. What concerns me are persons who are unable to see any picture at all. They try to learn to ski, but struggle with the sport in vain, frequently exceeding their physical and emotional limits, in the end to never ski again.

Once you're truly committed to learning to ski, and you've made the three connections among your body, mind, and spirit, there are more fascinating issues to resolve, through which you will develop more resolve to do well in the learning process.

## FOUR CHIEF MYTHS

The following myths cloud many people's attempts to learn to ski, stop others from even trying, and once resolved can be sources of inspiration.

### Myth 1: You Must Be Athletically Inclined to Learn to Ski

Fact: Prior athletic experience usually proves helpful in learning new sport skills when the new skills require the large muscle movements or eye-hand-limb coordination that were the essence of prior sport skills. So, although some persons find it easier to learn to ski due to their prior athletic experience, anyone who can walk a straight line, walk up and down stairs without

3

using railings, and hop a few hops on each foot can learn to ski.

## Myth 2: Learning to Ski Requires a Minimum Level of Cardiovascular or Aerobic Fitness

**Fact:** Running long distances, cycling for hours at a hearty pace, rowing across the lake, cross-country treks on Nordic skis—these are aerobic activities. Alpine skiing, particularly in the learning stage, is an anaerobic activity like golf, weight lifting, recreational tennis, or recreational volleyball. Learning to ski can make you tired—not because you ''run out of wind'' due to a lack of aerobic fitness, but because you expend a great deal of muscle energy on staying in balance and picking up yourself after falling.

## Myth 3: You Must Have Strong Arms and Legs to Learn to Ski

**Fact:** Learning to ski is full of muscular challenge at first, because you'll be climbing and walking around, getting up after tipping over, and poling across flat terrain from one place to another. All of these require muscular effort. It seems logical that the stronger you are, the easier it is to learn to ski; but strength is a relative concept, and although you may be strong when lifting weights, you might not be strong when pushing (i.e., poling) across flat terrain. It is wise to achieve a certain level of strength relative to the sport you intend to learn, but strength itself does not determine whether you can learn to ski or not, though it may make the process less fatiguing overall.

The stronger you are, the more physical ''abuse'' you can take while learning (so you can last longer), and the easier it will be to use your muscles to correct technical errors. This ''strength correction,'' unfortunately, may later impede your progress if you forsake technique for power. The essential connection between strength and learning to ski revolves around time: If you feel weak muscularly in the arms and legs, you may have to make adjustments in your time frame and take learning to ski a bit more slowly.

## Myth 4: Some People Can Never Learn to Ski

**Fact:** Anyone who can walk can learn to ski. (The physically impaired can learn to ski, as can persons with mental illness, cancer, or a number of other conditions.) Though at times it appears that certain people can't learn to ski because of a voodoo spell cast on them by a long-lost great grandparent, what in my estimation keeps persons from learning to ski is the chatter in their minds. With respect to learning more advanced skiing skills, however, it is true that some persons are more limited than others due to differences in sport preference, personality, attitude, and physical ability.

## THINK: FEET, NOT FEAT

You've heard the slogan used to advertise the ''Yellow Pages''—''Let your fingers do the walking'' (implied message: ''and not your feet''). In beginning skiing it's wise to think: Let your feet do the skiing (implied message: and not your legs). For perspective, think of ''feet'' as the sum of the principal anatomical parts within your boots that aid movement—your feet, ankles, muscles, and tendons. Consider the importance of your feet in skiing:

- You will use less energy to move your skis edge to edge, or to slide them to the side when you initiate the movement, if you focus first on the position of your feet (that is, how you move your feet, ankles, and lower legs to affect the position of your boots) to accomplish this movement.
- Your skis respond more immediately to messages from your feet, because they're connected to them.
- Messages sent to your skis from any part of your body must eventually go through your feet before your skis respond.
- As a beginning skier, you will find that your feet are the most active and vocal part of your skiing sensory system (i.e., neuromuscular response mechanism to sensory input received from touch, sound, inner ear equilibrium, proprioception, and vision). Your skiing sensory system will tell you what it feels like to be in or out of balance or to be moving fast or slow, the texture of the snow, the position of your skis on the snow, your degree of muscular effort or relaxation, and other information about your skiing.
- When you concentrate on moving your feet first, and your body remains relaxed and skeletally aligned in a solid skiing stance, the rest of your body follows the lead of your feet.

## THINK: SKIING IS SUBTLE

The complementary dimension of viewing skiing as more feet than feat is nestled between your ears. If you believe learning to ski is winning a tug-of-war with the mountain or defeating the enemy on the hill, learning will be a struggle. If you believe learning to ski is something you do with shortcuts, or that there's no process to learning to ski, you will not have the patience to learn basic skills. And believe me, taking the time to learn basic skills early on in your skiing will pave the way for a lifetime of improvement in your skiing.

By viewing skiing as a subtle sport, you acknowledge certain tenets:

- Learning sport skills cannot be rushed—that is, the biomechanics of movement are learned through repeated application. Trying to do more in less time doesn't necessarily mean faster skill development.
- You are not in competition with the mountain or anyone else.

- Almost every time you *force* a body part to conform to learned ski movements, you slow the learning process.
- Almost every time you get mad at yourself when learning to ski, you slow the learning process.
- You're working with the snow, not against it—learning to ski is a process that flows from one personal discovery to another. You are not learning a rigid set of mechanistic moves meant for application to all snow situations. You are not a robot; your style will emerge as an expression of your skiing preferences.
- Speed of learning does not equate with personal worth.
- Learning is process; skiing is process—there are no "end points"; rather, the points of transition are never-ending, and often exhilarating, when you believe in the subtlety of skiing.

Skiing is like many other sports in that you need certain basic equipment to participate. As well, you have basic apparel needs (and even these are seasonal within the ski season). For both equipment and clothing, you have a universe of options with respect to color, style, fit, and functionality.

Here's a list of necessities for your first full season of skiing. The first three items needn't be new. In truth, I recommend used skis for new skiers, and if available in your area, a season's lease for skis and poles, possibly for boots as well.

- One pair of ski boots.
- One pair of skis.
- One pair of poles. (Though an extra pair can be a boon, because some skiers find it's easy to break a ski pole by stepping on it with their skis.)
- Two pairs of ski socks. (White athletic socks are not recommended for skiing because as the foot sweats, boots fit more loosely and performance suffers. Ski socks are designed to be warm without being bulky, and to allow good foot-to-boot contact.)
- A good pair of sunglasses (UVA and UVB protective).
- A pair of goggles. (Extra-large goggles are available to accommodate the wearing of a pair of prescription glasses beneath them.)
- Cold weather gloves.
- Warm weather gloves.
- A ski hat or headband. (For comfort and a measure of safety, hats should be worn on very cold days, cold and windy days, and stormy days.)
- A head and neck gaiter. (A tubular stocking and hat material open at both ends so it can be slipped over the head, face, and neck as needed to protect from the cold. A head/neck gaiter will save you on many chair-lift rides.)
- Ski pants or ankle gaiters (tubular water-resistant overpant coverings that are worn over the calf and boot top to protect jeans or other pants from getting wet, and to keep snow from going into the top of the ski boot).
- Ski jacket. (Or other warm, water-resistant coat. One with a lot of pockets will be appreciated for years to come. Nylon zippers are a must.)
- Turtleneck long-sleeve shirt. (The turtleneck should fit snugly, but have a loose-enough neck to pull up over your chin and mouth when you need to.)

A number of optional items may add to your overall enjoyment of skiing:

- Cotton or thermal liner gloves. (Worn beneath gloves on very cold days.)
- A one-piece ski suit. (Easy on, easy off, the one-piece suit is comfortable and warm.)
- Wool sweater.
- Long underwear. (There are many varieties available, from very thin, silk-like underwear to the heavier, long-john type.)
- Vest. (A down-filled vest is very warm, and handy for chilly mornings that turn into warm days.)
- Powder shell with hood and lightweight shell pants. (Water-resistant materials are used to make lightweight jackets with hoods and pants to wear over sweaters or other clothing during snow storms, or while skiing in new-fallen snow.)
- Suspenders. (Great for holding up ski pants that don't fit just right.)
- Ski bag and boot bag. (These really are necessities if you travel with skis, boots, and ski gear.)
- Waist pack. (A waist pack is handy for carrying supplies, particularly if weather conditions are changeable and you want to be prepared.)

Of the items on the "necessities" list, none are more important than boots, skis, eyewear, and gloves. The former two are the foundation of skiing and skills acquisition; the latter two, the foundation of safety while learning. As such, each will be discussed in appropriate detail.

## BOOTS

You can lease or rent boots by the day or season (as some ski shops will do), or buy a pair of used boots. When you rent boots, you are fitted as well as possible, but the boots have often been worn and shaped by many other feet.

Nevertheless, when learning to ski or when making an occasional visit to the slopes, rented or leased boots may be as comfortable and responsive as you require. But when you become sure that skiing is for you and you want to invest money in your skiing, spend first on your boots.

Used boots offer very particular challenges. Without help or guidance, you may not know much about the quality of the boots, or which level of skiing they are best suited to. Extremely stiff racing boots would be a nightmare (and dangerous) for beginners, for example, as would boots with damaged buckles or excessively worn liners (inner boots), and older boots with a high ankle design that may lead to tibial fractures and breaks with torquing falls.

Generally, all high-performance boots, new or used, are inappropriate for beginning skiers. They are designed for more aggressive, skilled skiing, for precision moves that beginners are not yet capable of executing.

## Buying a Used Boot

Still, you can find a good pair of used boots at ski swaps (i.e., flea markets where the only merchandise is ski gear and clothing), at more generic flea markets, from private owners, and from ski rental shops at the end of the season. A good pair of used ski boots for beginners should be able to be used for at least two skiing seasons, regarding both wear and tear and ability to accommodate increased skill demand.

I consider a good used beginner boot to possess these qualities: the boot looks like new on the outside and on the bottoms of the boot, has very little wear on the inside, is priced anywhere from $50 to $100, is easy to put on and take off, and most importantly, fits you correctly. You can find these boots if you look, and by looking at different boots with an experienced friend or fellow skier, you can also get a feel for the difference between high-performance boots and more recreational boots.

Briefly, the high-performance boot is more versatile in terms of its rigid points and adjustments, makes the ski respond more quickly to stimuli because of its stiffness and adjustability, is often heavier, and is "aggressive looking." Recreational boots have fewer adjustments, are generally lighter in weight, don't trigger as quick a response in the skis, and are more subdued in their "look." The latter boot is definitely what you want when learning to ski.

Boots come in basically two styles: rear-entry boots and conventional lapover front-buckle boots. As well, there are boots that are a cross between rear entry and conventional front-buckle. The rear-entry boot is generally easier to put on, adjust, and take off, and thus more ideally suited to new skiers. There are high-performance rear-entry boots, but most high-performance racing-level boots are lapover front-buckle boots (see Figure E.1).

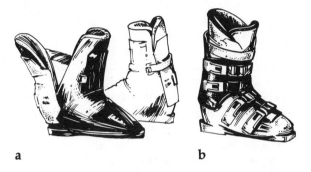

**a**        **b**

**Figure E.1** Rear-entry (a) and front-buckle (b) boots.

## How to Fit a Ski Boot

There are many ways to go about fitting a ski boot, but the least complicated, I believe, is to use these guidelines as they apply to you, whether you are buying new or used boots. With used boots, of course, your options are more limited, but apply all appropriate information.

**Guideline 1**—Take the size of your favorite athletic or comfort shoe, and pick out three pairs of boots: your shoe size, a half size larger, and a half size smaller. Because some boots are made more for thin feet, and others more for broad feet, different sizes will help you find the best fit for your foot.

**Guideline 2**—When trying on your boots, wear one pair of ski socks—not athletic socks and not two pairs of thin socks. It is not necessary to wear bulky socks under ski boots for warmth. Ski socks allow a good fit, and provide warmth by permitting natural body heat to escape inside the boot and be trapped around the foot by the insulation in the boot liner. Again, bulky socks lead to a poor fit, as do two pairs of thin socks. There are ways to pad and shave the boot lining to achieve a better fit. Some specially designed ski socks are made for a snug fit, with extra padding at the heel and toe; some are made a bit thicker yet fit snuggly; others are thin throughout.

**Guideline 3**—If possible, try on at least two brands of boot. You could try one on each foot, at the same time. Stand up, walk around, bend your knees; sidestep and hop with the boots. Wear them for 10 to 20 minutes. What do they feel like? You want the boots to feel very snug, almost tight, but you do not want any areas of pain, pressure, or pinching on your feet.

If the boots of your shoe size are very comfortable, perhaps almost too comfortable as may be the case with used boots of your size, try on a half size smaller. If the boots of your shoe size are very, very tight, almost numbing your feet, try on a half size larger. Never try on just one size and assume it's correct for you without trying another size up or down. Always err to the side that will lead to a snug fit! Boots will stretch out inside as skiing days increase. Boots can also be modified by ski shop staff to more closely fit your foot.

**Guideline 4**—When fitting the boot, you want to be fastened in the boot. You should be able to wiggle your toes slightly as you powerfully press your shin against the tongue of the boot, but your foot should not move laterally in the boot, and your heel should stay firmly in place.

**Guideline 5**—You don't want the boot to be too complicated to use. Easy entry and on-off mechanics are important for the beginner. Any adjustments you need to make must be easy to do with gloves on, on the slope. Some high-performance boots require special tools to make critical adjustments to the boot's action.

Let's face it, boots are critical to your skiing experience, and I recommend beginners who can afford it make a pair of ski boots their first investment. Rent the skis and poles, but your feet must feel good on and off the skis, and well-fitted boots that have been molded to your feet through wear are the best assurance of comfortable skiing.

## SKIS

If you had in mind the perfect ski for you—a ski that matched your ski outfit or graphic inclinations—you could probably find it at a large sporting goods store or specialty ski shop. However, when you are first learning to ski, such a find may be exactly the ski you don't want to own.

Why? For four main reasons:

1. Within months, for sure by next season, you'll likely outgrow the skis and will want a ski that is a little, or a lot, longer.

2. During the learning process and early skiing, you'll do every evil to the tops, edges/sidewalls, and perhaps even bases of your skis, turning them into pieces of scratch-and-groove art that doesn't always jibe with how you feel when you become a more accomplished skier.

3. After you have learned to ski, you may change your mind about what you want in a ski, and you may want another type or model. To be sure, when you begin skiing more of the mountain, what you want out of your skis becomes better defined.

4. If you buy new performance-oriented skis because they have the graphics and color you like, you'll spend a lot of money for skis you're not able to ski as designed, and skis that actually make learning to ski more difficult. Performance skis are performance oriented, and although more and more are made to be "forgiving" in various snow conditions, as a beginner you won't encounter the conditions or level of skiing that the skis' "forgiveness" is designed to accommodate.

A ski is forgiving when it can be maneuvered easily in challenging situations. An expert skier on high-performance, yet forgiving, skis, will, with crispness and style, ski out of conditions that less skilled skiers would find challenging. Less skilled skiers on the same skis will find that they don't need to ski as precisely as the expert to still look okay and feel okay about the conditions. Don't complicate learning to ski by buying as if you're already a performance skier; don't walk before you learn to crawl.

## New Skis or Used Skis?

Frankly, I discourage new skis for beginners for the reasons already noted, but if you do purchase new skis, look for wide, soft-flexing skis. Ask the salesperson to show you a number of recreational skis and ski packages. A ski package includes a pair of new skis, bindings (mounted on the skis to fit your boots), and a set of poles to fit your height. Ski packages are attractive because they deliver the "set" at a cost that's often lower than the cost of a pair of high-performance skis.

I encourage beginners to buy used skis if they plan to ski throughout the ski season and to rent skis if they plan a weekend or longer ski vacation during which they intend to learn to ski. Ski rental shops will provide boot and pole fitting, and most recreational rental skis are fine for beginning skiers. Let's suppose you are buying used skis. Consider the following tips:

- Have an experienced skier help you pick out your skis.
- Don't buy skis that appear to have damaged bases or sidewalls, particularly near the bindings, tips, or tails of the skis.
- Buy skis with modern bindings (i.e., metal working parts housed in hard plastic shells with hard plastic devices that bind the boot to the binding) and not bindings made with shiny chrome metal pieces to bind the boot to the binding. Ski brakes are a necessity. Don't buy skis with boot straps for brakes. Most modern bindings without metal chrome pieces can be remounted by a ski shop to fit your boots. Questionable bindings can also be remounted and tested for functionality and safety by ski shops, but you'll likely have to sign a damage waiver if you request a shop to remount non-indemnified (by the manufacturer) bindings.
- The base of the skis, and the metal edges and the state of their camber, are your main concerns. The bases shouldn't have any deep gouges in them (patched "welded" bases are fine), and the metal edges should not be separated from the sides or base of the ski, or broken so they stick up in places. The camber of the ski gives it some liveliness and shock absorption, so it's important even for the beginner—a "dead" ski moves on snow like a log moves in mud. The tops can be etched with ski lore or have topographical designs; this won't adversely affect learning. The importance of a ski's camber is explained and illustrated in Step 6.

You can expect to pay anywhere from $45 to $85 for a learning pair of skis and bindings when purchased at ski swaps, at flea markets, or from private parties. Paying any more for a used pair of skis on which to learn may not be cost-efficient. Remember, there's a good chance these learning skis will get banged up; and further, once you've learned to ski, you may want a longer, more performance-oriented ski, anyway.

Buy a pair of used skis, and then sell them a year later so another beginner can continue in the tradition. I believe new skiers should think of their first pair of skis as expendable training wheels.

## How Long Should Your Skis Be?

I have four guidelines for selecting skis for the first-time skier:

- If you are of average weight or thin for your height, and you are in good physical condition, your beginning skis should stand forehead high.
- If you are of average weight or thin for your height and in poor physical condition, shorten the skis to mouth level.
- If you are really overweight (you know if you are) yet have strong legs and arms, add 5 centimeters to the length of your skis.
- If you are really overweight and in poor condition, shorten the skis by 5 centimeters.

As you perfect your skiing skills and think about buying new skis (or newer used skis), you'll be rethinking ski length, because as your skills improve and broaden, ski length is determined by a number of other factors relative to the type of skiing you like to do, your overall body strength, your level of agility, and the time you have to ski.

Be sure you purchase alpine skis. Nordic skis with metal edges are not the same as alpine skis. Not only are the boots and bindings for each different, the technique for skiing each is different.

## How Should You Carry Your Skis (and Poles)?

Frankly, you should carry your skis any way that is comfortable as long as your skis are under control and not likely to hit another skier or passerby. To this end, there are several alternatives: shoulder, side, upright, and cross-abdominal (see Figure E.2, a-d). In each case, before you pick up your skis, make sure all is clear around you. Except for the cross-abdominal carry (which is not good in a crowd), carry your poles in your free hand.

## EYEWEAR

Never ski without eye protection, and inexpensive sunglasses that shade the eyes may not be enough. Protecting the eyes from both long UVA

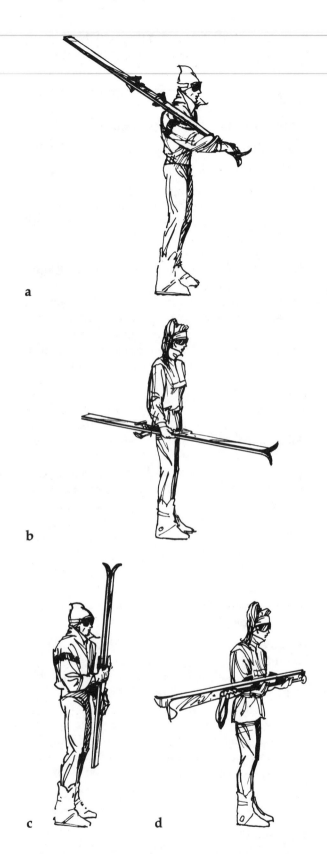

**Figure E.2** Four ways to carry your skis and poles: shoulder carry (a), side carry (b), upright carry (c), and cross-abdominal carry (d).

and short UVB rays is a must, and sunglasses that tend to wrap around the eyes may be a better selection than more conventional frames because they filter out the rays that come in from the sides. Whether it's sunny or not, UVA- and UVB-rated eyewear is important, particularly at higher altitudes where ultraviolet rays are more intense.

A "leash" can be purchased to attach to your glasses. As a beginner you won't need one until you're ready to start turning and picking up some speed, when a leash will control the whereabouts of your glasses should you take a tumble.

In stormy, windy, or cold conditions, goggles are a popular and effective alternative to glasses. Double-lens goggles tend not to fog up, although extraordinary muscular effort may foster foggy glasses and goggles. The fit of glasses and goggles is important. Take time to try on your eyewear—there are times when it may literally save your life! (Remember, goggles can be purchased to fit over prescription glasses.)

Sunglasses and goggles vary in price, but without question, the best time to buy either is at the end of the season or during preseason sales. Effective sunglasses and goggles may cost anywhere from $25 to $100+.

## GLOVES

You'll want two types of gloves: a warm pair for cold temperatures, and a lightweight pair for warm spring days. Cotton or linen liners can be worn under heavier gloves for added warmth. Warm gloves cost anywhere from $35 to $100+; spring gloves cost considerably less.

How should a glove fit? Snuggly, but with a little room in the fingertips. Try on different sizes of gloves to get an idea of the different fits in different sizes. The same size of glove by different glove manufacturers may fit differently. Don't buy a glove unless it feels like part of your hand, not something hanging on your hand. When you grip a ski pole or anything else with your gloved hand, you should be able to control the movements of all of your fingers, and have a strong grip. Liners are so thin that they'll fit under any properly fitted glove.

## SKI POLES

Choosing the correct size and style of ski pole is more critical for advanced skiing, but as a beginner it's important to choose a ski pole that will be functional during early skill development. These are the important characteristics of functional ski poles for beginners (see Figure E.3, a and b): straight grip with strap instead of molded grips; smaller baskets; sturdy shaft yet not bulky; and correct size.

To size a ski pole place the ski pole upside down with the top of the grip alongside and several inches to the outside of your toe. Grab the ski pole beneath the basket. Your hand should be around the shaft, and the basket should rest on top of your thumb and forefinger. Look at the angle created by your upper and lower arm at the elbow. The correct fit would be a 90 degree angle. If you must choose a pole with a smaller or larger angle, choose the larger angle because this will indicate a shorter pole. A shorter pole is easier to use than a pole that is too long for you. And a correctly sized pole is most ideal.

Although ski poles do not have a strict functional role in the actual mechanics of beginning skiing, they are, nonetheless, valuable aids to learning, due to their help in maneuvering on the snow and getting into position to perform various drills. If you were, alas, to lose your ski poles on the way to the mountains, you could still learn to ski without them.

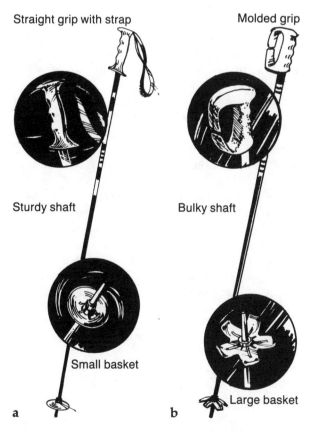

**Figure E.3** Ski pole grips, shafts, and baskets vary in size and style. Use depends on personal preference. More experienced skiers use type a.

There are many varieties of ski pole, from the more recreational pole to the more competitive racing series of performance poles. You can expect to pay anywhere from sales and swap prices of $10 to $15 to season prices of $20 to $50+ for a set of recreational ski poles, and more for racing poles.

## SKI LUGGAGE

Ski bags, boot bags, and soft-luggage skiwear bags are specially designed heavy-duty nylon and rubber or leather padded bags that are useful for airline, train, or bus travel. In fact, they make travel with ski equipment most accommodating. Prices range from $35 to $75 for ski bags and $20 to $35 for boot bags. Thought of as on-the-slope luggage, the waist pack is a specially designed pouch that attaches around the waist like a belt and is useful for carrying lip protection, sunscreen, goggles, handkerchief, hat, snacks, and other personal items. You can pick up a waist pack for as little as $5 for a small pack or up to $25 and more for larger name-brand packs.

## SKI CLOTHING

The purpose of ski clothing is protection against the (often changing) elements. Water- and wind-resistant clothing is the ideal. Manufacturers provide resistant clothing in numerous fashion designs, fabric combinations, and fills to provide warmth and insulation. As does ski equipment, ski clothing comes in recreational and performance varieties. Performance-oriented clothing, and skiwear with top-of-the-line materials, cost more.

*Given water- and wind-resistant qualities, with all ski clothing, the most important concern is fit.* When trying on skiwear, move around in it: stretch, bend, reach, and lift your knees. Are there binding points in the crotch, underarms, shoulders, chest, legs, or forehead? If so, try on another size, or another piece in the same size. As with regular clothing, size cuts differ, and size cuts from different manufacturers will vary, as will the size cuts of different styles. Ski hats vary in size depending on fabric and hat design.

**Ski pants**—There are many varieties of ski pants; find a pair that fits! Ski pants may be tight fitting and look like exercise tights, or they may be tight fitting with padded knees and shins. For most skiers, the padding is more an affectation than a necessity. What you wear to ski depends on what's comfortable for you. For learning to ski, I recommend very comfortable pants that are water resistant. You're going to be moving around a lot, and *tight restrictive pants may impede your learning to ski*. Cost: $50 to $400

**Ski jacket**—When first beginning to ski, you can wear whatever you like to stay warm, as long as you can move around in it; but if you want to stick with skiing, don't cut corners here. Invest in a good ski jacket (unless you go with a one-piece suit). A good ski jacket is warm, lightweight, and fully pocketed with inside and outside nylon-zippered pockets, has an integral hood tucked away in a collar that can be zipped up over the chin, and has arm sleeves and waistband with tight but comfortable cuffs. A good jacket will also comfortably accommodate a sweater and turtleneck beneath it. Cost: $150 to $450

**Ski hat**—You must have one; find a style and fit that you like. Cost: $10 to $35

**Headband**—This is useful for keeping your ears warm when it feels too hot for a hat, yet it's cool enough with the windchill to cover your ears. Fit is important; try on several types. Cost: $8 to $18

**Turtleneck**—Turtlenecks are made from many fabrics. Most important for you is a turtleneck that stays snug against your neck but can be pulled up over your mouth as an emergency faceguard during foul weather. Cost: $15 to $25

**One-piece suit**—Easy on, easy off; this is the magic of the one-piece suit. Warm, comfortable, accommodating—these are the traits so useful to beginning and expert skiers alike. So why not begin skiing with a one-piece suit? However, they may be too warm for many beginners, because of the muscular effort exerted when beginning to ski, and some people may find them too expensive.

One-piece suits are priced variably from $125 to $800, with special one-of-a-kind suits costing even more. Once you've learned to stop and have begun turning, an inexpensive one-piece suit is ideal for future skiing. Like ski pants and jackets, you must try on the one-piece suits and move around in them. If there are binding points,

don't buy them. Alterations may be difficult unless you own a one-piece shell.

**Wool sweater**—This should be snug fitting for warmth, but not so tight that a turtleneck doesn't fit beneath it with some room to spare, and never so tight that you feel restricted in your movements. You want air space between your undergarments, to trap pockets of warm air. Any wool sweater would work, although there are specifically designed wool ski sweaters. Prices vary greatly.

**Ankle gaiters**—These are water- and wind-resistant coverings that are fixed over the shins and boot tops to allow skiers to wear "street clothes" while skiing. Cost: $15 to $25

**Face mask; face gaiter**—These are very important for skiing in extreme cold and stormy conditions, when the face is vulnerable to frostbite and cracking. Face masks come in several varieties, as do face gaiters, which are soft fabric coverings that protect the face. Cost: $10 to $25

**Long underwear**—This is useful as long as it doesn't restrict movement.

**Ski vests**—These are handy when it's too warm for a jacket, yet there's a bit of a chill in the air and you want to dress light.

**Powder-shell upper and light shell pants**—These both have their places in skiing, but they are not necessary for beginners, although shell pants with a cotton lining are comfortable when learning to ski in warm weather.

**Suspenders**—These are handy when your ski pants are a bit loose around the waist and hips; suspenders are worn by both men and women skiers.

My suggestion for new skiers: Be prudent when buying skiwear and equipment. Spend more on learning and lift tickets than on new equipment and stylish clothing. What is most important are the necessities, and these have been discussed. You can spend a small fortune, or you can shop for bargains at season-ending sales, preseason sales, ski swaps, flea markets, or private-party sales. Go easy at first—and foremost, dress comfortably and have fun with this new adventure!

# Preparing Your Body for Success

Even though overall physical fitness is not an absolute prerequisite for learning to ski, your fitness level may well add to your overall enjoyment of first-time skiing. If you're fit, you'll be able to go farther on the same gallon of gas, and prevent some measure of the common fatiguing aspects of beginning skiing.

There are also two other reasons for considering your fitness level. First, your learning may be enhanced if your fitness allows you to spend more time on the slopes; and second, a higher level of fitness reduces the risk of injury by making the body more resilient in unexpected movements or falls. To attain a fitness level particular to skiing ("ski fitness"), there are four areas to focus on:

1. Building muscular endurance and stamina
2. Abdominal strength and stamina training
3. Increased muscle-tendon-joint flexibility and agility
4. Acquainting muscle-tendon-joint complexes with ski-related movement patterns

## COMMON FATIGUING ASPECTS OF BEGINNING SKIING

Skiing is, by necessity, performed on a slippery surface on which maneuvering is a constant process of learning and discovery while moving in and out of balance. So a tremendous amount of physical energy is used by beginning skiers, until they have learned how to "walk" and "glide" on the snow while muscularly relaxed. Befitting the nature of this sport, the following are associated with the onset of "beginner's fatigue."

- Falling and getting back up
- Climbing up slight hills to gain gliding experience
- Maneuvering and poling around on the flat terrain
- Excessive brain cell activity in trying to "think" muscles through movements
- Exaggerated muscle-joint-tendon activation to maintain balance and prevent falls

Fitness helps prevent fatigue and easy injury; generally speaking, the chance of having an accident is far greater for a tired skier. My studies and work with recreational and World Cup skiers, indicate that being conditioned for skiing yields many advantages: less injury, quicker recovery from injury, more resilience when confronted with unexpected changes in terrain and snow conditions, less fatigue after skiing long hours, and greater responsiveness on skis (i.e., quickness, agility, and flexibility).

The fastest track to conditioning is employing an integrated approach to fitness. If you live near the slopes, or in an area where skiing is a popular sport, many health clubs and fitness facilities offer ski conditioning and fitness classes in the late fall and early winter. If you are able to enroll in such a class, great; not only may the classes help you become more flexible, stronger, and more fit, they may add to your excitement about the sport you are about to learn.

Being active year-round is not a guarantee you'll be in shape for skiing. Although running, aerobics, jumping, swimming, weight lifting, cycling, rowing, and hiking are great for different parts of the body (and benefit overall fitness), these alone are not enough to "train" your body for the biomechanics of alpine skiing.

## PACING PRINCIPLES

The key to your conditioning program is pacing (i.e., a properly scheduled training program that includes planned days of rest). Whatever you devise for yourself (and you must do *your* program and not another's), realize it takes several different activities to achieve ski fitness.

Use the total training week (which may be 3 to 6 training days) to focus on different parts of your program, always allowing a day or two of rest from activities strenuously taxing to the large muscles and heart. During the first week or two, you may experience soreness, stiffness, and generalized aching in your muscle-joint-tendon complexes that are being exposed to new movements and stretches. Aches and pains that don't go away in a week or two are a sign of an injury that needs care, and you need to modify that aspect of your training.

## WARM-UP AND COOL-DOWN PRINCIPLES

Most importantly, prior to exercise and stretching routines, warm-up the muscles by engorging them with oxygen-rich blood. Do so by using activities that make the heart beat faster and large muscles work harder, but not excessively, for at least 5 to 10 minutes continuously. Once you've warmed up, engage in your chosen activity.

With respect to stretching for flexibility, be patient. Stretch until you feel a tingling sensation in the stretched area, hold the stretch for 10 to 20 seconds, and then relax the stretched area. As a rule, press into your stretches gently at first (never bounce), gradually increasing the length and duration of the stretch with each repetition.

Clearly, the best approach to flexibility gains is a daily program of moderate-intensity stretching. My rule of thumb for most stretches: The simpler they are to execute and the more familiar they are, the greater their benefit to you, provided they progressively challenge your body to elongate at the given areas of "stretch." You don't want to overstretch, but you want to effectively stretch key areas of your musculature to achieve flexibility. Specifically, the targets of flexibility stretching are muscles and the tendons that attach the muscles to your bones.

My six caveats for all stretches:

1. Don't bounce into the stretch; gradually push into it.
2. Don't forget to breathe while stretching, inhaling during the resting phase and exhaling during the work phase of the stretch.
3. Don't do exercises that require dynamic weight-bearing bending at the waist with your legs straight.
4. Don't do deep knee bends or full squats bearing weight to achieve stretching of the knee region.
5. Don't use weights with stretching unless you've received proper instruction.
6. *Effective stretches (that produce flexibility) lengthen your muscles and tendons beyond their normal resting state, yet don't force body parts beyond their normal ranges of motion.*

At exercise conclusion, cool down by engaging in activities that help your heart rate lower gradually, and thereby gradually return blood from the extremities, where it might otherwise pool and cause sluggish circulation, lightheadedness, and excess postactivity soreness.

## BUILDING MUSCULAR ENDURANCE AND STAMINA

Muscular endurance and stamina allow you to maintain strength and power during long periods of exertion, and are a product of cardiovascular conditioning. From training elite athletes, we've learned that muscular endurance and stamina can be targeted to different muscle groups in the body. Thus, to achieve muscular endurance and stamina in the legs, you must work the legs aerobically (e.g., in long-distance running or jogging, stairmaster, long-distance cycling, Nordic track skiing, or other activities that exercise the legs and heart for extended periods of time).

Similarly, upper body endurance and stamina would require working the chest, back, arms, and shoulders aerobically (e.g., in hill running with an arm pump, rowing, long-distance swimming, upper body aerobics). In all, endurance- and stamina-building activities should strive to produce a sustained heart rate 70% to 85% of your maximum heart rate (MHR) for at least 20 to 30 minutes, at least three times a week (MHR = 220 minus your age).

Another method for developing endurance and stamina is through "aerobic" weight training: lifting lighter weights at a high to very high number of repetitions (25 to 50), two to three sets of each lift, two or three times a week (*never* 2 days in a row on the same muscle systems, except for the first 4 days of a new lifting routine).

To add polish to the training systems noted above, you may strengthen muscles and joints through assorted resistance activities. *Isometric* and *isotonic* exercises are two such examples. With the former you hold a contraction without moving the muscles for a set time (e.g., 10 seconds); with the latter you hold a contraction for 5 to 10 seconds, then progressively relax the contraction while maintaining a measure of resistance as the muscle is moved to its relaxed position.

## ABDOMINAL STRENGTH AND STAMINA TRAINING

The abdominal muscles, along with the muscles of the lower back are the targets of this phase of strength training. Because these muscles are collectively responsible for helping to center the upper body over the hips and lower body (a key biomechanical advantage when skiing), their strength and stamina deserve independent attention. Your abdominal training program should include both stamina and strength work.

Stamina training takes time and dedication. Assuming correct form (i.e., lower back held against the floor/exercise mat most of the time, no yanking of the head and neck, feet on the floor most of the time, correct breathing rhythm, eyes focused on a fixed target), abdominal exercises should be done at a persistent but not sprint pace. Stamina training involves repetitious action stressing the different abdominal muscles. You can build up to many hundreds of repetitions of different abdominal exercises in sequence at one sitting, and this training can be done daily, if desired, but three times a week is effective.

### Abdominals

For abdominal strength, abdominal exercises should be done slowly and deliberately. There are many varieties of abdominal exercises, but I advise all exercisers to develop a baseline of strength, and in so doing to follow the safety precautions noted above. After achieving this basic strength of the trunk and lower back, you can explore the vast array of abdominal exercises and strength-building equipment. For example, sit-ups with your hands alongside your body but not touching your legs are more difficult.

As a matter of practice, to keep the lower back on the floor/mat, squeeze your abdominal muscles from the navel down before "lifting" your shoulders off the floor, or knees toward your chest. Full sit-ups are discouraged because of the strain they place on the back, and because they do not isolate the work in the abdominal muscles, relying on hip, leg, and back muscles as well. On the other hand, very small movements of 2 to 4 inches work quite well in

isolating the contraction and achieving positive results. These short contractions are strength builders!

## MUSCLE-TENDON-JOINT FLEXIBILITY AND AGILITY

Flexibility and agility make the learning of skiing skills easier, and they reduce the risk of injury during falls.

### Trunk

Think of the trunk as a region of your body to which upper and lower body are hinged. Flexibility exercises should focus on promoting the rotational properties of the lower back, spine, and abdominal muscles. Movements for these areas might include strengthening and slow rotational exercises, and exercises that encourage the gentle elongation and contraction of the spine with complementary action of the abdominals.

*Seated twists*: Sitting comfortably in an armchair or on a bench, keep your spine upright and one arm resting in your lap. Reach across your body with the other arm and slowly twist your entire upper body to one side, keeping your hips and legs stationary. Hold for 10 seconds and return to center. Do to the other side. Perform 5 to 10 times to each side.

### Feet and Ankles

Even though your feet and ankles are held securely within hard-shelled ski boots, they are both very active while skiing. Flexibility exercises should focus on supinating and pronating your feet, and on multidirectional flexion of your ankles.

*Seated ankle work*: Sitting in a swivel chair is best, but another chair or bench would suffice. Slowly rotate your feet laterally at the ankles, side to side. While one foot rolls to the outside (supinates) the other rolls inward (pronates). Hold for a 3-count to each side for 10 repetitions to each side, rest, and repeat again.

*Seated toe and heel raises*: Sitting in a chair or on a bench, feet flat on the floor, alternately lift your toes up, then down, and heels up, then down, to a set cadence (e.g., 1- and, 2- and, 1- and, . . . ). Perform the lift to exhaustion without straining, rest, and repeat once more.

### Calves and Achilles Tendons

Flexing and extending movements of the knees and ankles during skiing puts strain on the calves and achilles tendons. Effective skiing is achieved when ankles and achilles tendons move freely from flexed to more extended positions.

*Wall flex and stretch*: Stand approximately 3 feet from the wall, hands resting on the wall. First, round the back and flex or bend the knees forward, keeping your heels on the floor. Hold for 5 counts, then slowly straighten the legs and *lengthen* the spine; hold for 10 counts. Repeat the two-phase exercise 10 times.

### Quadriceps

The large muscles of the fronts of the thighs (along with the large buttock muscle) are among the chief movers in extending the body while skiing, and holding the lower body in a balanced skiing position.

*Lying on side quad stretch*: Lie on your left side, supporting your upper body on your left forearm. Bend your right leg and grab your right ankle with your right hand. Slowly pull the leg back until you feel a good stretch in your upper thigh. Being careful not to arch your back, hold the stretch for 5 counts. Holding the same position, gently bring your knee a little farther back for additional stretch. Don't hyperextend (overarch) your back. Hold for another 5 counts. Perform three repetitions for each leg.

## Hamstrings

These three muscles in the rear of the leg act as antagonists to the powerful quadriceps; they provide a stabilizing force to the flexion of the lower body while skiing as well as play a primary role in steering the inside ski.

*Straight-leg straddle*: Standing with both feet flat on the floor, separate your legs as far as possible without letting your heels rise. Keeping the spine straight, lean into the forward leg (as if taking a step forward), gradually working your chest toward your quad. Allow your front knee to bend *slightly* if this aids in the stretching. Hold the stretch for 10 counts. Perform three repetitions for each leg.

*Lateral one-legged hops*: Standing on one leg at a time, hop side to side over a ''line'' struck on the floor. To begin, take 3 hops to each side. Gradually build to 25. Perform this with both legs, and be patient—one leg may feel more balanced than the other.

## Knees

The knees are the essential hinges for the coordinated movement of the upper and lower leg. This movement is central to flexion and extension and dynamic balance. Exercises that create simultaneous coordinated movements of both knees side to side, inward movements, half-squat movements, and one-legged in-and-out movements are ideal.

*Lateral dips*: Standing in front of a mirror to watch your exercise form, keep your legs together and bend slightly at the knees. This is a two-phase exercise. The first phase works in a four-position (count) sequence. With hands on hips, press your knees to the right (position/count one), move them back to starting position (position/count two), press them to the opposite side (position/count three), and then back to starting position (count four). Phase two, do the same exercise moving from position one to position three. Perform phase one for 10 times, moving directly to phase two for 20 times. Perform the two-phase exercise twice.

## GETTING ACQUAINTED WITH SKI-SPECIFIC MOVEMENT PATTERNS

For the new skier, it's best to think of this phase of ski fitness as one in which general fitness activities are engaged in with an eye toward movement patterns that will acquaint the body with ski-related movements. As your skiing skills become more developed, your ski-specific moves during other activities will become more dynamic and selective. Consider what you can do while engaged in the following activities:

1. *Cycling*: Instead of leaning your upper body into a turn, try making turns where you keep your upper body fairly upright as you lean (''angulate'') your bicycle into the turn. Use your arms to control the lean of the bike into the turn.

2. *Stairclimbing*: Instead of walking up or down stairs the usual way; walk up sideways, one foot at a time. Do part of the stairway leading with your right foot, then part way leading with your left foot.
3. *Walking or jogging (not running)*: If you feel stable on your feet and surface conditions are predictable, step onto a curb, large rock or elevated structure, and then push off of it laterally. Walking and jogging through dried up riverbeds or creeks provides many opportunities for this activity.
4. *Hopping for dynamic balance*: Play hopscotch, or take walks where you must walk on cracks in the pavement or divisions in the sidewalk.
5. *Static balancing*: When you have to pick up something off the floor, do so by balancing on one leg.

As in skiing, these activities utilize angles created by the ankles, knees and hips—shoulders too—and help you learn to maneuver, walk, or jog through varied terrain. The use of varied terrain and activities to create ski-related movements is great for agility, quickness and balance, and for focusing on foot sensors and the sense of proprioception so important in skiing.

## ADAPT YOUR SKI CONDITIONING

Ideally, if ski conditioning is the path you choose, it ought to begin a solid 2 months before you go skiing. Nonetheless, this is not an ideal world we live in. Maybe you're going to start skiing next week or in a month; there is still something you can do; it's not too late to get in better shape for skiing.

Regardless of the time of the preseason, daily abdominal strengthening and flexibility exercise is more important than anything else. Stamina and endurance, if not already a part of your life (except for abdominals), are not likely to matter much to your learning. Flexibility, however, may preserve your enjoyment of life on and off the slopes.

*Note*. Drawing is based on a photograph of Inga Thompson, skier and world-class cyclist.

# *Step 1* Skiing With Safety In Mind

Safety first, skiing second. In this step you'll learn how to do a basic safety check of your equipment, how to familiarize yourself with your equipment, what your responsibilities are as a skier, how to learn about a ski area and read a ski area trail map, and how to ski safely and prevent injuries.

## WHY BE CONCERNED WITH SAFETY?

Skiing, like any other sport in which you are propelled at variable speeds on equipment to which your body is in some way attached, poses certain risks. Falling, running into other skiers, being run into, getting tangled up with your or another's equipment, even running into trees and other fixed objects are all potential risks of skiing.

The good news is that by preparing at home for your first day of skiing, and by following certain safety precautions on the slopes, you can greatly reduce your risk of injury. And by bringing good skiing sense to your new sport, you'll increase your enjoyment of skiing.

## BASIC SAFETY CHECK

The most important safety features of your equipment to check before going skiing are the boot bindings on your skis. I strongly urge you to have a binding check done at your local ski shop if your first pair of skis is used.

Ski technicians will set the bindings to your boots, making sure you have the correct forward pressure on your boot (i.e., the amount of pressure the heel piece exerts on the whole boot after it is bound into both toe and heel pieces; this pressure is critical to the proper functioning of your bindings). After this, technicians will check toe release clearance and anti-friction pads and then see if your bindings operate correctly at the release setting (''Din'' setting) that corresponds to your age, height, weight, and skiing ability. As a beginner, you have the skiing ability rating of 1 (see Figure 1.1).

Type 1 skier
- Ski conservatively
- Prefer slower speeds
- Prefer easy to moderate slopes

Type 2 skier
- Ski moderately
- Prefer a variety of speeds
- Prefer varying terrain, including most difficult trails

Type 3 skier
- Ski aggressively
- Prefer high speeds
- Prefer steeper and more challenging terrain

**Figure 1.1** Three types of skiers. Beginners (a) are Type 1; intermediates (b) are Type 2; and more advanced skiers (c) are Type 3. *Note.* Information courtesy of United Ski Industries Association, National Ski Retailers Association, and the suppliers of Ess Var, Geze, Look, Marker, Salomon, and Tyrolia ski bindings.

Here are some other safety checks you can do on your own:

1. Examine the metal edges of your skis for protruding sections. Edges are either continuous metal strips that run the length of the ski, or segmented metal strips that collectively run the length of the ski. Neither kind of edge should ever be separated from the base or sidewall of your skis. Similarly, holes in the bases of your skis that go through to sub-base material of any kind may cause an abrupt slowing of the ski, and left unrepaired may lead to further base damage.

2. Examine your boots. Check buckles, straps, tongue attachment of liner (soft inner boot), and general structure of outer boots. Any cracks or breaks? If so, don't use them.

3. Examine your ski poles. Check the baskets, grips, and straps. Is the pole bent? If so, try to straighten it—slowly—or don't use it.

4. Are you prepared for the day's conditions? Check for lip protection, skin protection, eyewear, gloves, hat, comfortable clothing, extra money, handkerchief, and other personal needs. Remember, protection from UV radiation is important whether it's sunny, cold, warm, or cloudy.

After completing your safety check, you're ready to actually begin skiing at home. Skiing begins with seeing yourself as a skier. Put on your ski clothes and take a look at yourself in the mirror. If you like the way you look, you'll feel better about walking out onto the slopes, and you'll take more pride in your effort.

The next step to skiing at home is actually putting on your equipment. Place a sheet on the carpet and go skiing in your living room.

### HOW TO PUT ON YOUR BOOTS

Unbuckle all buckles before putting on your boots. Pull apart the boot's hard shell with your hands, and guide your foot into the boot until your foot is resting fully in the bed of the boot. Pull the tongue up to get a comfortable fit on top of the foot. Close the hard shell flaps over the inner boot, making sure they overlap, without forcing them.

Be sure the outermost tongue flap overlaps the inner flaps. On front-buckle boots, first tighten the buckle that is second from the bottom. Then buckle the bottom buckle, and then the other buckles (see Figure 1.2). On rear-entry boots, tighten any adjustment near midfoot first, and the top ankle buckle last. Wear the

## Beginning to Ski at Home

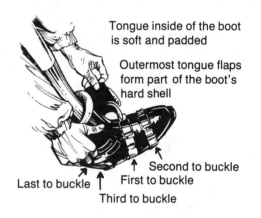

Tongue inside of the boot is soft and padded

Outermost tongue flaps form part of the boot's hard shell

Last to buckle
First to buckle
Second to buckle
Third to buckle

**Figure 1.2**  Parts of the ski boot.

boots for several minutes, and then tighten the buckle adjustments to create a snug fit.

### HOW TO STEP INTO YOUR BINDING

Place your skis on the sheet-covered carpet. The "heel shelf" of the heel binding must be in the "up" position. Using your poles for balance, place the toe of your boot beneath the toe holders of the toe piece, and lining up the heel of your boot in the middle of the heel shelf, press your heel down onto the shelf until the shelf drops to the top of the ski and the heel piece locks your boot in place. At this point, the ski brakes will be fully retracted. To take off your skis, use the tip of your ski pole to press down on the tip of the heel piece to release your boot from the binding (see Figure 1.3, a and b).

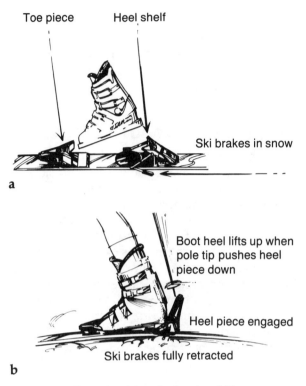

**Figure 1.3**   Engaging (a) and releasing (b) boot bindings.

If you don't correctly align your boot heel with the middle of the heel piece, the heel piece may clamp down when you press down, yet not latch over your heel. Reset the heel piece as if you were taking off your skis, and try again. Be sure your ski brakes retract off the floor (snow) when the heel piece is engaged. If they don't, the skis with the present bindings are unsafe to use. The brakes need repair or replacement.

## HOW TO ACTUALLY BEGIN SKIING AT HOME

After you've familiarized yourself with your equipment, take off your skis and put your ski-ing at home into high gear. Leave your boots on, and walk around the house. If you have stairs to walk up and down, all the better. Do housework with your boots on, take out the trash, go to the bathroom; do whatever you need to do around the house, but try to leave on your boots.

By wearing your boots at home in a variety of circumstances, you actually begin to learn to ski by

- exploring balance while moving in your boots;
- exposing your muscles and nerves to lateral pressures and movements, as well as changes in vertical position;
- exposing your feet and ankles to coordinated movements in response to lateral and vertical challenges;
- exposing your neuromuscular system to the need to adjust the position of the upper body to complement unique balance adjustments in the feet;
- exposing your leg muscles to the challenge of slowing down their coordinated response to these new movements in the feet and ankles, having already been conditioned to responding to faster, and more normal, foot and ankle movements so common in a hurried pace, walking fast, and running; and
- exposing your knee and hip joints to coordinated muscular and neural responses to what may appear as more truncated lower body movements.

All the while, your boot linings are molding to your feet and taking you a step closer to a more comfortable beginning skiing experience. By wearing your boots at home for several hours each of 2 days preceding your first day on the snow, your body is priming itself to more readily adjust to on-the-mountain challenges. Some of these originate from the skis on the snow, while other more fatiguing challenges originate from within your own muscle-control centers, where muscular effort is overused to accomplish on-snow tasks that require more feet than feat.

# Your Responsibilities as a Skier

The National Ski Patrol reminds skiers that there are elements of risk in skiing that common sense and personal awareness can help reduce. The following partial list of advice is endorsed by ski areas nationwide and should serve as a basic guideline for safe and responsible skiing.

1. Ski under control and in such a manner that you can stop or avoid other skiers or objects. Excessive speed is dangerous.
2. When skiing downhill or overtaking another skier, you must avoid the skier below you.
3. You must not stop where you obstruct a trail or are not visible from above (see Figure 1.4).
4. When entering a trail or starting downhill—*look before you begin to ski*—yield to other skiers.
5. All skiers shall use devices to prevent runaway skis—"ski brakes" are built into all modern downhill bindings.
6. You shall keep off closed trails and posted areas and observe all posted signs.

Add these to the list:

7. Be environmentally conscious: Don't litter!
8. Learn about the layout of the mountain: appropriate skiable terrain, restroom facilities, first aid stations, telephone, and food service, and more—learn to read a trail map!

## HOW TO LEARN ABOUT A SKI AREA

Every mountain or ski hill has its peculiarities and local flavor, and if you're going to ski at a new mountain, it behooves you to investigate it beforehand. The best way to familiarize yourself with any new mountain is a guided tour, but there's more to a ski resort than its skiing as depicted through the eyes of your guide.

Another source of information about the mountain and area is local residents who ski there, and who share both the glitter and the grime about the mountain. Yet another method of discovering a mountain is through the printed media: newspapers, magazines, books—

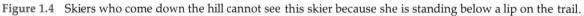

**Figure 1.4**   Skiers who come down the hill cannot see this skier because she is standing below a lip on the trail.

and mountain brochures, the number one source of printed information.

Marketing and public relations divisions of ski areas put their area's best foot forward in these brochures, and along with a trail map, these are excellent reviews of the mountain: its terrain; services; accessibility by auto, bus, train, and airline; and much, much more. Information covered might include the following:

- General resort information
- 24-hour snow phone (call for the day's ski conditions)
- Reservations line
- Guest services office
- Parking shuttles
- On-project transportation
- Transportation from local airports or bus depots
- Lift-ticket prices and multiday packages
- Ski-school prices and lesson options
- Special program notices (e.g., video analysis, race clinics, high-performance clinics, *special first-time skier packages*)
- Rental and repair shop services
- Retail shops on project
- Dining and entertainment opportunities
- Fitness and spa options
- Off-project shuttles and activities
- Cooperative arrangements with neighboring mountains
- Local sites of interest
- A trail map rendering, and description of the mountain as a ski hill

## HOW TO READ A TRAIL MAP

On the map you'll find a legend on the symbols (e.g., "Map Key" or "Key to Symbols") used to detail the location of different facilities on the hill, as well as the location of different chair lifts and the trails or ski runs they service. Chair lifts are generally marked by solid, straight, colored lines (usually red) and are often named on the map. A question in the "Safety Test" at the end of this step will give you an opportunity to learn about the meaning of various map symbols.

Many ski areas will remind you that the degree of difficulty of their runs is classified according to the difficulty within their ski areas, and their rating is to be used as a general reference, noting that weather and snow conditions may alter (often increase) the difficulty of a slope.

The ski runs are generally marked in three colors: black, blue, and green. In the United States, Canada, and Europe, black diamond runs (♦) are the most difficult runs on the mountain, and called advanced and expert runs. Blue square (■) runs are more difficult than beginner runs, and called intermediate runs (in Europe, red runs are intermediate). Green circle (●) runs are the easiest runs on the mountain and are called beginner runs (in Europe, blue runs are the easiest).

Many mountains with extreme steeps and highly challenging terrain lable some runs double black diamond (♦♦) and are for experts only, with extreme caution advised.

Ski maps usually indicate the names of the mountains on which ski runs are cut, indicate elevations, name individual runs, indicate the easiest way down from the top, show boundaries of the ski area's skiable terrain, indicate any closed areas within the boundaries, and offer assorted descriptors of restaurant and snack shop locations on the mountain. Some maps note which lifts may be downloaded—that is, lifts on which you can ride down the hill instead of skiing down. See Figure 1.5, a and b, for two different ski maps.

Some maps will advise you clearly that your right to ski may be revoked at any time due to reckless, out-of-control skiing, or for not obeying posted signs (e.g., skiing in closed areas or skiing out of bounds). The latter may result in a federal citation and U.S. Forest Service fine. Safety first: *Read your trail map!*

## HOW TO SKI SAFELY AND PREVENT INJURIES

The faster you ski and the more demanding the terrain, the greater the risk of higher speed falls, collisions, and overuse sprains and strains. Certainly, the most common injuries for advanced skiers are sprains and strains to the knee.

For beginners, the falls and collisions are of the slow-speed variety. Most are harmless, although slow-speed falls and the like that cause your body to twist and compress into unnatural positions are almost always injury makers. Thumbs are banged up, bumps and bruises may ensue, shoulders get wrenched, legs get pinched, sometimes knees are sprained and banged up, shoulders may even be dislocated.

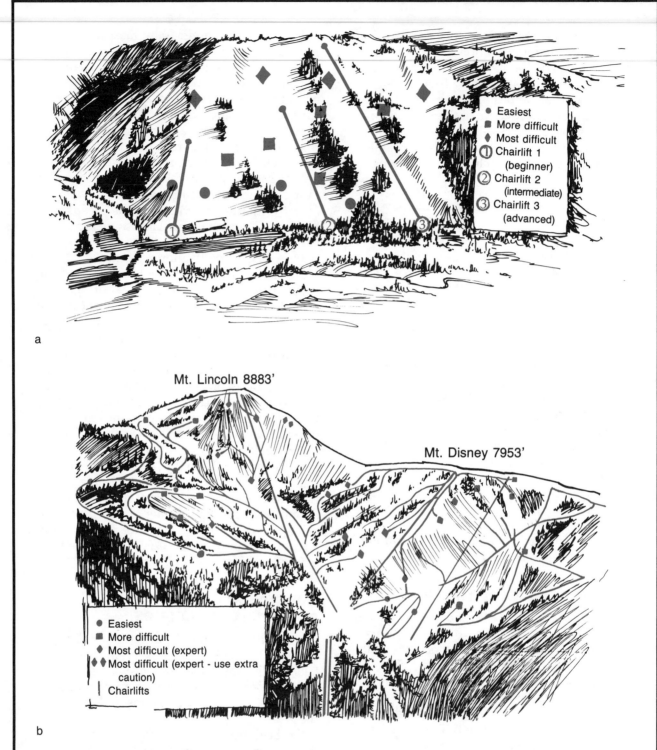

**Figure 1.5** A simple ski map (a) compared to a complex ski map (b).

Bone fractures of the lower extremity are rare among beginners.

Most injuries can be prevented, and not going skiing is not one of the methods. I believe that most injuries in beginning and new skiers are the product of (1) a lack of commitment to learning the sport (which leads to distraction and lack of focus, and the taking of shortcuts); (2) persons exceeding the limits of their present level of physical conditioning and ski readiness (which leads to pushing too hard and too long and creating fatigue at a time when you need alertness and strength, perhaps stamina); and (3) persons attempting to ski beyond their skill level (which leads to taking chances on too-challenging terrain and relying on survival tactics that may lead to injury).

Overall, when the mind is not focused and muscles are slow to respond to myriad stimuli, injury occurs. I advocate eight principles of injury prevention for beginning and new skiers:

1. Follow the guidelines for safe and responsible skiing.
2. Know how to fall and several methods of getting up.
3. Don't ski tired; better to rest and be last than be first to be injured.
4. Be knowledgeable about how your equipment works, and make sure it's properly fitted to your body.
5. Use plenty of sunblock, and use it repeatedly during early days on skis.
6. Check the forecast for the day's weather, and dress appropriately; carry along ''extras'' in case the forecast is wrong.
7. Wear gloves even when it's warm.
8. Listen to your body, respect your present level of fitness, and don't overdo it. Your skiing days may seem short at first; they will get longer.

# Safety Test

It is desirable to know the principles of skiing with safety in mind before embarking on your adventure with downhill skiing. Falls, collisions with other skiers, equipment entanglements, and other possible mishaps are all potential risks. Learn the principles of safety on skis, and you'll make the slopes more enjoyable for you and those with whom you share the mountain. Use the following questions to check your safety knowledge.

## Equipment

1. What's the most important safety feature of your equipment to check before going skiing?
2. What are the components of this feature that are most important to check?
3. What would be a danger sign with respect to the bases or edges of your skis?
4. What should you examine when checking out your boots?
5. What should you examine when checking out your ski poles?
6. Make a checklist of the items you'd need with you on the mountain:
   a. On a cold, cloudy, windy day
   b. On a stormy day
   c. On a bright sunny day
   d. On a bright, sunny, cold day

## Skiing at Home

7. What should you know about putting on and tightening your boots?
8. What should you know about adjusting your boots for a snug fit?
9. What part of your boot goes into the binding first?
10. What position should the heel piece of your binding be in before you step into the binding?
11. How should your ski brakes work when the heel piece is engaged?
12. Is it best to wait until you go skiing to break in your ski boots?
13. Is there any value in getting used to your boots at home?

## Skier Responsibility

14.-18. What are the five responsibilities that apply more to your safe and courteous interaction with other skiers on the mountain?
19.-21. What are the three responsibilities that apply more to your safety and courtesy alone on the mountain?

## The Ski Area and Ski Hill

22. What kinds of information should you want to know about a ski area, and how would you get this information?
23. How do you use a trail map to find out about the best terrain for you to ski? What about how to determine the terrain you should avoid?
24. What other information might you expect to get from a trail map?
25.-40. Match the following trail map symbols with the appropriate meaning:

A. Ski patrol and first aid

B. Emergency telephone

C. Public Restrooms

D. Expert only—use extreme caution

E. Public telephone

F. Most difficult

G. Restaurant

H. Easiest

I. Ticket office

J. More difficult

K. Key lockers

L. Ski accessories

M. Child care

N. Gondola

O. Ski equipment and rental

P. Double chair lift

## Skiing Safely

41. What are the most common injuries for beginning skiers?
42. Can certain injuries be prevented by planning ahead?
43.-49. In addition to the Skier Responsibility Code, what seven other practices can you follow to make your skiing a safer experience?

**Success Goal** = 49 correct answers

**Your Score** = (#) _____ correct

## Answers to Safety Test

1. Boot bindings on your skis.
2. That you have the correct forward pressure created by the heel piece. That you have the correct toe piece clearance between boot and binding. That you have antifriction pads on the bindings' toe pieces. That you have the correct ''Din'' settings on toe and heel pieces.
3. Bases—holes or grooves that go through to the sub-base material. Edges—any sections that are bent or protruding out away from the normal shape of the edge.

4. Cracks or breaks in the hard plastic outershell are a no-no. Check buckles and all fastening attachments, and check the tongue attachment on the inner boot.
5. Any bends in the poles? Are the baskets attached to the poles? What's the condition of the grips?
6. 

|  | a. | b. | c. | d. |
|---|---|---|---|---|
| Lip protection | / | / | / | / |
| Skin protection | / | / | / | / |
| Eyewear | / | / | / | / |
| Gloves | / | / |  | / |
| Hat | / | / |  | / |
| Goggles | / | / |  | / |
| Warm jacket or skiwear | / | / |  | / |
| Lightweight gloves |  |  | / |  |
| Headband | / |  |  | / |
| Face mask |  | / |  |  |
| Neck/head gaiter | / | / |  |  |

7. First open all buckles and fastenings. Pull apart the hard shell to slip your foot into the boot. Pull up the tongue of the inner boot until the boot fits comfortably around your foot, which should be resting on the footbed of the boot. Close the hardshell flaps over the tongue of the inner boot, and correctly overlap the hardshell flaps over each other so the buckles tighten easily. The same principles of correct overlap of hardshell parts and inner boot parts apply to rear-entry boots.
8. On buckle boots, tighten the second from the bottom first, then the bottom buckle, and then the other buckles. On rear-entry boots, tighten any adjustment near midfoot first and the top buckle last. Wear the boots for several minutes, then retighten for a snug fit.
9. The toe.
10. In the "up" position, with the heel shelf exposed.
11. The ski brakes should be tucked up above the ski's edge and next to the heel piece (or, in some bindings, above the edges near the toe piece).
12. No, begin breaking in ski boots at home by wearing them during ordinary household activity.
13. There are many good reasons to begin wearing ski boots at home:
    a. To explore balance while moving in boots
    b. To expose muscles and nerves to lateral pressures and movements and changes in vertical position
    c. To expose feet and ankles to coordinated movements
    d. To expose the neuromuscular system to the need to adjust the upper body to complement balance adjustments in the feet
    e. To expose leg muscles to the challenge of slowing down their response to new movements in the feet and ankles
    f. To expose knee and hip joints to coordinated muscular and neural responses to lower body movements
14. Ski under control and in such a manner that you can stop or avoid other skiers or objects. Excessive speed is dangerous.
15. When skiing downhill or overtaking another skier, you must avoid the skier below you.
16. You must not stop where you obstruct a trail or are not visible from above.
17. When entering a new trail or starting downhill—look before you begin to ski—yield to other skiers.
18. All skiers shall use devices to prevent runaway skis.
19. You shall keep off closed trails and posted areas and observe all posted signs.
20. Be environmentally conscious; don't litter!
21. Learn about the layout of the mountain: skiable terrain, restrooms, first aid, telephone, and other services; learn to read a trail map!

22. How to get there, the variety of terrain, general snow conditions, cost, availability of services like child care, ski school, parking shuttles, food services, ski rental and repairs. Reputation of the mountain. Printed materials, resort brochures, direct contact, magazine and newspaper stories, and personal recommendations are ways to find out about a ski resort.

23. When using a trail map, first consider your level of skiing. If you're a beginner skier, you'll want to examine only beginner terrain (green circle trails). Then when you get on the mountain and feel more comfortable, you may be able to elicit advice from resort personnel on appropriate low-intermediate terrain. You should always avoid terrain where you have no option for getting down if the hill turns out to be too intimidating; be sure of your skills before attempting unknown hills.

24. The location of a vast array of services might be on a trail map, as well as the names and locations of different lifts and ski trails. Visually the map will tell you how you might be able to hook up with different lifts to get around the mountain. Importantly, the map will show you the locations of ski patrol and first aid stations.

25.-40. P, D, E, B, C, F, J, H, N, A, I, K, G, M, L, O

41. Banged-up thumbs, bumps and bruises, wrenched shoulders, slight knee sprains, shoulder dislocations.

42. Many injuries can be prevented by keeping focused on learning, not pushing yourself too far beyond your present level of physical conditioning, and avoiding terrain that's too challenging for your skill level.

43. Know how to fall and several methods of getting up.

44. Don't ski tired.

45. Know how your equipment works and make sure it's properly fitted to your body.

46. Use plenty of sunblock.

47. Check the forecast for the day's weather and dress appropriately.

48. Always wear gloves!

49. Listen to your body; don't overdo it.

# Step 2   Hit the Flats

As a beginner, your mountain should be a molehill—if not literally, then at least figuratively. You can learn so much about how to ski by effectively utilizing almost level terrain. Add to this a slight 20- to 30-foot incline, and you've got the makings of great first-day learning terrain.

In this step, you'll learn to walk and stand "full-footed" in your boots, and to swivel your boots. You'll learn how to maneuver on level terrain. You'll learn to use the edges of your skis to provide support and control slippage as you walk up or down slight hills, you'll learn the difference between a "flat" (easy gliding) ski and an "edged" (controlled gliding) ski, and you'll discover the most balanced position for your body when skiing.

## WHY IT'S IMPORTANT TO HIT THE FLATS

It's difficult to learn the basics of skiing, which are really offensive in nature, when the body is stuck in a defensive posture. Starting out on the "flats" provides comfortable, safe terrain and reduces the influence of gravity that propels skiers downhill. Be certain: You don't need a chair lift, lift ticket, ski instructor, or for that matter, a ski resort to learn to ski by my method. All you need to begin is a patch of snow-covered ground the size of a school bus and a giant-size molehill.

Beginning skiing does not mean steep hills, long chair-lift rides, lightning speeds, and rough-and-tumble falls. All of these scare prospective skiers and have little or nothing to do with the kinds of experiences needed to begin skiing. The skills you must acquire to learn to ski are learned best, and most safely, on flat terrain.

As I refer to them, the "flats" are that school bus-size piece of snow-covered real estate on which you will learn most of the basics of maneuvering on your skis. For my daughter, our driveway was her first ski school, and I, her first surface tow. Although this is not absolutely necessary the first time out, it would be beneficial if the flats included a 20- to 30-foot-long hill of slight descent (i.e., if you rolled a ball down the hill, it would travel very slowly and not appear to pick up much speed). This slight hill will round out the learning environment such that you'll learn flatland maneuvers better and be able to use the same piece of real estate for the lessons in Steps 3, 4, and 5.

## HOW TO STAND "FULL-FOOTED" IN YOUR BOOTS

When you're moving on skis, your feet feel different pressures depending on how you've positioned your feet within the boots and how balanced you stand on your skis. When standing full-footed in your boot, you have the most control and stability when walking in boots alone or when stepping and gliding with skis underboot.

When standing full-footed in your boots, you feel pressure along your whole foot in the bottom of the boot, with pressure about equal in the toes and heels and along the arch and ball. To accomplish full-footedness, you must relax your thighs so your knees will relax and bend slightly forward, and you must relax your ankles so they can accommodate the settling of your feet. As well, you must relax your feet.

Full-footedness is the most important skill to develop at this time. As you progress, you will learn to selectively manipulate the position of your hips, legs, and feet to create different pressures in your boots at diferent times during skiing. Still, your basic home base while skiing at all levels is standing full-footed in your boots (see Figure 2.1).

*Figure 2.1  Keys to Success:*
*Standing Full-Footed in Boots*

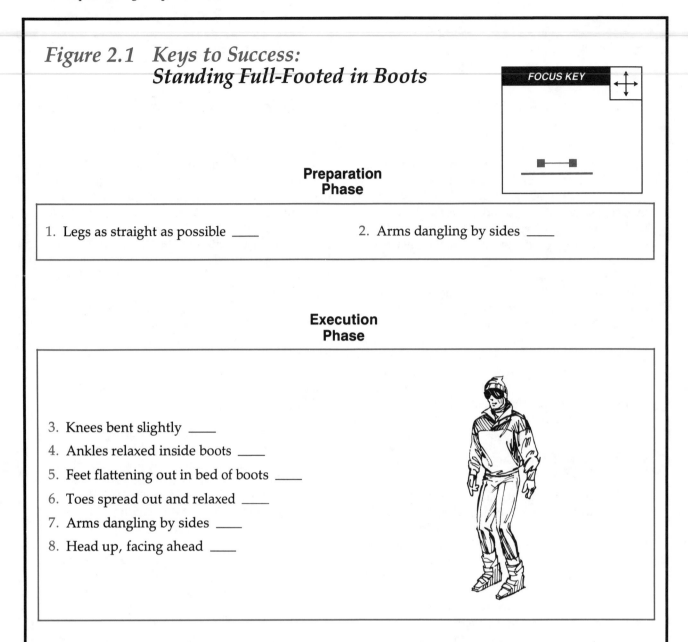

FOCUS KEY

**Preparation
Phase**

1. Legs as straight as possible ____

2. Arms dangling by sides ____

**Execution
Phase**

3. Knees bent slightly ____
4. Ankles relaxed inside boots ____
5. Feet flattening out in bed of boots ____
6. Toes spread out and relaxed ____
7. Arms dangling by sides ____
8. Head up, facing ahead ____

# Detecting Errors in Full-Footedness

Errors in developing full-footedness in the boot are usually due to poor boot fit, lack of ankle and foot flexibility, and too rigid a body from the knees up.

| ERROR ⊘ | CORRECTION |
|---|---|
| 1. Your boots are too tight. | 1. Have the boots widened at a ski shop; have footbed work done to the boots at a shop; wear a thin pair of socks. |
| 2. Your boots are too big. | 2. Try to get another boot; footbed work might help. |
| 3. You lack flexibility. | 3. Do daily flexibility exercises for your feet and ankles. |
| 4. Your knees, legs, and upper body are rigid. | 4. Use poles for balance; use mind and body relaxation techniques; open your frame of reference to ease your psychological fear (see Appendix). |

## HOW TO USE YOUR SKI POLES ON THE FLATS

To put full-footedness into practice with skis on, you must first learn how to use your ski poles to maneuver on the flats, assist gliding forward and in reverse, and climb and descend slight hills.

In general, there are basic guidelines to using ski poles to accomplish the above goals:

1. Hold your poles on top, in the way you'd grip a gearshift knob, with the tip of the pole grip against the middle of your palm (see Figure 2.2).

**Figure 2.2**  Pole grip used on the flats.

2. When you are moving forward, put the tips of your poles in the snow 3 to 6 inches to the sides and behind your boots.
3. When you are moving in reverse, put the tips of your poles in the snow outside of and near the tips of your skis.
4. When you have stopped and are facing down a decline, place the tips of your ski poles in the snow well in front of you, and brace yourself by locking your elbows, or resting your elbows against your midsection while gripping the poles in maneuvering position.
5. When you are stopped on an incline, with your back facing downhill, place the tips of your ski poles in the snow well behind you, and brace yourself by locking your elbows or resting the grips of the ski poles against your buttocks.

Figure 2.3 shows how to use your ski poles to assist gliding both forward and backward.

*Figure 2.3  Keys to Success:*
**Maneuvering With Poles on the Flats**

FOCUS KEY

Face forward ———→

Face backward  ←———

**Preparation
Phase**

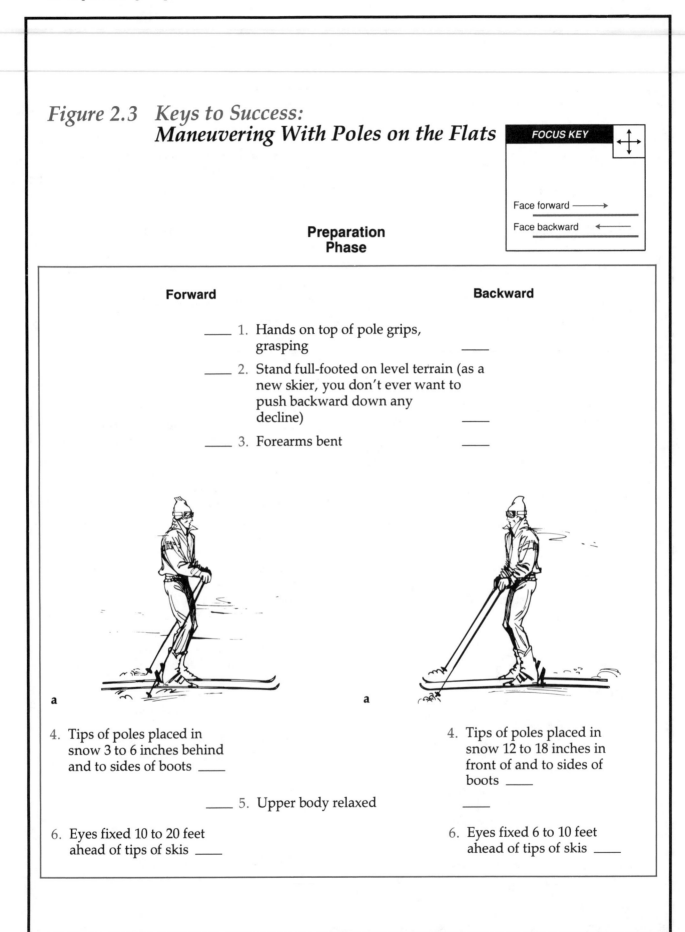

**Forward**                                      **Backward**

_____ 1. Hands on top of pole grips,
grasping                        _____

_____ 2. Stand full-footed on level terrain (as a
new skier, you don't ever want to
push backward down any
decline)                        _____

_____ 3. Forearms bent                           _____

a                                                a

4. Tips of poles placed in          4. Tips of poles placed in
snow 3 to 6 inches behind          snow 12 to 18 inches in
and to sides of boots _____        front of and to sides of
boots _____

_____ 5. Upper body relaxed          _____

6. Eyes fixed 10 to 20 feet          6. Eyes fixed 6 to 10 feet
ahead of tips of skis _____         ahead of tips of skis _____

## Execution Phase

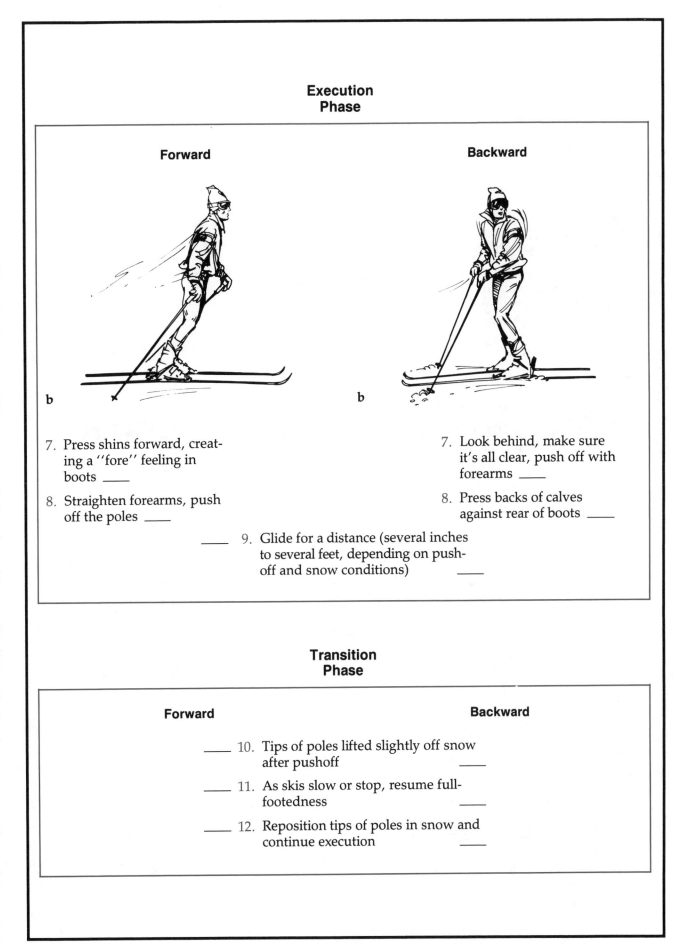

**Forward**

**Backward**

b

b

7. Press shins forward, creating a "fore" feeling in boots ____

8. Straighten forearms, push off the poles ____

7. Look behind, make sure it's all clear, push off with forearms ____

8. Press backs of calves against rear of boots ____

____ 9. Glide for a distance (several inches to several feet, depending on push-off and snow conditions) ____

## Transition Phase

**Forward**

**Backward**

____ 10. Tips of poles lifted slightly off snow after pushoff ____

____ 11. As skis slow or stop, resume full-footedness ____

____ 12. Reposition tips of poles in snow and continue execution ____

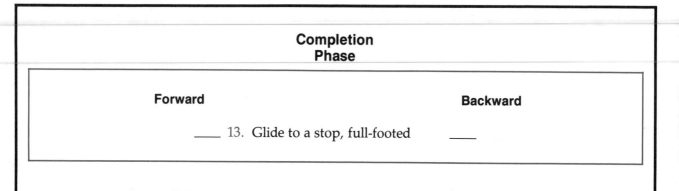

**Completion
Phase**

| Forward | | Backward |
|---|---|---|
| ____ | 13. Glide to a stop, full-footed | ____ |

## HOW TO INTEGRATE THE ELEMENTS OF FULL-FOOTEDNESS AND EDGE CONTROL

Skiing is the controlled movement of metal-edged skis on a snowy surface. Because you are bound to the skis, you are the instrument of control—you make skiing happen! Full-footedness helps you control your skis on level terrain. Then, you can use your edges to create platforms (as in the sidestepping drills) to control your movement on inclines and declines (see Figure 2.4).

Put the two skills together with the pivoting of your boots, and you near the moment when you'll be ready to start gliding, stopping, and turning. Learn the difference, now, between a "flat" ski and an "edged" ski, and you'll learn the basics of gliding on skis in control.

*Figure 2.4   Keys to Success:
Maneuvering With Poles on
Slight Hills*

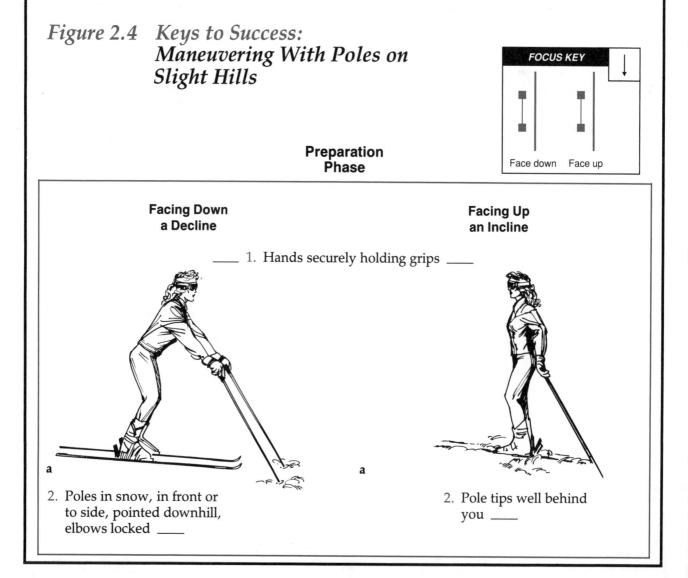

**Preparation
Phase**

FOCUS KEY

Face down    Face up

| Facing Down a Decline | | Facing Up an Incline |
|---|---|---|
| ____ | 1. Hands securely holding grips | ____ |

a

a

2. Poles in snow, in front or to side, pointed downhill, elbows locked ____

2. Pole tips well behind you ____

## Execution Phase

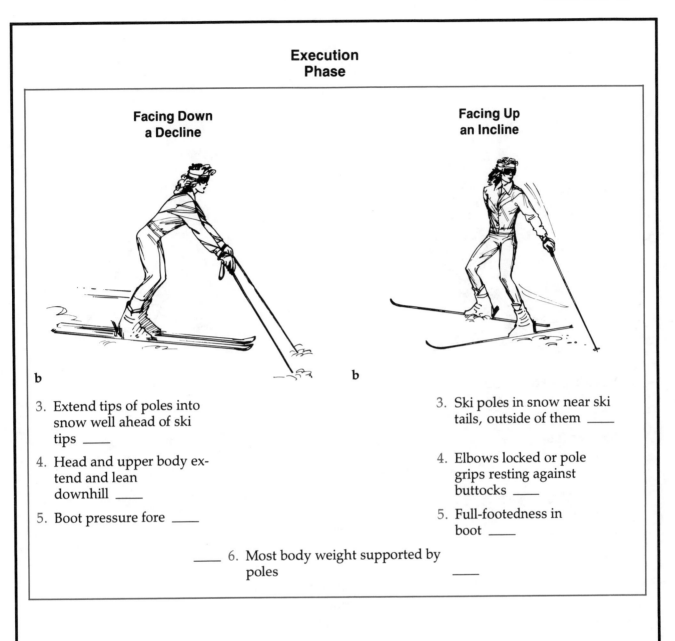

**Facing Down a Decline**

**Facing Up an Incline**

b

b

3. Extend tips of poles into snow well ahead of ski tips ___

4. Head and upper body extend and lean downhill ___

5. Boot pressure fore ___

___ 6. Most body weight supported by poles

3. Ski poles in snow near ski tails, outside of them ___

4. Elbows locked or pole grips resting against buttocks ___

5. Full-footedness in boot ___

___

## Transition
## Phase

### Facing Down
### a Decline

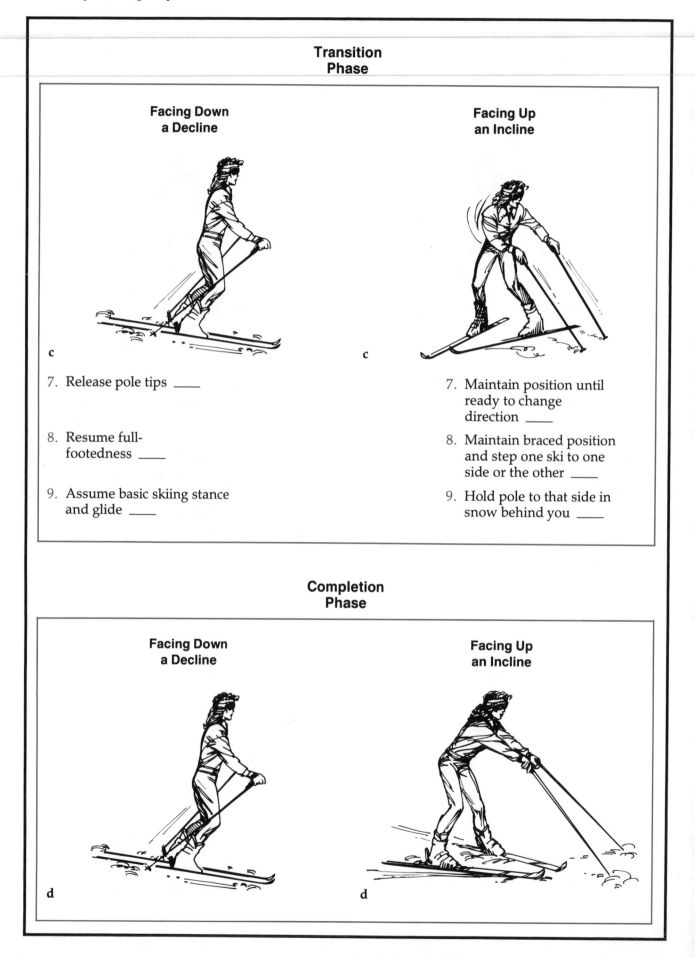

c

7. Release pole tips ____

8. Resume full-footedness ____

9. Assume basic skiing stance and glide ____

### Facing Up
### an Incline

c

7. Maintain position until ready to change direction ____

8. Maintain braced position and step one ski to one side or the other ____

9. Hold pole to that side in snow behind you ____

## Completion
## Phase

### Facing Down
### a Decline

### Facing Up
### an Incline

d

d

| **Facing Down a Decline** | **Facing Up an Incline** |
|---|---|
| 10. Glide to a stop, full-footed ____ | 10. Twist upper body around to side of stepped ski and swing around other pole to position facing down a decline ____ |
| | 11. Lock elbows and hold position ____ |

# Detecting Pole-Use Errors

Pole-use errors usually relate to the placement of the poles relative to the position of the skis.

**ERROR**

**CORRECTION**

| ERROR | CORRECTION |
|---|---|
| 1. Your push lacks power. | 1. Your poles may need to be farther behind your boots or closer to the tips of your skis; check your pole grip; strengthen your forearms. |
| 2. Your glide is short. | 2. Make sure you're standing full-footed and give a good forearm push; lengthen your arm when pushing backwards. |
| 3. The tips of your poles get caught under your skis. | 3. Keep your poles positioned wide; look up and well in front of and behind you. |
| 4. You are slipping on hills. | 4. Keep your elbows locked when facing downhill and when your poles are braced against your buttocks; your poles are not far enough downhill, either in front of or behind you. |
| 5. Your stance is unstable. | 5. Extend your upper body and arms down the hill. |

# Full-Footedness and Maneuvering Drills

## 1. Fore-Aft Boot Walk

With ski boots on, take a leisurely walk on the snow, taking 10 paces forward and 10 paces in reverse.

With emphasis on placing your body weight toward the front of your boots (fore), bend your knees and press your shins against the tongue of the boot. You want to feel your toes and the tops of your feet pressing into the front portion of the boot. Take 10 paces forward with your weight fore.

With the emphasis on placing your body weight toward the back of your boots (aft), bend your knees and press the backs of your lower calves against the rear of your boots. At the same time, point your toes toward the front of your boot. Your foot should feel elongated in your boot, with your body weight aft. Take 10 paces forward.

Stand upright. Stand fore, then aft, then back in the middle. Stand full-footed and walk forward and in reverse.

**Success Goals** = 8 steps full-footed forward and 4 steps full-footed in reverse

**Your Scores** =

  a. (#) _____ steps forward

  b. (#) _____ steps in reverse

## 2. Ball of Foot Pivot

Focusing on the movement of your boots while standing "full-footed" in them, pivot off the heels of your boots as you swivel out and in; keep your boots in parallel association, and swivel your toes. Do this until you synchronize the movement of both boots and can do it both quickly and slowly. Use your poles for balance as needed.

**Success Goals** = 5 pivots to each side

**Your Scores** =

  a. (#) _____ pivots to right side

  b. (#) _____ pivots to left side

## 3. Level Sidestep

Gripping your poles for maneuvering on the flats, place them in the snow well to the sides of your skis, and use them to aid balance as needed. On flat terrain, and at all times maintaining full-foot-edness, take lateral parallel steps with your skis, one ski at a time, to the left, then back to the right. To execute the stepping, lift the entire length of the ski you want to step several inches off the snow, and step it 4 to 10 inches to the side and place it back on the snow. Think of stepping over a thick rope that's as long as your ski.

The task is to keep the boot and ski you're step-ping, parallel to the ski remaining on the snow. To do so, maintain full-footedness as you direct the outside of your knee and the outside edge of your boot to move laterally. To complete a step, main-tain full-footedness with the trailing foot, and as you step the ski, focus on directing the inside of the knee and boot to follow the lead of the first ski. In a very real way, these movements are rudiments of dynamic skiing.

**Success Goals** = 8 side steps to the right and 8 side steps to the left

**Your Scores** =

   a. (#) ____ of side steps to right

   b. (#) ____ of side steps to left

## 4. Sidestep Up

Using your poles for balance (see ''How to Use Your Ski Poles on the Flats'') apply the lateral step-ping movement to ascending a slight hill or incline. To ascend the incline, take short (3- to 6-inch) lateral steps up the hill. To keep the ski that's not stepped from slipping when the other is lifted off the snow, you must create a platform on the snow beneath it. To keep the lead ski from slipping when the follow ski is lifted, it too must have a platform be-neath it.

Staying full-footed, use your ankles to control the lateral position of your skis. By tilting your ankles and knees into the hill, you create two plat-forms that edge your skis in the snow, give you stability, and prevent you from slipping down the hill.

As with the lateral step, step first with the leg that's headed up the hill, as if you're stepping over a thick rope, tilting your ankle into the hill as you lift your knee. As you lift your uphill knee, it's essential to maintain the platform beneath your other ski, the downhill ski, by keeping that ankle tilted into the hill. This movement pattern is known as sidestepping, and it is a reliable method of climbing hills at all levels of skiing.

**Success Goals** = 5 side steps up an incline to the right and 5 side steps up an incline to the left

**Your Scores** =

a. (#) _____ of side steps to the right

b. (#) _____ of side steps to the left

## 5. Sidestep Down

Do as in Drill 3, except step down a hill, using platforms to control descent. Again, these are rudiments of dynamic skiing. The degree to which you tilt your ankles, knees, and even hips into the hill depends on the steepness of the hill. The steeper the hill, the more the tilt of the ankles (and knees and hips).

**Success Goals** = 4 side steps down to the right and 4 side steps down to the left

**Your Scores** =

a. (#) _____ of side steps to the right

b. (#) _____ of side steps to the left

## 6. Creating "Flat" and Edged Skis

On level terrain, with skis on, stand with skis hip-width apart. Using your poles for balance, put your skis on edge by tilting both ankles and knees to one side, then the other.

The inside edge of your ski is the edge next to your big toe; the outside edge, the edge next to your little toe. When your skis are on neither inside nor outside edge, they are "flat" and have the greatest gliding ability. Sometimes you want your skis to be flat, sometimes slightly edged, sometimes dramatically edged. Full-footedness allows you to control all of these situations, and move in and out of them as needed. In sequence, practice putting your skis on edge, making them flat as you

stand full-footed in your boots, pushing yourself forward with your poles to glide a short distance on your skis. Remember to maintain a flat ski. The muscular feeling of skiing on a flat ski, full-footed, is one of relaxed legs and feet.

**Success Goal** = To glide as far as you can on a flat ski (3-foot glide—okay, 5-foot glide—good, or 8-foot + glide—excellent)

**Your Score** = (#) _____ feet

## 7. *Fore-Aft Experiment With Flat Skis*

When maneuvering on beginner terrain, your body will be exposed to many variations in slope and challenges to your balance. You will find yourself "fore" and "aft" on your skis in the process of getting used to moving in balance. It's most important for you to teach your body the feeling of being centered and full-footed over your skis. Use the following sequences to explore the extremes of fore and aft on skis. You will find both of these extremes uncomfortable, particularly when maneuvering. Still, you need to feel this discomfort to find your most balanced point on your skis. This is the position from which you will learn to ski.

a. Assume a fore position on your skis by leaning forward, straight-legged, with shins against your boots. From this exaggerated (uncomfortable?) position forward, maintain a flat ski, push, and glide forward. Next, try to take lateral steps in this fore position.

b. Assume an aft position on your skis by leaning back, straight-legged against the back of your boots. From this exaggerated (uncomfortable?) position aft, maintain a flat ski, push, and glide. Next, try to take lateral steps in this aft position. Try lateral steps without poles.

c. Continue to experiment with fore and aft positions, and find the most comfortable position for you to push and glide and to take lateral steps. This position should be one of full-footedness and be comfortable, because it is the basis of your skiing stance from which all beginning skills will emerge.

**Success Goal** = Subjective feeling of balance and the ability to position yourself full-footed on command

**Your Score** = _____ Awareness of balance and ability to position full-footed on command (yes or no)

# Maneuvering Skills
# Keys to Success Checklists

Ask a friend who skis to observe your ability to step laterally on the snow: level, uphill, and downhill. The observer can use the checklist items in Figures 2.1, 2.3, and 2.4 to evaluate your progress. Ask this same observer to examine the way you use your poles to assist your maneuvering. Do you appear balanced; are you able to move at will on the flats?

# Step 3   Downs and Ups of Falling

Three concerns of beginning skiers are (1) "If I fall will I get hurt?" (2) "If I fall will I be able to get back up?" and (3) "If I fall will I look foolish?" The answers, in truth, are that (1) it's possible but not likely; (2) most certainly yes, but you must know how in more than one language; (3) only to persons who can't remember when they learned to ski.

In this step you'll learn what to expect from falling and the situations most associated with falling for beginning skiers and how to prevent them. As well, you'll learn how to fall safely, and four methods for getting up after falling on a hill.

### WHY FALLING ISN'T FOOLISH

In expert-level race training, for example, falling is looked on not as curse, but as counsel. Racers are not foolish for falling, because they are exploring the dimensions of their racing edge. They are going for it in varied conditions under as many different race situations as they can. They want to be just as strong on the "perfect" course as they are on the "devil's" course. They are not embarrassed to fall when they look to the fall as a teacher; they are, of course, disappointed when they believe they didn't need to fall, and variably distraught when a fall takes them out of the money.

Skiers who get embarrassed when they fall are still doing too much of the skiing with their ego. Consequently, they have taken away the teaching potential of falling. As a beginner, you will find it valuable to remember that falling is expected—that many watching your fall have fallen too, and likely, continue to fall. The best skiers in the world fall in practice, and they fall in World Cup and Olympic competition. If you want to learn to ski, don't think about not falling, but about including falling as a normal—and safe—part of your skiing experience.

### WHAT TO EXPECT FROM FALLING

Generally, falling in beginning skiing is more like toppling over than burning in a fiery crash.

One of the common feelings beginners experience once they're on their way down is one of being powerless to do anything to stop their fall. In a way, this feeling of powerlessness is a blessing, because to fall well in skiing, you must not resist the fall.

It is unwise to ski with the idea of preventing all falls, because it tends to make you ski tense and static. Nevertheless, it is good to resist a fall when muscular and joint strength can prevent the fall. To be sure, most injuries to beginning skiers happen during slow-speed falls where the skier tries to resist the impetus of the fall once the body has passed the point of no return and the fall is inevitable.

### HOW TO FALL SAFELY

Most of the time, you realize you are about to fall, and when you accept this, you can use a very brief, often instinctual, movement to minimize ill effects of the fall (see Figure 3.1). To protect your wrists, I've found it helpful for persons to make a fist (but not to tense the arm) as soon as they feel they're headed down. At the same time, you've got to let the fall happen; "relax, don't resist" are three important words.

In general, you want to direct your body away from your skis and poles. It can be dangerous to try to kick or otherwise slide your skis away from your body as you're falling, because this makes it difficult to relax the rest of your body. Most of the time this means fall to the side of your skis, preferably uphill of your skis. Do not sit down on the tails of your skis, or the skis might scoot ahead out of control. You want to fall with a limp body. Loose and limp legs will accommodate many distortions incurred by skis getting caught up in the snow. To protect body joints, try to roll away from the skis if it's likely you're about to fall on them.

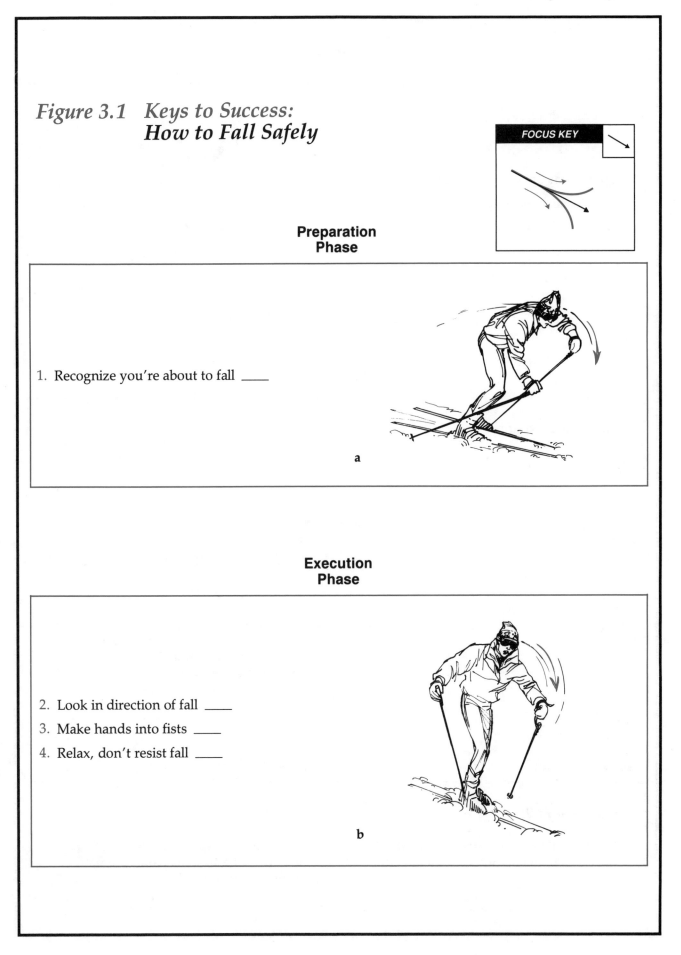

*Figure 3.1  Keys to Success:*
*How to Fall Safely*

**FOCUS KEY**

**Preparation
Phase**

1. Recognize you're about to fall ____

a

**Execution
Phase**

2. Look in direction of fall ____

3. Make hands into fists ____

4. Relax, don't resist fall ____

b

## Transition
## Phase

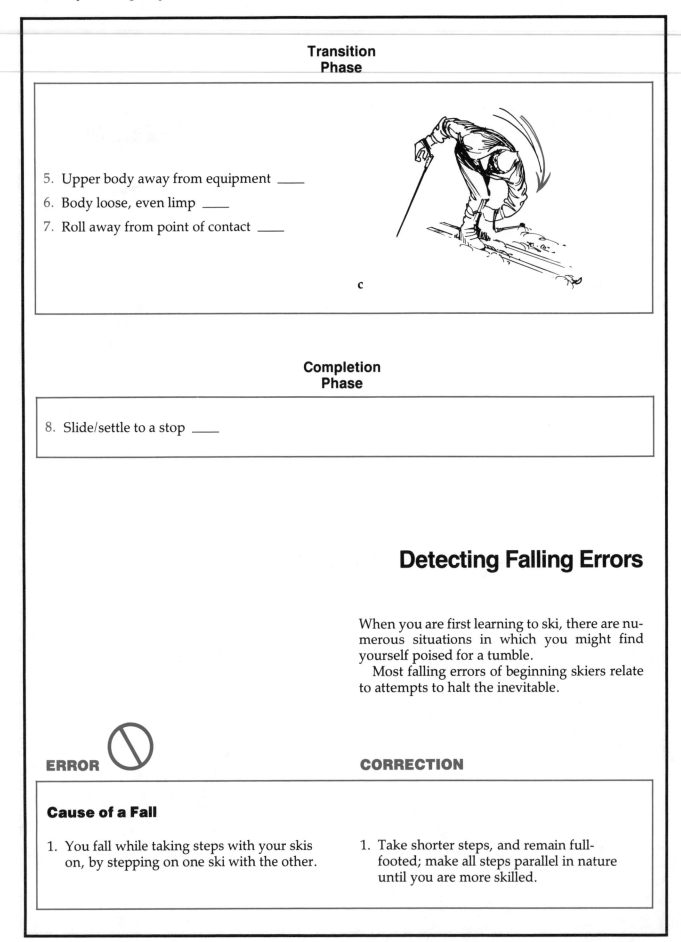

5. Upper body away from equipment ____
6. Body loose, even limp ____
7. Roll away from point of contact ____

c

## Completion
## Phase

8. Slide/settle to a stop ____

# Detecting Falling Errors

When you are first learning to ski, there are numerous situations in which you might find yourself poised for a tumble.

Most falling errors of beginning skiers relate to attempts to halt the inevitable.

**ERROR**                                    **CORRECTION**

### Cause of a Fall

1. You fall while taking steps with your skis on, by stepping on one ski with the other.

1. Take shorter steps, and remain full-footed; make all steps parallel in nature until you are more skilled.

ERROR

**ERROR**                                          **CORRECTION**

2. You fall when a pole tip gets caught under an advancing ski.

2. Keep your pole tips well to the sides of your boots, and pull the tips slightly off the snow during poling.

3. You fall out of fear of speed; your skis get too close together.

3. Be patient with challenges; don't put yourself in situations where you'll move too fast without the ability to slow and stop.

4. You fall because skis aren't "flat" at the same time; one is "edged" and the other flat, leading to misdirection.

4. Practice making a "flat" ski, an "edged" ski, and gliding "full-footed."

5. Your ski tips cross while gliding.

5. Keep your upper body relaxed; maintain full-footedness; look ahead and not at your skis.

## Reaction to a Fall

1. You are trying to break the fall with your hands.

1. Make fists with your hands.

**ERROR**                                    **CORRECTION**

2. You grab your sunglasses and other gear to protect them from damage.

3. You try to halt the fall with your poles.

2. Let the glasses and gear fall where they might; wear leashes for glasses.

3. Give in to inevitable falls, and forget about trying to stop yourself with your poles—this leads to injury.

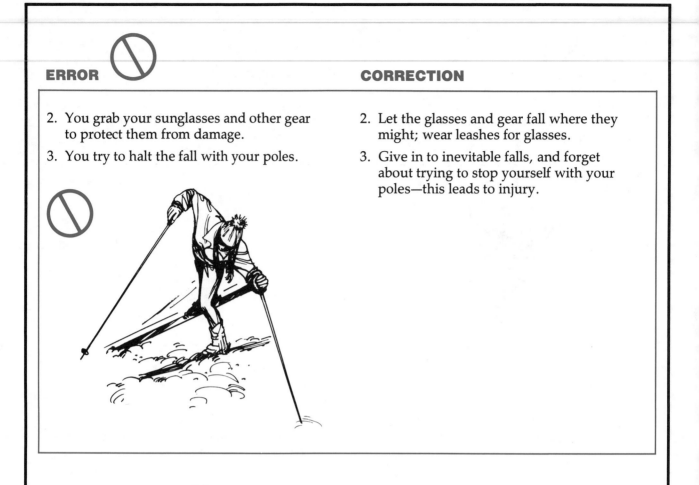

## HOW TO GET UP SAFELY

It's just as important to get up safely after falling as it is to safely fall. After the snow has settled, think over how you want to get up. Untangle yourself from equipment, and gather any obvious belongings within reach (e.g., glasses, hat, earmuffs). On beginner terrain, you might find that taking off one or both skis is the best method available. There are two other methods, however, that you should learn, because as soon as you get off of beginner terrain, taking off a ski or two may be more dangerous than convenient.

When getting up, the most important thing to do is minimize slippage. Do so by placing your skis on their edges down the hill from you and across the hill as when you are sidestepping (see Figure 3.2). If only one ski is on, place it in this position for support. If both skis are off, and you must put one on, and you're on a hill, you have to dig out a small trough into which the ski can be placed so you can put it on. Place the ski in the trough, and using your poles for support, step into the binding. Then as you stand braced on this ski, you can put on the other ski. Always make sure the second ski you put on is uphill, and you are using the downhill ski for support.

Most times when you get up, you want to first position yourself close to the middle of your skis in a crouched position, your hips uphill of the skis. From here you can either walk your hands around to the tips of your skis and push yourself up, or use your poles as an aid to leveraging yourself up off the snow. In both methods, after maneuvering yourself into position to actually rise up, you want to take a deep breath and then exhale forcefully as you exert to push yourself up, either to a semicrouched position or to a completely upright position. After you get up, it's important to do an equipment check. Make sure boot buckles are closed, boots are properly in bindings, poles are not bent, glasses or goggles are not broken. Pick up anything that may have fallen out of your pockets or off you during your fall.

## Figure 3.2 Keys to Success:
### How to Get Up Safely

FOCUS KEY

### Preparation Phase

1. Choose how to get up ____

2. Get free of equipment ____

3. Position skis or single ski ____

4. Make trough in snow if needed ____

### Execution Phase

#### Method 1

1. Take off one ski ____

2. Secure it on the snow ____

3. Brace yourself with hands or poles ____

4. Edge ski downhill for support ____

5. Use free leg to stand up ____

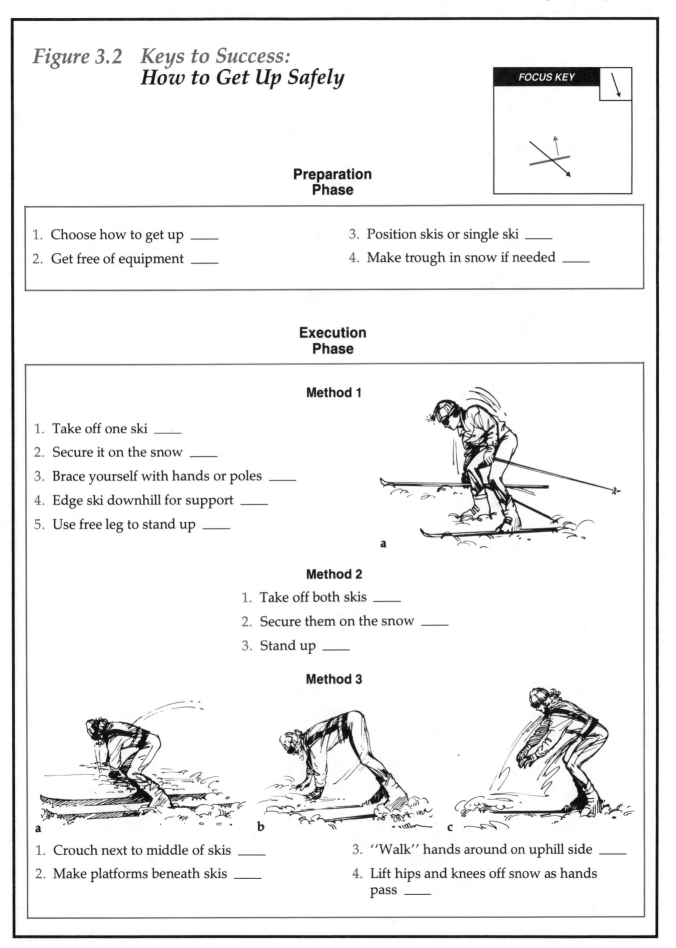

a

#### Method 2

1. Take off both skis ____

2. Secure them on the snow ____

3. Stand up ____

#### Method 3

a          b          c

1. Crouch next to middle of skis ____

2. Make platforms beneath skis ____

3. "Walk" hands around on uphill side ____

4. Lift hips and knees off snow as hands pass ____

5. Straighten arms as you "walk" hands to ski tips ___

6. Exhale as you rise up ___

7. Simultaneously push off with hands ___

8. Right the body by contracting buttocks ___

**Method 4**

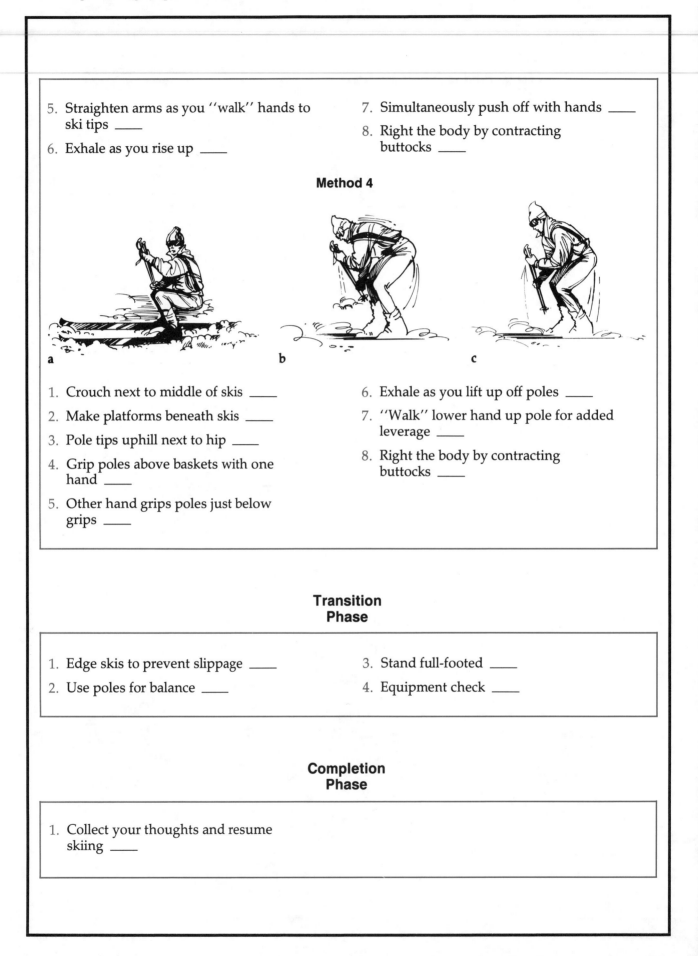

a            b            c

1. Crouch next to middle of skis ___

2. Make platforms beneath skis ___

3. Pole tips uphill next to hip ___

4. Grip poles above baskets with one hand ___

5. Other hand grips poles just below grips ___

6. Exhale as you lift up off poles ___

7. "Walk" lower hand up pole for added leverage ___

8. Right the body by contracting buttocks ___

**Transition Phase**

1. Edge skis to prevent slippage ___

2. Use poles for balance ___

3. Stand full-footed ___

4. Equipment check ___

**Completion Phase**

1. Collect your thoughts and resume skiing ___

# Detecting Errors in Getting Up on a Hill

Most problems are related to improper preparation and positioning when readying yourself to get up.

**ERROR** 🚫

**CORRECTION**

| ERROR | CORRECTION |
|---|---|
| 1. You are sliding backward or forward when getting up. | 1. Make sure your skis are across the fall line. |
| 2. You lack momentum when you rise and lift up; your lift is awkward, and you lose your balance. | 2. Your pushoff point is too fore or too aft of your hips and midsection. |
| 3. You experience repeated failure to rise and get up after falling. | 3. This is a wrong method for you; try an easier method. |
| 4. Your poles fall or slip. | 4. Plant poles firmly and hold tightly above the baskets and on the grips. |
| 5. You fall downhill over your skis. | 5. Keep your body uphill of your skis. |
| 6. You can get only part way up. | 6. Strengthen your quadriceps; review technique; use a more forceful execution. |

# Getting Up After Falling Drill

## 1. The Get-Up!

Although I don't favor practicing what you really want to avoid (i.e., falling), it is useful to start from the fallen position and practice getting up. Go through methods 1, 3, and 4 on variable terrain, and method 2 for getting up on flat terrain.

**Success Goal** = If it takes you only one attempt to get up, for each method, you've scored excellent; 2 or 3 attempts is good; 4 or 5 attempts suggests you need more practice with technique and perhaps more muscle power

**Your Score =**

Method 1 _____

Method 2 _____

Method 3 _____

Method 4 _____

# Getting Up After Falling
# Keys to Success Checklists

Ask a friend to observe your skills at getting up using the four methods on a variety of terrains. Checklists in Figures 3.1 and 3.2 will assist your observer's evaluation of how safely you approach the risk of falling, and how safely you get up, and thus provide corrective feedback for you. The areas of chief concern to safely falling are protecting your wrists, having a loose and relaxed body, and directing your body away from equipment. The areas of chief concern to safely getting up are a stable base of support to prevent slippage, a focus on what you need to do to get up, and a coordinated effort to get up with a distinct moment of exertion when actually getting up.

# Step 4   Using a Basic Skiing Stance

Anyone can stand up on skis—at least for a moment—and then try to glide down a mild or more challenging descent. The difference between anyone slapping on the skis and trying it, and you trying it, is that you've gone through Steps 1, 2, and 3, and others may not have. Onlookers will attest to the different look you and others will have when making a downhill glide on skis. You will look confident and balanced, while the "unschooled" may look like they're in an ongoing struggle with balance, or like they're using their arms to help guide their skis.

In this step you'll learn the importance and *essentials* of a basic skiing stance and how to develop it. You'll learn a new method for climbing hills that adds great versatility to your use of beginner terrain, and you'll learn how to take a downhill glide on skis, comfortably, balanced and fully in control.

## WHY YOU NEED A BASIC SKIING STANCE

Our bodies are balanced during movement by a series of levers and joints: feet hooked to legs through ankles; lower legs to upper legs, through knees; and so forth. Balance is created when various levers and joints align themselves according to the demands of the situation. In skiing, basic (as well as advanced) skill development evolves from the same foundation of a basic skiing stance. If that foundation is strong, subsequent skiing skill development will flow more easily and be long-lasting. Conversely, if that foundation is shaky, skill development will be fragmented and inconsistent and short-lived.

The basic skiing stance you'll learn in this step was designed with the goal of creating balance and stability through the alignment of various levers and joints. The good news is that all the calculations have been done for you, and all you have to do is connect the dots to create a basic skiing stance for yourself.

The *essentials* to a strong foundation are these:

- "Full-footedness"
- Appropriate use of ski poles for maneuvering

- Fore-aft balance
- Ski maneuverability
- The ability to make skis flat as well as make them edged to form platforms
- Relaxed upper body with slight forward curve in the spine
- Slight forward flexion of the knees and ankles
- Balanced arm and hand position
- Scenic eyes
- Slight forward hip projection

## WHY ARE THE ESSENTIALS SO IMPORTANT?

"Full-footedness" is the cornerstone of stability on skis. When you are able to make a ski flat, you can better control its gliding and, ultimately, its turning. Similarly, when you can edge a ski, you can create platforms and thus control maneuvering on hills and, ultimately, the quality of your turning and stopping.

An upright body with rounded back and slight forward hip projection and lean help you regulate the pressures applied to your ski from your weight as well as from outside forces, like gravity, that pull you down the hill. Moreover, it helps you maintain balance over your skis, and it is the kind of basic skiing stance you need to develop as a skier. When skiing downhill, you will find it easier to shift your balance fore or aft as needed for better ski control and turning if your stance displays the foregoing *essentials*.

Fore-aft balance neutralizes the ill effects of too much weight on either end of the skis, and aids in your adaptability to different conditions and on-snow challenges. The position of your hands and arms with ski poles in hand regulates the position of the upright upper body and degree of lean, and assists coordination between upper and lower body.

Your "scenic eyes" help to keep you focused on looking ahead rather than staring at the tips of your skis in a telekinetic trance, hoping to influence their direction through mind alone. Further, "scenic eyes" keep you focused on the skiing environment, particularly other skiers, and thus promote safer skiing.

## HOW TO EXECUTE
## A BASIC SKIING STANCE

With skis on, stand on level terrain, skis parallel and 6 to 10 inches apart. Think of your skis as two balance points. Stand tall, legs stiff, eyes ''scenic.'' To form a basic skiing stance, allow your legs to relax enough at the knees and ankles to create the feeling of full-footedness and a fore-aft balance. Grip your poles for skiing by grasping the grip handles with your palms, your fingers wrapped around the grip as if you were gripping a bicycle grip. With molded grips, grasp the grip with its soft rubber flaps resting against the backs of your gloves. With poles with straps, place your hand through the bottom side of the strap, and grasp the grip so the strap is between your palm and the grip.

Let the poles dangle by your sides next to your hips. Move your hands 6 to 8 inches away from your hips, and with elbows locked, raise up your hands and arms to a point where the tips of your poles have been dragged to a position alongside the middle of your boots.

Leaving your poles in the snow 6 to 8 inches to the sides of your boots, unlock your elbows, let your arms bend slightly, and relax your wrists, hands still gripping the poles for skiing. The present position of your hands and arms is the desired position for a basic skiing stance.

To complete the stance, maintain hand and arm position and use your forearms and wrists to lift the tips of the poles several inches off the snow. There is no exact distance the poles need to be off the snow, and as your skills improve, this distance will vary depending on many factors you'll discover as you progress in the sport.

Next, tighten your abdominal muscles and project your hips slightly forward. Round off the spine of your upper back just enough to relax any pressure, and maintain ''scenic eyes.'' Take a deep breath. As you exhale, shake loose your arms and make little bounces up and down like there are springs in your knees and ankles. Return to a basic skiing stance, relaxed and balanced (see Figure 4.1).

## Figure 4.1  Keys to Success:
## Basic Skiing Stance

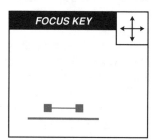

**FOCUS KEY**

**Preparation
Phase**

1. Upright on skis, 6 to 10 inches apart ____

2. Maneuvering grip on poles ____

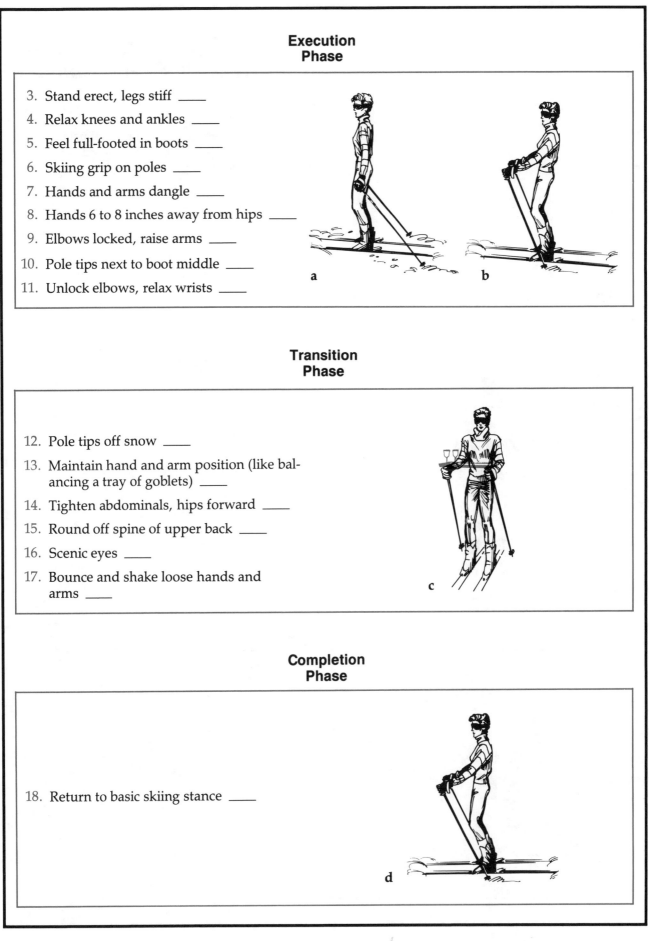

## Execution Phase

3. Stand erect, legs stiff _____
4. Relax knees and ankles _____
5. Feel full-footed in boots _____
6. Skiing grip on poles _____
7. Hands and arms dangle _____
8. Hands 6 to 8 inches away from hips _____
9. Elbows locked, raise arms _____
10. Pole tips next to boot middle _____
11. Unlock elbows, relax wrists _____

a

b

## Transition Phase

12. Pole tips off snow _____
13. Maintain hand and arm position (like balancing a tray of goblets) _____
14. Tighten abdominals, hips forward _____
15. Round off spine of upper back _____
16. Scenic eyes _____
17. Bounce and shake loose hands and arms _____

c

## Completion Phase

18. Return to basic skiing stance _____

d

# Detecting Errors in a Basic Skiing Stance

Most errors relate to a lack of overall balance in the position of body parts distributed over the skis, and a stiffness in muscles.

**ERROR**                                     **CORRECTION**

1.  Your hands and arms are too low.

1.  Readjust your stance and check where your ski pole tips touch the snow.

2.  Your back is slouched over too much.

2.  Look up; think of ''scenic eyes''; tighten your abdominal muscles and project your hips forward.

**ERROR**                                          **CORRECTION**

3. Your lower body and hips are leaning back.

3. Relax your knees and ankles; put your hands and arms in position; check your upper spine for forward curve; tighten your abdominal muscles and project your hips forward.

4. Your arms and shoulders feel too tight or stiff.

4. Unlock your elbows, relax your wrists.

## WHY CLIMBING SKILLS ARE IMPORTANT

Very often during your skiing experience you'll have to negotiate slight hills in either direction to enter chair-lift lines, maneuver to a different trail, make a restroom stop, or gain access to other mountain facilities. When beginning to ski, you need to know how to climb hills so you can gain access to good learning terrain without having to ride a chair-lift or surface tow.

## HOW TO EXECUTE THE HERRINGBONE WALK

In Step 2 you learned how to sidestep up and down slight hills. These are effective hill climbers, but as you gain more confidence and want to ascend hills more quickly, there is another approach to climbing that blends all of the skills you've learned thus far: the herringbone walk (see Figure 4.2).

With the herringbone walk, you're using the inside edges of your skis to form platforms that are like steps you use to walk up a hill. Knees and ankles must be relaxed and slightly bent. Your ski poles are gripped for maneuvering and used both to help propel you up the hill and to protect you from slipping down the hill—so they are always behind you and down the hill from your skis.

Form a "V" with your skis and, leaning slightly into the hill, begin stepping one ski at a time, lifting the ski 3 to 5 inches off the snow and stepping 3 to 8 inches up the hill. As the incline increases, roll your ankles and knees to the insides of the skis to create more edging and sturdier platforms beneath the skis. As each ski is stepped, the pole that corresponds to that ski is simultaneously moved accordingly up the hill. In these moments of transition, brace your weight entirely on the opposite ski and pole. It is important that you look up the hill to your intended destination, and not down at your skis.

## Figure 4.2   Keys to Success: The Herringbone Walk

FOCUS KEY

### Preparation Phase

1. Basic skiing stance ____
2. Maneuvering grip on poles ____
3. Tips of poles behind boots and skis ____
4. Body leaning slightly forward ____

### Execution Phase

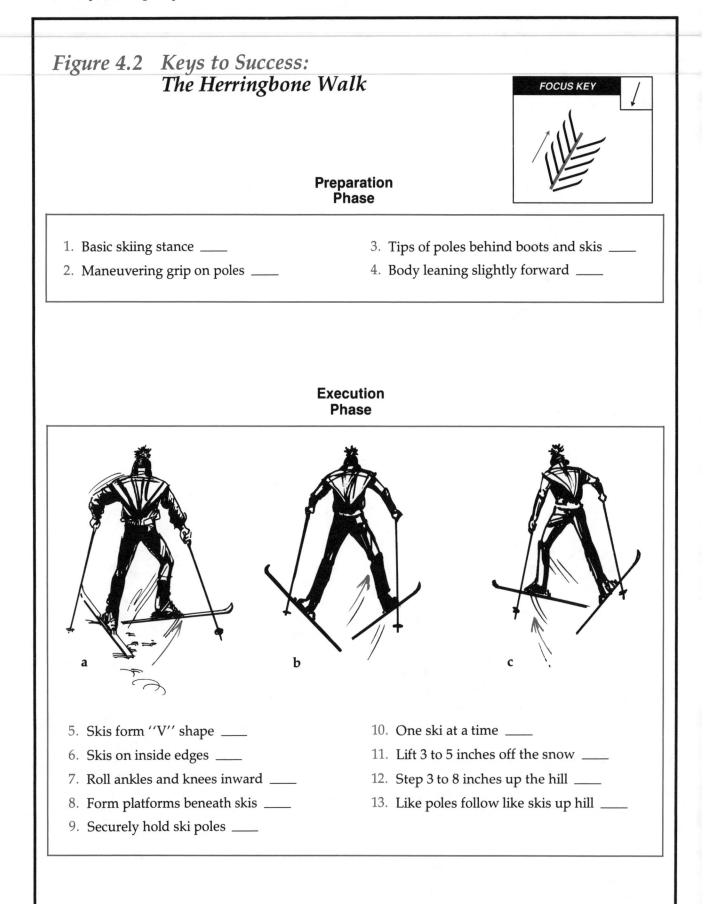

a                    b                    c

5. Skis form ''V'' shape ____
6. Skis on inside edges ____
7. Roll ankles and knees inward ____
8. Form platforms beneath skis ____
9. Securely hold ski poles ____
10. One ski at a time ____
11. Lift 3 to 5 inches off the snow ____
12. Step 3 to 8 inches up the hill ____
13. Like poles follow like skis up hill ____

**Transition
Phase**

14. Head up, scenic eyes ____

15. Skis stepped sequentially ____

16. Rhythmic breathing ____

**Completion
Phase**

17. Destination is reached ____

18. Appropriate maneuvering skills applied ____

# Detecting Errors in the Herringbone Walk

Most errors are related to timing and coordination, and practice time is essential to remedy these.

**ERROR**

**CORRECTION**

1. You are tripping over your skis by stepping one ski onto the other ski's tail.

2. You are stepping on your ski poles.

3. You are dropping your ski poles.

4. Your skis are getting caught on the inside edge when being stepped uphill.

5. Your skis are slipping downhill between steps and while you are stepping.

1. Take slower, more deliberate steps.

2. Keep your poles well to the side of and behind the skis.

3. Keep a firm grip on the poles.

4. Lift your skis higher off the snow; don't drag your skis uphill.

5. Make sure your skis are edged on the inside when they are on the snow and as soon as they touch the snow.

## WHEN TO PUT YOUR BASIC SKIING STANCE INTO ACTION

There are five prerequisites for safely gliding downhill on beginner terrain:

1. A basic understanding of your responsibilities as a skier.
2. The ability to get into a basic skiing stance on demand (this assumes that you are comfortable and balanced on your skis, and that your body has "memorized" the feel of the basic skiing stance).
3. The ability to climb slight hills and control slippage on inclines and declines through the use of your poles along with appropriately edging your skis.
4. The ability to make your skis "flat" while moving.

5. The proper selection of terrain on which to test your basic skiing stance.

## HOW TO GLIDE ON SLIGHT HILLS

This is very specific: Your first glides on skis should be on slight hills that level off at the bottom and allow you enough room to glide to a stop without having to do anything but stay in your basic skiing stance. Hills that have no "runout" tempt you to control your body and equipment in any way you can to stop or slow yourself at glide's end, and this is counterproductive to learning to ski comfortably in a basic skiing stance. Figure 4.3 shows the Keys to Success for a straight run and glide on a slight hill.

## Figure 4.3  *Keys to Success: The Straight Run and Glide*

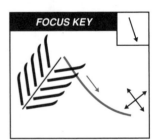

**Preparation Phase**

1. Climb hill of your choice \_\_\_\_

2. Position yourself at top \_\_\_\_

3. Get into basic skiing stance; check balance \_\_\_\_

4. If hill so dictates, brace yourself with poles in front until ready to begin glide \_\_\_\_

a

## Execution
## Phase

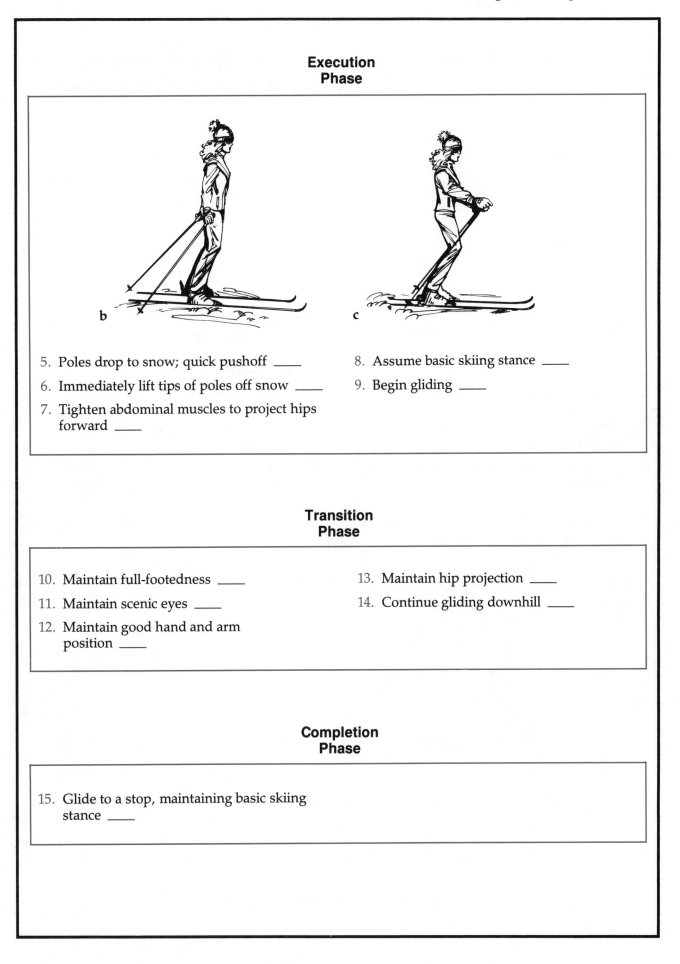

b

c

5. Poles drop to snow; quick pushoff \_\_\_\_

6. Immediately lift tips of poles off snow \_\_\_\_

7. Tighten abdominal muscles to project hips forward \_\_\_\_

8. Assume basic skiing stance \_\_\_\_

9. Begin gliding \_\_\_\_

## Transition
## Phase

10. Maintain full-footedness \_\_\_\_

11. Maintain scenic eyes \_\_\_\_

12. Maintain good hand and arm position \_\_\_\_

13. Maintain hip projection \_\_\_\_

14. Continue gliding downhill \_\_\_\_

## Completion
## Phase

15. Glide to a stop, maintaining basic skiing stance \_\_\_\_

# Detecting Errors in Gliding in a Basic Skiing Stance

The principal problems relate to balance being jeopardized by the lack of proper body-part positioning in response to the variables *movement* and *acceleration*.

**ERROR**                      **CORRECTION**

1. Your hands and arms drop.

2. Your eyes and head are facing the tips of your skis.

3. The tips of your skis cross, or your skis collide in front of you.

4. You feel you're being pulled out of control by the skis.

5. Your ski poles are picking along in front of you; you're in a defensive posture.

1. Check the positions of your poles.

2. Look up; have scenic eyes.

3. Make a wider stance, with your skis starting farther apart.

4. Relax your knees and ankles; curve your upper spine forward; keep your hips forward; check your fore-aft balance.

5. Resume proper hand and arm position; relax and glide.

6. Your skis turn; they won't go straight.

7. One leg or foot dominates the other, causing your body to lean and the skis to go crooked.

6. Seek full-footedness; make both skis ''flat.''

7. Redistribute your body weight more evenly to both skis.

# Climbing and Gliding Drills

## 1. Slow Herringbone Walk and Glide

Select a slight 15- to 20-foot hill and begin climbing with the herringbone walk technique (review Figure 4.2). Make sure that you take deliberate steps up to avoid stepping on your skis or poles or slipping downhill because of lack of edging.

Then glide down the hill using the straight run and glide technique (review Figure 4.3). Use your basic skiing stance both during your glide and while slowly coming to a stop.

Take a brief break, and repeat this process as many times as you need to achieve what feels to you to be (a) error-free climbing, and (b) a comfortable and balanced glide.

**Success Goals** =

   a. 5 unimpeded climbs up the hill

   b. 5 comfortable and balanced glides to a stop

**Your Scores** =

   a. (#) ____ unimpeded climbs up the hill

   b. (#) ____ comfortable and balanced glides to a stop

## 2. Fast Herringbone Walk

Repeat the previous drill, except ask a partner to time your climbs from preselected start and stop locations. Climb as quickly as you can to the top. Then, glide down using correct technique. Switch roles with your partner so that you become the timer while your partner climbs and glides to a stop. Use the timing of climbs to test your ability to coordinate arm and leg movements while maintaining balance.

**Success Goals** =

   a. 5 quick, unimpeded climbs up the hill

   b. 5 comfortable and balanced glides to a stop

**Your Scores** =

   a. (#) ____ quick, unimpeded climbs up the hill

   b. (#) ____ comfortable and balanced glides to a stop

## 3.  *Fast Herringbone Walk and Glide*

Move to another hill that is steeper or longer. Repeat the previous drill, now asking your partner to time both your ascent and your descent. Try to go as fast as you can (your time for this should be less than your time in the previous drill). Remember to alternate roles with your partner between each trial.

**Success Goals =**

   a.  5 quick, unimpeded climbs up the hill
   b.  5 quick, comfortable, and balanced glides to a stop

**Your Scores =**

   a.  (#) _____ quick, unimpeded climbs up the hill
   b.  (#) _____ quick, comfortable, and balanced glides to a stop

## 4.  *Glide for Distance*

Select a steeper hill yet to climb. Push off the glide in balance, using the basic skiing stance for as far as you can before coming to a stop. Use an approximate distance to measure the length of each glide, for example, five ski lengths, or seven ski lengths, and so forth.

**Success Goals =** Record the longest distances of 5 out of 10 glides

**Your Scores =**

   a.  (#) _____ ski lengths
   b.  (#) _____ ski lengths
   c.  (#) _____ ski lengths
   d.  (#) _____ ski lengths
   e.  (#) _____ ski lengths

# Basic Skiing Stance
# Keys to Success Checklists

Ask a friend to use the checklist items within Figures 4.1 through 4.3 to evaluate your balance points in the basic skiing stance while you are motionless, while you are climbing, and while you are gliding. The areas of most concern are a stable upper body, skis held hip-width apart, and "scenic eyes" maintained.

# Step 5  Learning to Slow to a Stop

Suppose you were on the road alone, in wide-open spaces—what would it be like to ride a bicycle or drive an auto there without brakes? Wild, perhaps dangerous, maybe scary. What about riding a bike or driving a car without brakes on a crowded road? That would be dangerous, scary, and irresponsible. Not only would you place your life and limb at risk, you'd be doing likewise for anyone within striking distance.

In this step you will learn additional responsibilities of the beginner skier, and why learning to slow to a stop is a crucial step in learning to ski. You will be introduced to the essential turning skill of steering. Using steering, you will learn how to make a wedge skiing stance. From this skiing stance, you will learn how to control your downhill glide and how to slow to a stop. At this point in your learning to ski, the wedge is the single most important transition from feeling like a beginner to feeling like a skier.

## BEGINNING SKIER'S ADDITIONAL RESPONSIBILITIES

As soon as you consider taking your skis to the mountain, you must assume the responsibility to ski safely and courteously. The Skier Responsibility Code in Step 1 is a useful guide for your days on the mountain as a skier. In the early learning process, you have additional responsibilities:

1. *Know how to stop*! Until you learn to slow to a stop, you are a hazard on the mountain. If you cannot stop, you should not be skiing!
2. Be courteous.
3. Look around you before you move, whether carrying skis, attempting drills, or skiing.
4. Learn how to use surface lifts; don't expect it to be automatic.
5. Learn how to use chair lifts, but don't use chair lifts until you know how to glide, turn, and slow to a stop.

## WHY IT'S IMPORTANT TO KNOW HOW TO STOP

The importance of knowing how to stop seems self-evident, but many beginners think skiing is all about moving down the hill. Beginning skiing is gliding, turning, and slowing to a stop, just as expert skiing is some form of gliding, turning, and stopping. Knowing how to slow to a stop is the foundation for acquiring a host of skiing skills, and knowing how to control your speed helps you learn in several ways:

- It allows you to feel more confident and less afraid of going down hills.
- It makes you freer to explore more of the beginning terrain in control and thereby further develop skills that manipulate gliding speed without your having to stop.
- It assists you in learning to turn by modifying stopping skills.
- It introduces you to basic upper level skills that will be important weeks and months later.
- Because it helps you control your skiing speed, you are more able to familiarize yourself with the skier traffic on the hill, as well as make yourself a safer skier.

## WHY STEERING IS IMPORTANT TO STOPPING

The manipulation, direction, or guiding of edged and flat skis with the feet and lower legs is the turning skill called *steering*, and is **the most important turning skill used at all levels of skiing**. Learn to steer skis with feet and lower legs, and you will be able to guide skis into, through, and out of turns, whether the skis are flat, edged, or in the air.

In earlier steps, you learned that a flat ski moves easily on the snow, forward, backward, or to either side. You also know that the position of your feet and legs influences the flatness of a ski. When your ankles are perpendicular to the slope of a hill, your skis are flat. When your ankles are tipped into the slope, or tipped to resist the pull of gravity or the pull of centrifugal force, they are edged. Thus, sometimes an edged ski is more important to your balance, stability, and movement than a flat ski. For example, you need edged skis to climb hills, to turn, for getting up after falling, and to slow to a stop!

## WHY THE WEDGE IS CRUCIAL TO STOPPING

Certainly, one way to stop is to intentionally fall, but this is ill-advised most of the time because you're often out of control once you "bail out" of your skiing stance. Slowing to a stop from a wedge skiing stance is the preferred method to learn, because it incorporates the same basic skiing skills that are the foundation of polished skiing style.

To learn to slow to a stop, you must learn to steer your skis into a wedge skiing stance. When you want your skis to move with the least resistance, you want them to be flat; flattened skis are more easily steered while in motion. When you want to slow the movement of gliding skis, you must alter their degree of flatness.

When you press your body weight down onto your skis through the flexing of your knees and ankles, there's a higher concentration of pressure on your skis. If you tip your ankles slightly up the slope, or into the hill (anywhere but down the hill from you), at the same time as you direct your skis across the slope of the hill, you create edging that will control speed.

Conversely, when you want to reverse the slowing process, you must release the pressure on your skis and neutralize the edging by extending your legs and making your ankles (boots) perpendicular to the snow, thereby flattening your skis. The manipulation of both your feet and your lower legs, knees included, will assist the righting of your boots and flattening of your skis. In the end, all manipulation of skis from edged to flat to fore to aft is the product of or prerequisite to steering to stop or to turn.

## HOW TO EXECUTE A WEDGE SKIING STANCE

A wedge skiing stance begins with skis flat, 6 to 8 inches apart, in parallel position on level terrain. Stand on an 8-foot-by-8-foot patch of smooth snow. Icy or clumpy snow or terrain with ridges would make the formation of the wedge more difficult to control. Grip your poles on top and place their tips in the snow well to the sides of the forebodies of your skis for balance. Look up with scenic eyes and stand relaxed in a basic skiing stance, knees and ankles flexed slightly forward.

To form a wedge, extend your legs as you steer the tips of your flat skis together, a few inches apart. At the same time, steer the tails of your skis 2 to 4 feet apart, forming a wedge or "A" shape (the distance between the tails will vary depending on size of the wedge, your height, and the length of your skis).

The focus in making a wedge should be on your feet! Twist your feet—toes in, heels out—and if your skis are flat, you will make a wedge. But you cannot twist only your toes, or brush out only your heels; they must be steered together. To make a wedge, steer your skis slowly, not abruptly, to simulate the formation of a wedge as it occurs when gliding (see Figure 5.1). Make a wedge in slow motion, and experience the steering power in your feet!

Because of your position on level terrain, your skis should be only faintly on their inside edges with your legs only slightly angled toward the inside of the wedge. To complete the wedge formation, let your knees and ankles settle back to a slightly flexed position (basic skiing stance) and place your hands and arms in a basic skiing stance.

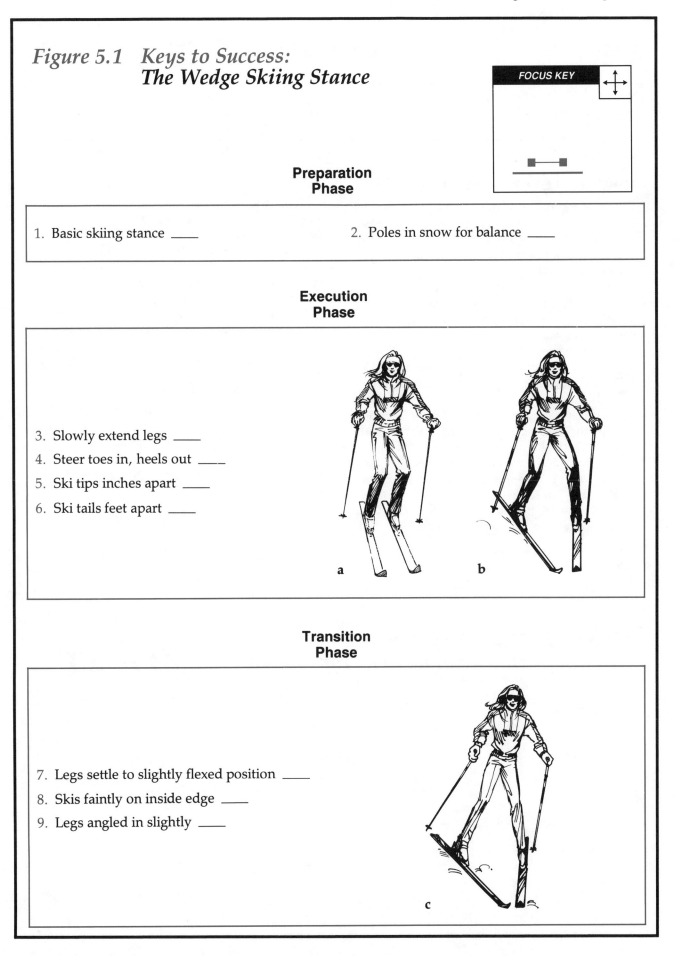

## Figure 5.1 Keys to Success: The Wedge Skiing Stance

**FOCUS KEY**

### Preparation Phase

1. Basic skiing stance ____

2. Poles in snow for balance ____

### Execution Phase

3. Slowly extend legs ____
4. Steer toes in, heels out ____
5. Ski tips inches apart ____
6. Ski tails feet apart ____

a          b

### Transition Phase

7. Legs settle to slightly flexed position ____
8. Skis faintly on inside edge ____
9. Legs angled in slightly ____

c

## Completion
## Phase

10. Return to basic skiing stance \_\_\_\_

11. Flatten skis \_\_\_\_

### HOW TO SLOW TO A STOP

When you glide or ski down a hill, you are in a basic skiing position. The basic skiing stance was a learning tool for stationary practice and laid the biomechanical framework for how you should stand while skiing. So, henceforth, any reference to ''skiing stance'' is a reference to stationary balance; any reference to ''skiing position'' is a reference to gliding or skiing with the body balanced.

From a basic skiing position, glide 15 to 20 feet down a slight slope (e.g., your practice hill), and gradually steer your skis into a wedge with the intention of slowing to a stop. As you do, concentrate on distributing your body weight through your lower legs to the inside edges of both skis at the same time. Just as you divide your body weight when kicking a ball, divide your body weight between your legs and apply it to your skis.

As the wedge is formed, gradually flex your knees and ankles slightly inward and forward. In this way you create more pressure on your edged—and wedged—skis, and greater slowing. You are using another turning skill, angulation, to keep your body weight uphill of the edged skis. Keeping the bottoms of your skis between your body and the downslope of the hill creates moving platforms beneath your skis that serve to slow your descent.

When you form these braking platforms gradually by slowly steering your skis into a wedge, you slow to a stop. The more abruptly the wedge is formed, the more immediate the halting of the skis. Abrupt wedges may lead to unnecessary falls. The more gradually the wedge is formed, the easier it is to control gliding speed (see Figure 5.2). Learning to steer the skis to different degrees of edging while gliding in a wedge skiing stance is the central skill necessary for gliding in control and slowing to a stop.

## Figure 5.2   Keys to Success:
### How to Slow to a Stop

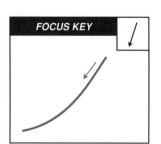

FOCUS KEY

## Preparation
## Phase

1. Downhill glide in basic skiing position \_\_\_\_

## Execution
## Phase

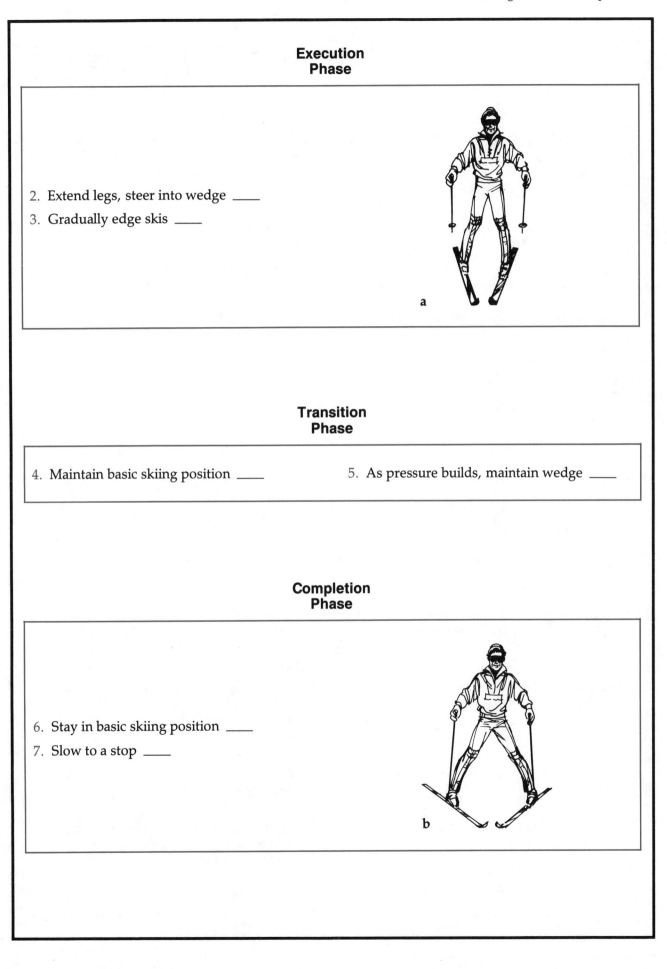

2. Extend legs, steer into wedge ____
3. Gradually edge skis ____

a

## Transition
## Phase

4. Maintain basic skiing position ____          5. As pressure builds, maintain wedge ____

## Completion
## Phase

6. Stay in basic skiing position ____
7. Slow to a stop ____

b

# Detecting Wedge, Gliding, and Stopping Errors

Errors in making a wedge usually relate to a lack of physical commitment to steering both skis and improper timing of the flattening of the skis prior to making the wedge. Errors in gliding and stopping usually relate to a fear of speed (see Appendix A) that leads to panic and stress that cause skiers to lock up muscularly and forget what they need to do.

**ERROR** 🚫                                   **CORRECTION**

1. One ski is less wedged than the other.

2. Your skis get caught on their outside edges when they are brushed apart.

3. The tips of your skis cross, or your skis collide at their forebodies.

4. Your wedge is too narrow; your skis don't slow.

5. Your wedge is ineffective; fear sets in, and you crash.

1. Practice brushing out that one ski only; then try both skis again.

2. Keep your ankles and knees flexed slightly inward as you brush them out; extend your legs to begin; make sure your skis are flat.

3. As your toes go in, your heels must be brushed out; keep your legs apart, knees under hips; don't look at the ski tips; your skis should not be overly edged on inside edges (see Figure 5.1).

4. Make a larger wedge; place the skis on their opposing edges (their edges are your brakes).

5. Maintain a toes-in, heels-out position; remain full-footed, and control the entire length of your skis.

| ERROR | CORRECTION |
|---|---|
| 6. Your hands and arms appear to be chasing equilibrium, and they look like they're being used as rudders. | 6. Relax your knees and ankles and stay full-footed; separate your skis into a wider stance; maintain scenic eyes and keep your hips projected forward. |
| 7. You panic and lock up. | 7. Go to a flatter hill; practice wedge and slow-to-a-stop basics. |
| 8. One ski is dominant over the other, causing it to cross over the other. | 8. Evenly steer your skis; balance your hands and arms; project your hips evenly. |
| 9. You have no control over the tips of your skis. | 9. Stand more forward (you're aft if this is happening). |
| 10. You are yanking or lifting your skis to form a wedge. | 10. Be patient with the steering power of your feet/boots. |
| 11. You are using your ski poles as brakes or steering aids (which will lead to poor skill development and injury). | 11. Position your ski poles in basic skiing position; go back to the basics and a flatter hill. |

# Wedge and Stopping Drills

## 1. Single-Ski Circular Walk

With one ski on and using ski poles and your free boot to propel you, step and glide, step and glide, until you cover 20 feet, and then make a circle with the ski to the outside. With your right ski on, you'll make a counterclockwise circle; left ski on is a clockwise circle. As you make the circle, you'll have to twist your boot (toe-in, heel-out) to move the ski around the rim of the circle. This will help your lower leg and foot muscles, nerves, and tendons learn this subtle steering maneuver.

After completing the circle, glide another 20 feet and make another circle. Repeat this several times until you're making a twisting motion with each step around the circle. It's not enough to start twisting your toe inward, or heel outward. You want to steer your ski with your whole foot (toe in, heel out), and add power to this twisting action with your knee and lower leg as the large bone of the thigh (femur) rotates inward.

**Success Goals** = Complete one full circle clockwise (left ski on) and one counterclockwise (right ski on) in balance and in control

**Your Scores** =
   a. (#) _____ of attempts it took to achieve success goal with the right ski
   b. (#) _____ of attempts it took to achieve success goal with the left ski

## 2. Wedge Extremes

Stand with skis hip-width apart, poles in the snow for balance. Let your knees and ankles flex slightly forward. Repeatedly make any size of wedge you'd like, but the wedge must be large enough to slow your descent and eventually stop you on a hill. Each time you make a wedge, complete it by returning to the parallel starting position.

Do this to a cadence: "into a wedge" (wedge is formed), "out of a wedge" (back to parallel). Repeat this again and again until it becomes automatic. Next, slow down the process of wedge formation, and form wedges as slowly as you can, in rhythm. You need to develop both safe and effective skiing habits.

Ask a friend to assist you in this drill, and announce the kind of wedge you are to form: fast wedge, slow wedge. Next, have your friend time you and rate the quality of the wedges you form on demand (and how completely you return to parallel after each wedge), and thus determine how many minutes it has taken for you to form five "perfect" wedges.

**Success Goals** = Ability to make 5 symmetrical wedges, returning to parallel after each one, (a) quickly, then (b) slowly

**Your Scores** =

   a. (#) ____ minutes to quickly form 5 symmetrical wedges, returning to full parallel after each one

   b. (#) ____ minutes to slowly form 5 symmetrical wedges, returning to full parallel after each one

## 3. Wedge Variations

After you are proficient at forming fast and slow wedges with your poles in the snow for balance, take the tips of your poles out of the snow and assume a basic skiing stance. Maintaining hand and arm position, make a series of fast and slow wedges (again, of a size sufficient to slow your descent and stop you on a hill), mixing them: 2 fast, 2 slow; 2 fast, 1 slow; 3 slow, 2 fast; and so forth.

A fast-forming wedge will help you to stop abruptly; a slow-forming wedge will help you control gliding speed, come to a gradual stop, and when ready, make fluid turns. Early on in your skiing it's more important to perfect the slow-forming wedge with hands and arms in skiing position. Abrupt wedges, although effective brakes at slow speeds, have little value in furthering your skiing.

**Success Goals** = In a series of 5 attempts where you make a wedge then return to the parallel stance after each attempt, form 5 fast and 5 slow wedges starting from a basic skiing stance and not using your poles for balance

**Your Scores** =

   a. (#) ____ of symmetrical wedges formed in 5 attempts at slow speed

      5 of 5 (excellent)

      4 of 5 (good)

      3 of 5 (more practice needed)

b. (#) ____ of symmetrical wedges formed in 5 attempts at fast speed

5 of 5 (excellent)

4 of 5 (good)

3 of 5 (more practice needed)

## 4. Downhill Glide to a Stop

Using your ''training hill'' to begin, mark a place 20 to 30 feet down the hill (with a cloth). This will be your stopping place. Begin gliding down the hill in a basic skiing position, skis parallel and hip-width apart. After gliding 10 to 15 feet, start making a wedge to slow yourself. As you near the cloth marker, increase the size of your wedge (and you slowing), and try to stop at the cloth marker.

The steeper the hill or the faster the speed, the more edge you'll need on your opposing edges to slow you to a stop, and the wider the wedge. Conversely, the flatter the hill and slower the speed, the less edge you want on your opposing edges.

*Variation:* Take a downhill glide that's twice as long as what you've already done. Experiment to alternately do a glide and a wedge before slowing to a stop.

**Success Goal** = 10 stops at the cloth marker

**Your Score** =

(#) ____ of times you stopped at the marker in 10 tries

9 of 10 (excellent)

7 or 8 of 10 (good)

6 of 10 (marginal)

5 or fewer (much more practice is needed)

# Wedge and Stopping Keys to Success Checklists

Ask a friend to observe you making a wedge with your hands and arms in basic skiing position while you are stationary and while you are moving slowly, using the checklist in Figure 5.1 to evaluate your performance and provide corrective feedback. Have your friend observe you gliding, slowing, gliding, and stopping at a mark, using the checklist in Figure 5.2 to evaluate your performance and provide corrective feedback. Corrective feedback may also be provided from reviewing correction sections relevant to demonstrated errors depicted in ''Detecting Wedge, Gliding, and Stopping Errors.'' The areas of greatest concern are hand and arm position, equal body-weight distribution to the skis, gradual steering of the skis into a wedge, and slowing to a stop.

# *Step 6*   Turning and Chair-Lift Riding

Now the good news! If you have learned to stop in a wedge, it will be very easy for you to turn in a wedge. Better yet, the ability to make wedge turns (in which skis are on their opposing edges—the left edge of the right ski; right edge of the left ski) opens a whole new world of sport and leisure adventure for you to enjoy.

Your first series of successful wedge turns will most definitely be exhilarating, though tempered by the nagging question, "Will I be able to turn again the next time out skiing?" More good news: After you've learned the basic stopping and turning skills, and practiced stopping and turning, you won't have to worry about how to ski easy to moderate terrain.

In this step, you're going to learn why skis are designed the way they are, and how to use the design of the ski, along with the turning skills you've already learned, to make wedge turns to either side. To complement your turning skills, you'll learn how to select appropriate terrain on which to practice turning, and how to connect or link together your turns. You will also learn how to get on and off chair lifts and surface tows.

## WHY SKIS ARE DESIGNED THE WAY THEY ARE

For the new skier, it is particularly helpful to understand three basic elements of ski design as these relate to turning: camber, sidecut, and ski body (tip, shovel, waist, and tail).

## Camber

Camber is a prestressed arc built into skis so a skier's weight is distributed evenly over the entire length of the ski. Camber is the feature of the ski that makes full-footedness so important. When you stand full-footed on a cambered ski, the full length of the ski is available to you (see Figure 6.1).

A cambered ski also helps you adapt to sudden depressions in the snow or terrain, by bending and reversing its camber while the waist of the ski is in the depression, and then rebounding back to normal when you come out of the depression.

Camber of ski (exaggerated)

**Figure 6.1** Expert skiers use camber intentionally to influence ski performance. Ski will bend on bumpy terrain then spring back due to its camber.

## Sidecut

The sidecut of a ski determines its native turning radius, given other constant turning skills and the flex pattern in the ski's design. Looking at the ski from tip to tail, you will see an arc on each side of the ski—making, overall, an hourglass affect.

Not all skis have the same sidecut, and depending on level of proficiency, ski demand, and personal preference, skiers choose the sidecut that suits them. Today's recreational and sport skis favor a semislalom-like sidecut (greater arc) for quick turning, but there are special ski designs for all types of skiing. More advanced skiers are, as well, interested in the flex of a ski, tip and tail stiffness, torsional rigidity, base construction and texture, edge construction, damping, pressure dispersal, waist dimensions, and assorted other esoteric concerns.

Recreational skis are often softer in flex, with a modest sidecut, a broad shovel, and a tail that is a bit narrower to provide plenty of stability and ease of turning at slow to moderate speeds. When you put sidecut and camber together with ski-body design and steering, you get turning and stopping.

## Ski Body

Ski-body design promotes turning. With a broad shovel, narrow waist, and wide tail (though narrower than the shovel), the ski is designed to turn on an arc when directed to do so. The ski goes where the toes (i.e., the tips of the skis) point. Add balance, steering, and variable weight distribution to the ski while it's gliding downhill, and you can manipulate edge angle on the ski and turn it in a variety of ways.

The ever important complement to this scenario is the basic skiing position!

Ski design is particularly useful when you are learning to turn, because the broader size of the shovel creates more friction than either the waist or the tail, and thus if you continue steering your toes where you want to go, the tip of the ski will "slow" as the waist and tail skid around and help make the turn (see Figure 6.2).

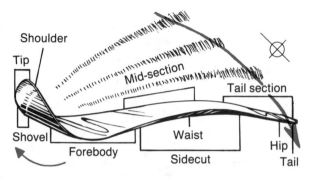

**Figure 6.2** Steering with toes to the right causes the waist and tail of the ski to skid around and help make the turn.

## HOW TO MAKE WEDGE TURNS

Foremost it's your use of ski design that affects turning; ski design itself does not turn the skis. The dual advantage of using the wedge skiing stance to learn to turn is that it provides a stable base of support during gliding, and your outside ski (your dominantly edged ski for turning) is already pointed in the direction of the intended turn when in the wedge skiing stance (see Figure 6.3).

To turn your skis to the left, your right ski is the outside, or dominantly edged, ski. Begin gliding down your practice hill in a controlled wedge in basic skiing position. After gliding 10 to 15 feet, look left with your head and eyes (not shoulders and upper body) to where you want to turn. I call this act "early initiation." At this point, extend your legs to flatten your skis, and point your right hip to the left (i.e., *hip influence* left) as you steer your right ski into the turn by brushing out your right heel 3 to 5 inches, as if you were making the right side of the wedge 3 to 5 inches wider. Hip influence to either side is a technique I recommend to boost the effectiveness of foot and lower leg steering.

As you brush out the tail of the right ski, you must also point the tip of the right ski in the direction you want to go. Do this by steering the right ski as you concentrate on pointing your right big toe in that direction. At the same time, try to flatten the left ski so it moves easily on the snow, but at all times keep it in its wedged position.

You make the left ski flat by making your left boot perpendicular to the slope of the hill. This may mean you'll need to move your left knee a bit downhill to accommodate your boot being perpendicular to the slope. To fully use ski design to turn, redistribute your weight so most of it is on the right ski. If you lighten the left ski (leaving it on the snow), it will be easier to hold it in a wedge as you flatten and steer it through the turn.

Always focus on steering both skis through the turn. Aiming your boots to the left will help. You may also find that favoring a slight angling of your right knee uphill as you take on more weight to this ski will make control all the better. It is important that if you angle your knee into the hill, you keep your chest and shoulders upright with a slight lean down the hill.

You don't want to lean your whole body into the hill while turning; the subtle action of your feet and lower legs is all you need for this kind of beginning turn. As your turn appears nearly complete, your right ski will be edged much more than the left, yet both skis will continue to be steered left and up the hill until you come to a stop.

*Figure 6.3* **Keys to Success:**
**Wedge Turn to the Left**
**(Reverse Directions for a**
**Turn to the Right)**

FOCUS KEY ↓

**Preparation**
**Phase**

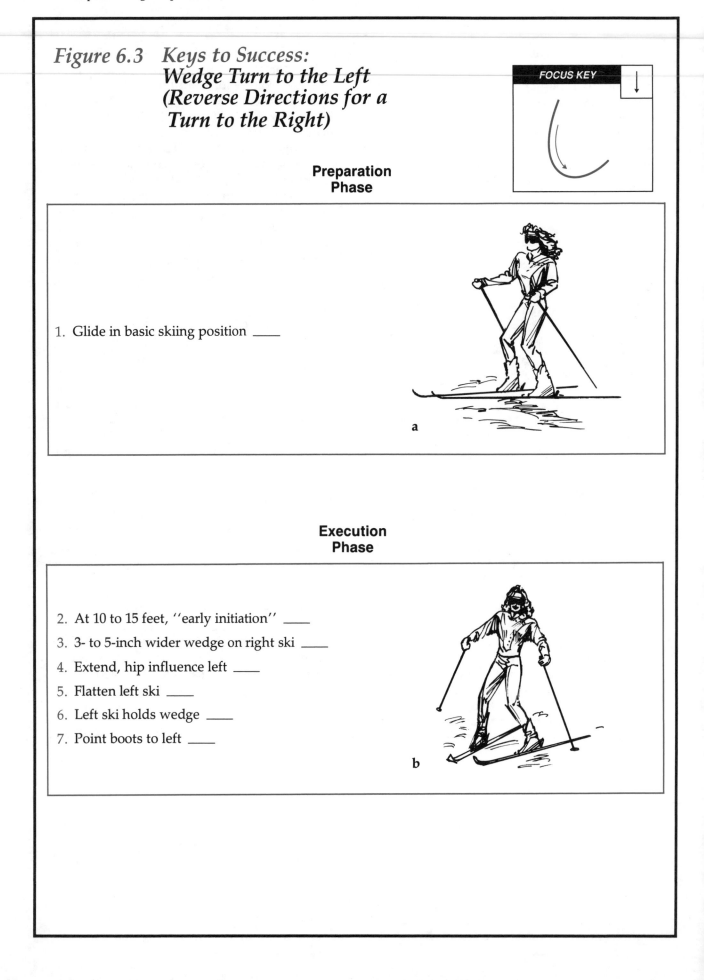

1. Glide in basic skiing position ___

a

**Execution**
**Phase**

2. At 10 to 15 feet, "early initiation" ___
3. 3- to 5-inch wider wedge on right ski ___
4. Extend, hip influence left ___
5. Flatten left ski ___
6. Left ski holds wedge ___
7. Point boots to left ___

b

**Transition
Phase**

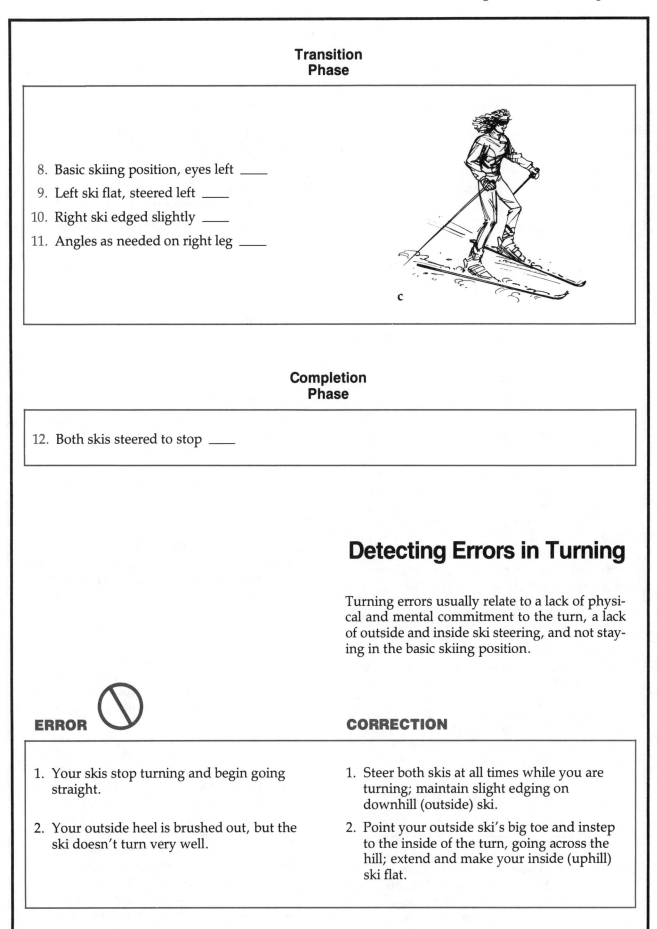

8. Basic skiing position, eyes left ____
9. Left ski flat, steered left ____
10. Right ski edged slightly ____
11. Angles as needed on right leg ____

c

**Completion
Phase**

12. Both skis steered to stop ____

# Detecting Errors in Turning

Turning errors usually relate to a lack of physical and mental commitment to the turn, a lack of outside and inside ski steering, and not staying in the basic skiing position.

**ERROR**

**CORRECTION**

1. Your skis stop turning and begin going straight.

2. Your outside heel is brushed out, but the ski doesn't turn very well.

1. Steer both skis at all times while you are turning; maintain slight edging on downhill (outside) ski.

2. Point your outside ski's big toe and instep to the inside of the turn, going across the hill; extend and make your inside (uphill) ski flat.

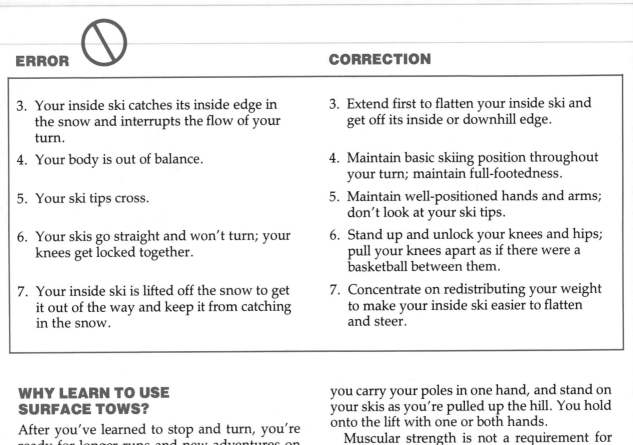

**ERROR**

**CORRECTION**

3. Your inside ski catches its inside edge in the snow and interrupts the flow of your turn.

3. Extend first to flatten your inside ski and get off its inside or downhill edge.

4. Your body is out of balance.

4. Maintain basic skiing position throughout your turn; maintain full-footedness.

5. Your ski tips cross.

5. Maintain well-positioned hands and arms; don't look at your ski tips.

6. Your skis go straight and won't turn; your knees get locked together.

6. Stand up and unlock your knees and hips; pull your knees apart as if there were a basketball between them.

7. Your inside ski is lifted off the snow to get it out of the way and keep it from catching in the snow.

7. Concentrate on redistributing your weight to make your inside ski easier to flatten and steer.

## WHY LEARN TO USE SURFACE TOWS?

After you've learned to stop and turn, you're ready for longer runs and new adventures on beginning terrain. There are a variety of means of on-the-mountain transportation to get you to new terrain without your having to hike to it. There are aerial trams and gondolas (enclosed cabins that transport skiers with skis off) that may carry you to beginner terrain. These require no instruction to use, except to say, "Follow the person in front of you."

Surface tows, on the other hand, come in several varieties, and may be the principal means of transportation to some beginner terrain. These require instruction on loading, riding, and unloading. Learn to ride these lifts early, and you'll supercharge your learning by lessening your fatigue and increasing your practice time. Something you should know: it's easy to ride these lifts; millions of skiers did it (and still do) at one time or another.

## HOW TO RIDE A SURFACE LIFT

Before using any means of mountain transportation, study how other skiers use it. Be familiar with how lift attendants assist skiers, and generally how skiers board the lift. If possible, watch how they get off as well. The three most common surface lifts are surface tows ("tow rope"), T-bars, and poma lifts. On all three,

you carry your poles in one hand, and stand on your skis as you're pulled up the hill. You hold onto the lift with one or both hands.

Muscular strength is not a requirement for riding surface lifts, although some tows require a greater application of strength to ride them repeatedly (see Figure 6.4). The essentials for riding surface lifts are proper form, patience, balance, and letting the lift pull as you stand relaxed and hold on. Two standard rules are these: Cooperate with the lift attendant, and don't pull and yank on the surface lift. When you do, you usually fall.

When being towed by the lift, stand tall with a slight bend in your knees and ankles. Standing tall helps keep your skis flat, which makes it easier to be towed. A slight bend in the knees and ankles makes it easier for you to absorb any deviations in the path over which you travel on the lift.

When getting off surface tows, you must take a big step away from the path of travel and the lift itself, and if you're on a hill, you must get your skis across the slope of the hill and edged so you don't slip sideways, backward, or forward. As soon as you step away, use your poles for additional support and balance. When getting off T-bars and poma lifts, you must release the respective device at lift's end, and simply ski off the slight down ramp. Watch the people in front of you; even though they may not always be good examples, they will be instructive.

## *Figure 6.4   Keys to Success: Surface-Lift Riding*

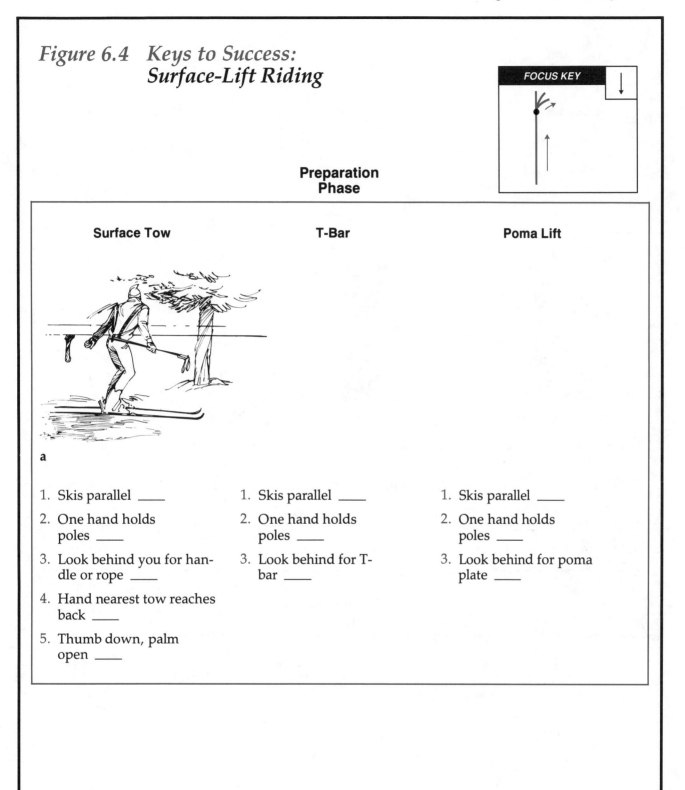

FOCUS KEY

**Preparation Phase**

| **Surface Tow** | **T-Bar** | **Poma Lift** |
|---|---|---|

a

| **Surface Tow** | **T-Bar** | **Poma Lift** |
|---|---|---|
| 1. Skis parallel ____ | 1. Skis parallel ____ | 1. Skis parallel ____ |
| 2. One hand holds poles ____ | 2. One hand holds poles ____ | 2. One hand holds poles ____ |
| 3. Look behind you for handle or rope ____ | 3. Look behind for T-bar ____ | 3. Look behind for poma plate ____ |
| 4. Hand nearest tow reaches back ____ | | |
| 5. Thumb down, palm open ____ | | |

## Execution
## Phase

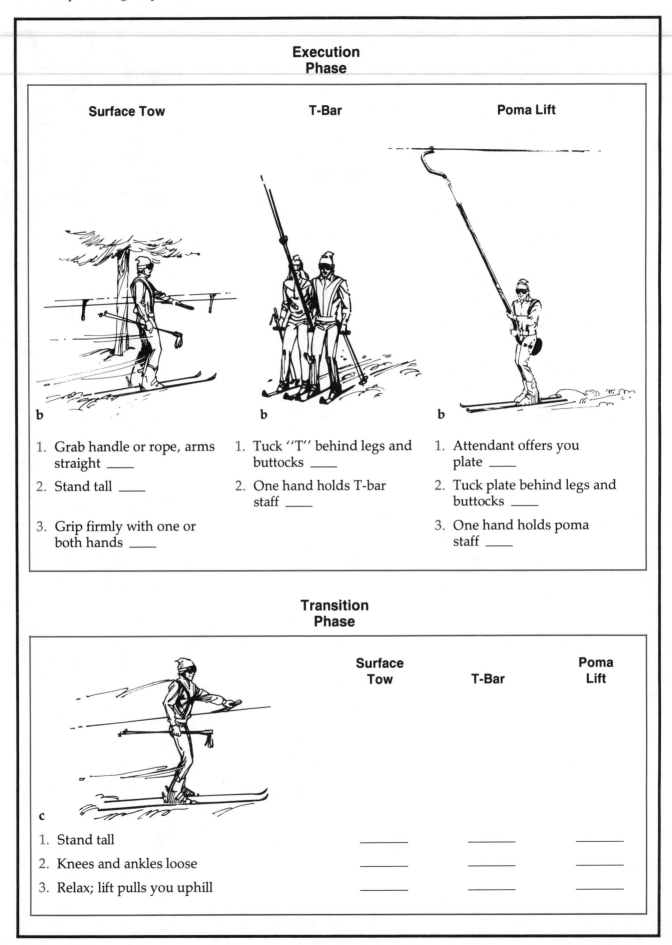

| Surface Tow | T-Bar | Poma Lift |
|---|---|---|

**b**

**Surface Tow**

1. Grab handle or rope, arms straight ____
2. Stand tall ____
3. Grip firmly with one or both hands ____

**T-Bar**

1. Tuck "T" behind legs and buttocks ____
2. One hand holds T-bar staff ____

**Poma Lift**

1. Attendant offers you plate ____
2. Tuck plate behind legs and buttocks ____
3. One hand holds poma staff ____

## Transition
## Phase

**c**

|  | Surface Tow | T-Bar | Poma Lift |
|---|---|---|---|
| 1. Stand tall | ____ | ____ | ____ |
| 2. Knees and ankles loose | ____ | ____ | ____ |
| 3. Relax; lift pulls you uphill | ____ | ____ | ____ |

**Completion
Phase**

**Surface Tow**

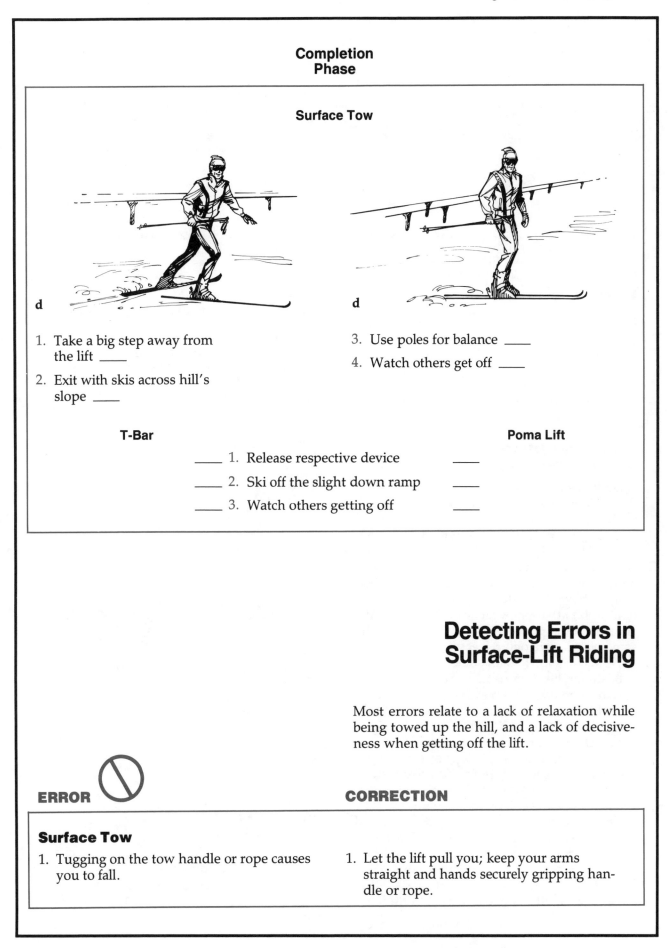

d

1. Take a big step away from
   the lift ____
2. Exit with skis across hill's
   slope ____

3. Use poles for balance ____
4. Watch others get off ____

**T-Bar**                                                                          **Poma Lift**

| | | |
|---|---|---|
| ____ | 1. Release respective device | ____ |
| ____ | 2. Ski off the slight down ramp | ____ |
| ____ | 3. Watch others getting off | ____ |

# Detecting Errors in Surface-Lift Riding

Most errors relate to a lack of relaxation while being towed up the hill, and a lack of decisiveness when getting off the lift.

**ERROR**                                                                          **CORRECTION**

**Surface Tow**

1. Tugging on the tow handle or rope causes you to fall.

1. Let the lift pull you; keep your arms straight and hands securely gripping handle or rope.

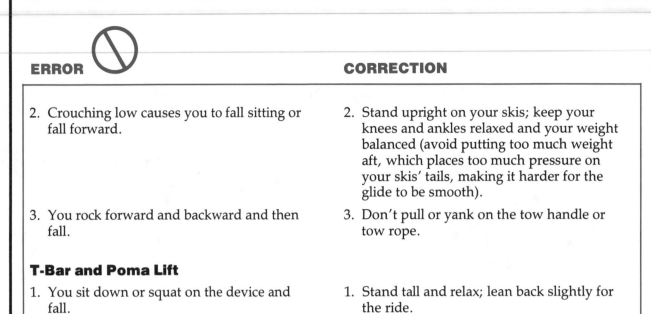

**ERROR**

**CORRECTION**

2. Crouching low causes you to fall sitting or fall forward.

2. Stand upright on your skis; keep your knees and ankles relaxed and your weight balanced (avoid putting too much weight aft, which places too much pressure on your skis' tails, making it harder for the glide to be smooth).

3. You rock forward and backward and then fall.

3. Don't pull or yank on the tow handle or tow rope.

**T-Bar and Poma Lift**

1. You sit down or squat on the device and fall.

1. Stand tall and relax; lean back slightly for the ride.

2. You swerve off the track and fall.

2. Keep your knees and ankles loose, skis parallel; look up, not down at your skis.

## WHAT YOU SHOULD KNOW ABOUT RIDING A CHAIR LIFT

Chair lifts vary greatly, but when all is said and done, skiers ride all chair lifts the same: you sit in the chair lift, poles in hand, skis on, alone with a space next to you, or with 1 to 3 other skiers. The chair in which you ride is attached to a cable that's suspended between lift towers and driven by large motors. Lifts vary in their height above the surface of the snow. I've ridden on lifts that one year were 30 feet off the snow in some places, and another year in the same places were only 3 feet off the snow. It all depends on snowfall, for some lifts.

Beginner lifts are usually two-person lifts, and they are usually run at a slower speed than other lifts. This is to accommodate ease in loading and unloading, and to keep down the swaying of chairs that sometimes accompanies the quick takeoffs and abrupt stops of chairs moving at a faster pace. Beginner lifts are generally closer to the surface as well, and have a very gradual slope to ski down at the end.

Chairs for two have two basic designs, and before boarding, know which kind of chair you'll be riding (see Figure 6.5, a and b). Not only will it be a safer boarding for you, it will protect your partner as well, and be another small but significant boost to your confidence

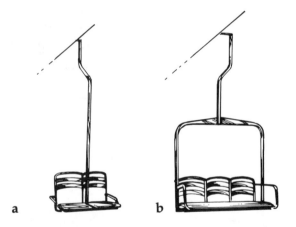

**Figure 6.5**   Chair lifts with a center pole (a) are divided in the middle and seat only two people. Chair lifts with side poles (b) are open in the middle and seat two, three, or four people.

as a skier, actually making it easier for you to unload.

## HOW TO SELECT THE CORRECT CHAIR LIFT

Looking at your trail map, choose only chairs that lead to green-sphere ski runs. It's perfectly sound advice to stop by the ski school, which is almost always near beginner terrain or near access to it, and ask where the easiest and more difficult beginning terrain is, and which chair lift to use to access this terrain.

As soon as you've demonstrated a basic command of gliding and stopping skills on your practice hill and made rudimentary turns to each side, you need to expose yourself to the kind of beginning terrain at chair lift's end. Once you have a grasp of the gliding and stopping basics, and you are placed on more wide-open beginning terrain, your learning curve will accelerate—and you'll give your legs and arms a break from the climbing and poling.

## HOW TO RIDE A CHAIR LIFT

As with surface lifts, study how other skiers use the chair lift, and watch lift attendants. While in line to get on the lift, make sure your pole straps are off your wrists. Walk through the line and grip your poles for maneuvering. When you get to the front of the line, you'll come to a ''boarding gate'' marked by poles or plastic boards flush with the snow. Wait there until the lift attendant signals you forward. Usually the lift attendant expects you to be ready to board as soon as the person in front of you has boarded.

Push out to the boarding area and stand next to the attendant, skis parallel and pointed uphill. The chair will be a center-pole or side-pole variety (review Figure 6.5). Hold your poles in the hand you won't be using to grab the chair

lift pole when you board. In the boarding area, there is often another plastic board on which you can stand. Its color scheme will parallel the color scheme of boards at the boarding gate. When the chair arrives, grap it with your free hand and sit down, sit back, and enjoy the ride. Keep your skis parallel until you lift off of the snow, and then allow them to dangle—they'll seek a comfortable position.

Near lift's end, a sign will announce, ''Prepare to unload.'' Another may read, ''Keep ski tips up.'' This is your signal to get your poles in one hand (usually your outside hand, so you don't get them tangled with the skier next to you. Holding the lift with one hand, scoot your body a bit forward in the chair just before getting to the landing before the unloading ramp. As your skis come into contact with the landing, scoot more forward and place your free hand on the lip of the seat.

Let your knees and ankles be loose for this short section of landing. At the end of the landing there may be another sign that reads, ''Stand up at this point.'' When it's time to stand, push off from the lip of the chair with your free hand and stand tall and project your hips and chest down the ramp. Reach with your hands as well, so you keep your weight forward. Glide parallel down the ramp. As you get used to getting off of chair lifts—and you will do so quite readily—you will develop your own style. Figure 6.6 shows the Keys to Success for riding a chair lift.

## Figure 6.6  Keys to Success: *Chair-Lift Riding*

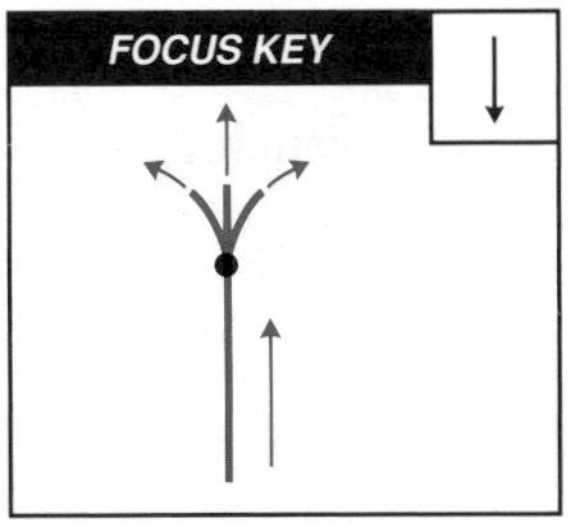

**Preparation Phase**

1. Watch others board ____

2. Pole straps off wrist ____

## Execution Phase

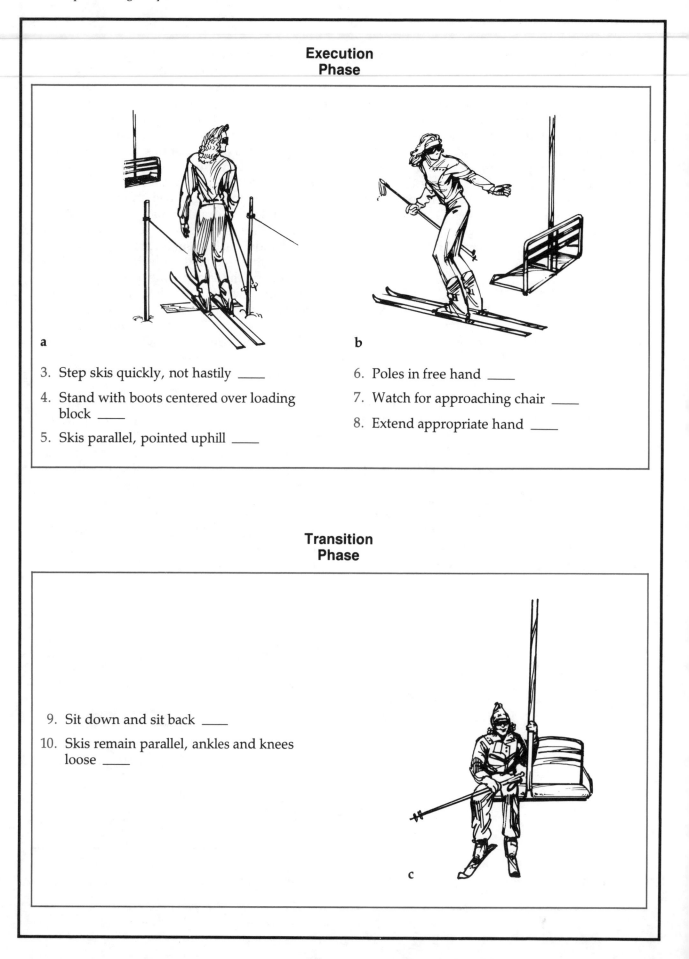

a

3. Step skis quickly, not hastily ____

4. Stand with boots centered over loading block ____

5. Skis parallel, pointed uphill ____

b

6. Poles in free hand ____

7. Watch for approaching chair ____

8. Extend appropriate hand ____

## Transition Phase

9. Sit down and sit back ____

10. Skis remain parallel, ankles and knees loose ____

c

**Completion
Phase**

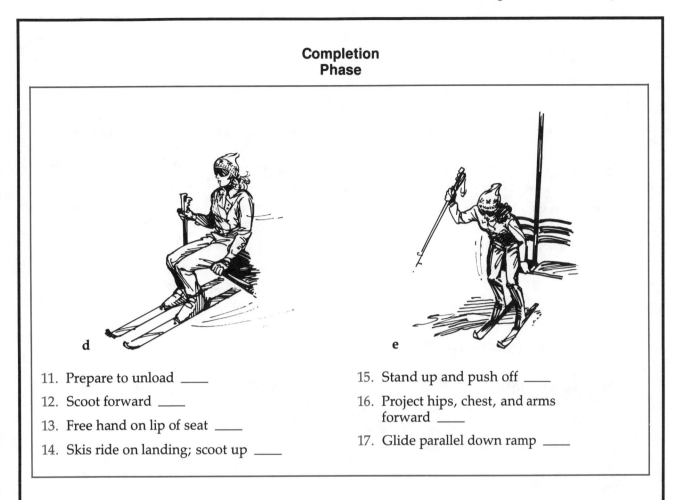

d

e

11. Prepare to unload ____

12. Scoot forward ____

13. Free hand on lip of seat ____

14. Skis ride on landing; scoot up ____

15. Stand up and push off ____

16. Project hips, chest, and arms forward ____

17. Glide parallel down ramp ____

# Detecting Errors in Riding a Chair Lift

Most errors in riding a chair lift are mental errors that lead to physical entanglements or falling at the beginning or end of a lift ride. These are generally the result of inexperience and anxiety about the mechanics of getting on and off the lift. Some skiers are worried about falling off the lift; others are afraid of heights. Ridden correctly, lifts are very safe! Yes, some lifts are higher off the snow than others, but beginner lifts are generally close to the snow.

**ERROR** 🚫

**CORRECTION**

1. You drop a pole or poles when boarding.

2. You are out of position on the loading block.

1. Grip your poles tightly before sitting in the chair.

2. Get to the loading block early enough to wait for the coming chair.

## ERROR

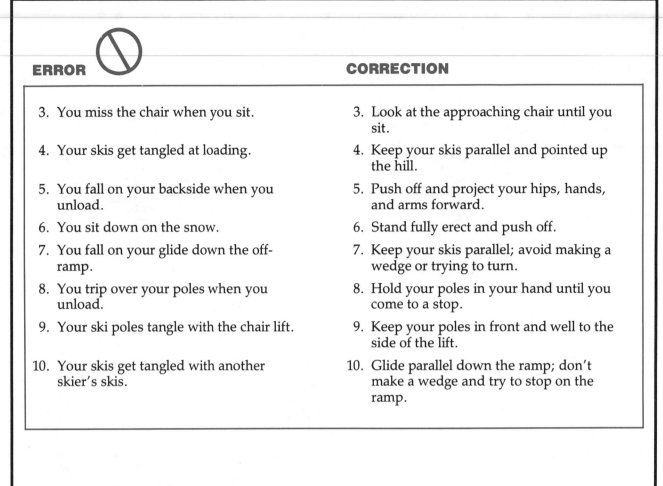

## CORRECTION

3. You miss the chair when you sit.

4. Your skis get tangled at loading.

5. You fall on your backside when you unload.

6. You sit down on the snow.

7. You fall on your glide down the off-ramp.

8. You trip over your poles when you unload.

9. Your ski poles tangle with the chair lift.

10. Your skis get tangled with another skier's skis.

3. Look at the approaching chair until you sit.

4. Keep your skis parallel and pointed up the hill.

5. Push off and project your hips, hands, and arms forward.

6. Stand fully erect and push off.

7. Keep your skis parallel; avoid making a wedge or trying to turn.

8. Hold your poles in your hand until you come to a stop.

9. Keep your poles in front and well to the side of the lift.

10. Glide parallel down the ramp; don't make a wedge and try to stop on the ramp.

## HOW TO USE THE FALL LINE

After you've learned to glide and stop on easy terrain, you'll need to venture up the hill a bit to engage new learning terrain. At all times during skiing, your use of the fall line is an important component of control. Again, when your skis are pointed across the fall line and platforms have formed beneath them, you can hold your position on the slope.

Similarly, when you glide down a slope at an angle that crosses the fall line, you control speed. The smaller the angle, other than straight down, the faster you travel; the greater the angle (in degrees) across the fall line, the slower the speed. As a reference to controlling your descent down the fall line as well as a reference to starting positions in drills in this and subsequent steps, I've developed a numbering system for using the fall line.

Fall line exercise positions (FLEP) #1 through #6 are used to achieve certain speeds for different exercises (see Figure 6.7). For general speed control purposes, the higher the FLEP number, the faster the speed. If you encounter a hill that appears too steep for what you want to do, try

to position yourself in a low FLEP number. If you feel a hill is too steep for you to ski comfortably the way you like to ski, which is normally in a FLEP of, say, #4, then position yourself in a traverse position at FLEP #2, and try making long, slow turns until the terrain feels more comfortable. Then maybe move to FLEP #3 and perhaps #4.

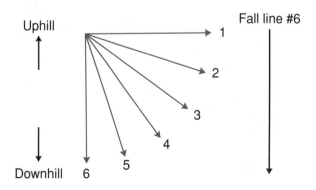

**Figure 6.7** Fall line exercise position (FLEP). Degree of difficulty is on a scale of 1 to 6. Position 1 is the easiest and results in the slowest speeds. Position 6 is the most challenging and results in the fastest speeds.

## WHY IT'S IMPORTANT TO LINK OR CONNECT TURNS

A time will come when you'll be on a slope and you cannot easily lower the FLEP number, because the slope isn't wide enough or there are too many skiers. It's important you learn another far more reliable and ultimately more stylish way to work with intimidating fall lines—turning. When rhythmically connected, turns are the most efficient decelerators of skiing speed and the greatest navigational controls on the hill. Clearly, both speed control and navigational ability are essentials for safety in skiing and enjoying the thrill and command in playing with the mountain. Learning to connect or link turns one after the other is a skill that begins with the wedge turn and continues throughout all of skiing.

The essential reference you must have when using turns to control your speed and intended use of the mountain (i.e., to go where you want to go and at the speed at which you want to travel), is rhythm and fluidity in your skiing. Put simply, one turn flows into the next: The END of one turn becomes the BEGINNING of the next turn. Indeed, linking turns like this when skiing the fall line takes you to a new level of thrill and excitement.

## HOW TO LINK TURNS

Think of linking turns as a musical beat, each turn being a note connected to another note; each run beginning to end like a sheet of music. Your intention when skiing is not to turn, then stop, then turn, then stop, but to always keep turning. Link together a series of turns, not a series of stops.

Start by linking a pair of turns (see Figure 6.8). Use terrain on which it's easy for you to turn in control, and mark off an area 30 to 50 feet long and wide enough for you to turn. This is your practice field. Start by making a left turn, but as soon as you come across the fall line, begin your "early initiation" for a right turn.

As soon as you are committed to the right turn visually, extend your legs and go into the motions to make a right turn and continue through the turn until you come to a stop. The most important feature of this beginning linkage of turns is making an early visual commitment to turn.

*Figure 6.8   Keys to Success:*
   *Linking Turns*

(*Safety note*: Before attempting this, be able to stop!)

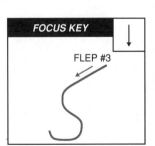

**Preparation
Phase**

| 1. Visually set up practice field ____ | 2. FLEP #3 facing right for left turn ____ |

**Execution
Phase**

a

b

3. Glide 10 to 15 feet, turn left ____

**Transition
Phase**

4

c

4. Early initiation for right turn ____

d

5. Extend and make right turn ____

**Completion
Phase**

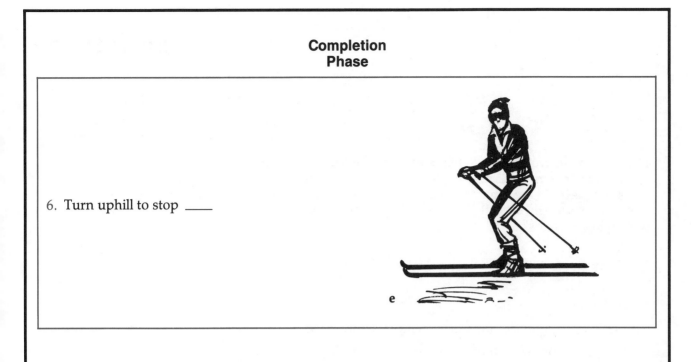

6. Turn uphill to stop ____

# Detecting Errors in Linking Turns

The basic errors in linking turns are in timing, turn shape, and physical commitment to turn, which are often the result of yet immature wedge turning skills. Fear of speed is also an error trigger for some skiers.

**ERROR** | **CORRECTION**

| ERROR | CORRECTION |
|---|---|
| 1. Your transition to the new turn is ragged. | 1. Be sure you make an early initiation. |
| 2. You have too much speed between turns. | 2. Make turns more rounded; keep your skis out of the fall line. |
| 3. You have lazy skis. | 3. Practice full-footedness with both feet; relax your knees and ankles. |
| 4. Your turns are sloppy and awkward. | 4. Go back to basics, Figure 6.3; don't over-edge the outside ski. |
| 5. Your turns lack rhythm. | 5. Think cadence; switch the ''work'' from the right ski to the left ski. |
| 6. Your outside ski is way ahead of your inside ski. | 6. Slow the work of the outside ski and speed up the work of the inside ski. |

## 1. *Making First Turns*

Herringbone up your practice hill, and from the top, vigorously push off and descend the hill making only one right turn. Complete the turn by steering both skis to the right until you come to a stop. Next, do the same to the left. In turning exercises, you need to develop some measure of speed to properly execute the steering of the skis, and some degree of pitch to effectively use the edging of your skis.

**Success Goals** = 5 smooth, controlled turns to the right and then to the left

**Your Scores** =

    a. (#) _____ controlled turns in 5 attempts to turn right

    b. (#) _____ controlled turns in 5 attempts to turn left

## 2. *Traversing After a Chair-Lift Ride*

When you unload from the chair lift for the first time, you may feel that the terrain looks intimidating. It may appear steeper than you thought, but if you can turn and stop, you can handle it. To acquaint yourself with the pitch, however, without committing yourself to point 'em down the hill and go, you are going to learn to traverse (go across) the hill.

Begin full-footed at FLEP #2 with both skis parallel and platforms beneath them. Standing there you look like you're sidestepping up the hill, with your uphill leg shorter than your downhill leg.

Begin to traverse the hill with most of your weight on the downhill ski, using your uphill ski for balance. Flex your knees and ankles slightly while maintaining good hand and arm position. If you keep the angle across the hill slight (e.g., at FLEP #1 or #2), you'll keep your speed quite low.

When you come to a stop on the other side and you wish to reverse yourself and go back the other way, you must either turn or employ a more complicated but effective method for changing directions on slopes when you don't feel you can make an easy turn. Start with the tips of your poles reaching downhill for support, and take a series of small steps inside the confines of the arc created between the ends of your skis and the tips of your poles. Maintain rigid arms as you step your skis around, and keep your head faced downhill at all times. Once your skis are facing the other way across the hill, you're ready to begin a new traverse (see Figures a-e). If you'd like, complete the entire run with a series of traverses, and then after the next chair-lift ride, you can try traversing with a turn.

**Success Goals** = Traverse the slope in balance and under control

**Your Scores** =

a. (#) _____ traverses right to left

b. (#) _____ traverses left to right

c. (#) _____ traverses and turns without slipping sideways, right to left

d. (#) _____ traverses and turns without slipping sideways, left to right

## 3. Traversing With a Turn

Set up for the traversing drill, except at the end of the traverse make an early initiation of a turn down the fall line, and try to make a wedge and turn down the hill, steering your skis around until you come to a stop.

**Success Goals** = Complete the following series of 3 skills: traverse, turn, and stop to each side

**Your Scores** =

a. (#) _____ times successful to the right

b. (#) _____ times successful to the left

## 4. Linking Wedge Turns

Take a chair-lift ride to beginning terrain. Make a series of three linked turns. If it works for you, repeat the sequence to the bottom, or ski until you get tired and stop. Remember ''early initiation''!

**Success Goal** = Link together a series of 3 wedge turns down the beginner slope (turn shape and distance traveled between turns is not important now)

**Your Score** = (#) _____ times a series of 3 turns were linked on a single run down the trail

## 5. Maximum Linking of Turns With Cadence

Use a counting rhythm, and start down the hill in a controlled wedge. At the point of early initiation, say ''*and*'' (aloud or to yourself), and begin turning, counting 1—2—3. By ''3'' the turn should be over, and you say ''*and*'' to begin the early initiation for your next turn, and then begin steering your skis into your next turn, counting 1—2—3.

You could also say ''Right—2—3—*and*—left—2—3,'' meaning that your right leg works the outside ski *and* then your left leg works the outside ski. Cadence and rhythm are integral to skiing; learn them now at the most basic level of performance, and the habit will aid you greatly as you learn new skills.

**Success Goals** = Follow a cadence to link your turns, recording (a) the maximum number of linked turns in a single episode, and (b) the total of linked turns in 3 runs

**Your Scores** =

a.  maximum (#) _____ of linked turns in a single episode
b.  total (#) _____ of linked turns in 3 runs

# Turning and Chair-Lift Riding Keys to Success Checklists

Ask a friend to observe you making both right and left wedge turns with your skis on your practice hill as well as on beginner terrain accessed via chair lift or tow. The observer can use the checklist items in Figures 6.3, 6.4, and 6.6 to evaluate your performance and provide corrective feedback.

Then ask your friend to observe you making a series of three, then five or more, linked turns—at any speed, making any shape of turn. Your performance can be evaluated by referring to the checklist items in Figure 6.8, and your observer can offer you corrective advice. Important areas of focus when turning and linking turns are balanced stance, early initiation, mental and physical commitment to the turn, rhythm, and continuous motion.

# *Step 7* Inside-Ski Steering and Sideslipping

You've learned to stop and turn, and hereafter you'll be enhancing your performance of both as you progress in your skiing. To perfect skiing skills, as with skills in any sport, it's not enough to log in time with practice, practice, practice. Rather, you need to invest time in perfect practice, and to do so you need a clearer understanding of the changing roles your skis play in downhill turns.

In this step you'll learn more about the importance of free skiing and about the turning relationship between your outside and inside skis. You'll learn more about inside-ski steering and why you should actively steer the inside ski. You will also learn about how to control your skis while they are slipping sideways (i.e., sideslipping, a planned maneuver) and how to use sideslipping to further develop your turning and stopping skills.

## WHY FREE SKIING IS IMPORTANT

Free skiing is going out with friends and family and just skiing. It's time on the slopes that is free of the need to give attention to learning; there are no scores to tabulate. Although your primary success goal is to have fun on the mountain, free skiing leads to a great deal of learning.

The skills learned from study and drills are not ignored during free skiing. Rather, they are allowed to "flex" a bit as your body makes natural biomechanical adaptations to the application of these skills in myriad on-the-mountain situations. Free skiing is the "drill" that develops your overall skiing style. After you've learned to stop, turn, and subsequently, link a series of turns, plenty of free skiing should be on top of your "To Do" list. The free skiing will provide time for your body to "memorize" these skills, and thereby lay the groundwork for new skills. Free skiing is a great testing ground for inside-ski steering practice.

## THE TURNING RELATIONSHIP BETWEEN THE OUTSIDE AND THE INSIDE SKI

I like to conceptualize the relationship between the outside and inside ski thusly: The outside ski is the brawn that does the lion's share of the work; the inside ski is the brain behind the operation that decides which ski needs to be steered, and by just how much. In other terms, the inside ski is the warm-up act for the main event—the inside ski leads you into a turn, and the outside ski takes you through it to completion.

There are inside and outside skis at all times during all turns. The skis simply play a game of changing roles at the END and BEGINNING of each turn. Admittedly, many skiers think only of the outside ski in their skiing, and just take the inside ski along for the ride. To be sure, inside-ski steering is a subtle sport most of the time, though there are more dynamic applications in racing and more advanced and expert skiing. Nevertheless, by beginning early to actively use your inside ski along with your outside ski during turning, you can avoid what many new skiers fight for many years—an inside ski that seems like an anchor you have to drag along behind you, and one that has the power to submerge you at any time.

When you are learning to ski, and during recreational skiing, you mustn't rely solely on the outside ski, or you'll develop a lazy attitude about the inside ski. Skiers who don't start early in their skiing to make the inside ski an active part of turning end up making turns where the inside ski actually chases after the outside ski. The result: a lot of abruptness in their turning, ragged speed control, limited terrain choice, and a weak foundation for learning new skills. Remember this throughout your skiing: Both skis are steered through every turn: wedge turns, parallel turns, and racing turns.

Actively use the inside ski, and it can be the first ski to go into each new turn. The goal of working on incorporating inside-ski steering into your skiing from the start is to train your nerves, muscles, tendons, and joints to deliver *inside-ski steering* whenever appropriate, without first thinking it through. When learning to steer with the inside ski, however, you must think about it and use mental reminders to steer, guide, or lead with the inside ski, during both practice drills and your free skiing.

## WHY ACTIVELY STEER THE INSIDE SKI?

Through its "brain" the inside ski applies the appropriate amount of steering to (1) help keep your body weight inside the turn—between the platform beneath your outside ski and the hill; (2) co-steer with the outside ski to help maintain the platforms and thus control your speed of descent and the shape of your turns; and (3) prepare itself to become the new outside ski as soon as you're ready to make another turn. In other words, as turns are linked, so too are the changing roles of your skis, outside to inside, inside to outside (see Figure 7.1).

The active use of your inside ski in steering helps you make smoother wedge turns of different shapes, make better stops, ski with a smaller wedge, learn to ski parallel, advance to skiing more challenging runs, and develop more style in your skiing.

You must continually put the inside ski into perspective: All directional and steering movements of the inside ski presented thus far, and those that will follow in subsequent steps, are important components of actively steering the inside ski.

Actively steering the inside ski will make it easier for you to progress in your skiing, because you'll be more stable on your skis while turning. As you learn to use inside-ski steering, it will be easier to integrate other turning skills into your skiing: countered upper body added to early initiation; early weight transfer added to extension; upper body projection added to hip projection; edge set added to flexion; skidding (steering while sideslipping) added to sideslipping; simultaneous steering (necessary for parallel turns) replacing sequential steering (the status of wedge turning).

## HOW TO ACTIVELY STEER THE INSIDE SKI

First, distinguish the difference between an actively steered inside ski and an inside ski that is steered passively. Active steering implies you make very direct and intentional adjustments of the inside foot and lower leg through every stage of the turn. Active steering suggests leadership in turning. Passive steering implies you make the necessary adjustments of the inside foot and lower leg to accommodate the turning action of the outside ski.

In earlier steps, the inside ski has been steered, although the implication has been more passive than active. It's time to change this focus and accelerate the pace of learning. The direction you're turning always dictates which ski is your inside ski: left turn, left ski; right turn, right ski. When you're ready to turn one way or another, you begin the turn with early initiation. This signals other events, one of which is a lightening of your inside ski to make it easy to complete the turn you're making.

As soon as you finish this turn, your inside ski becomes your outside ski for the next turn, and your old outside ski now becomes the inside ski that will lead your hips and upper body into the next turn. It does so by your directing the knee and lower leg of the inside ski in the direction of the turn.

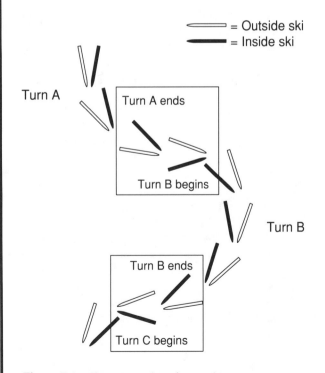

= Outside ski
= Inside ski

Turn A

Turn A ends

Turn B begins

Turn B

Turn B ends

Turn C begins

**Figure 7.1**  Changing roles of your skis.

As the turn begins to take a definite shape, you supercharge the inside-ski steering by directing the little toes of your inside foot to try to escape from the boot. As well, you exert more conscious control of the movement of the inside ski on its uphill edge (the skill you borrow from sideslipping).

All the while your outside ski is being steered and edged to support the turn. All the way through the turn, the inside ski is continually being steered and guided by the foot and lower leg. Your skis are working independently but cooperatively. The change in roles for the skis is more dramatic and better defined, turn to turn (see Figure 7.2).

## Figure 7.2  Keys to Success: Active Steering of the Inside Ski

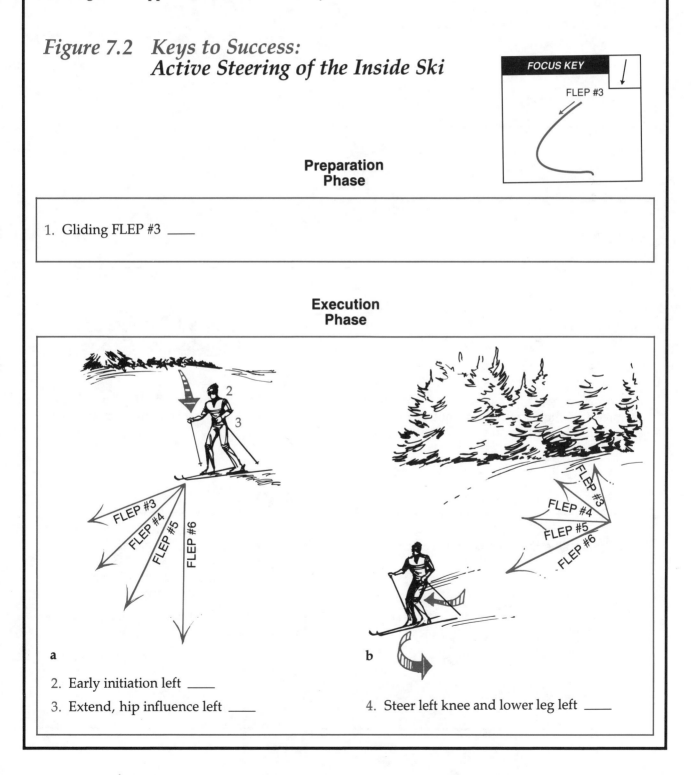

**FOCUS KEY**

FLEP #3

**Preparation Phase**

1. Gliding FLEP #3 ____

**Execution Phase**

FLEP #3
FLEP #4
FLEP #5
FLEP #6

a

FLEP #3
FLEP #4
FLEP #5
FLEP #6

b

2. Early initiation left ____

3. Extend, hip influence left ____

4. Steer left knee and lower leg left ____

## Transition Phase

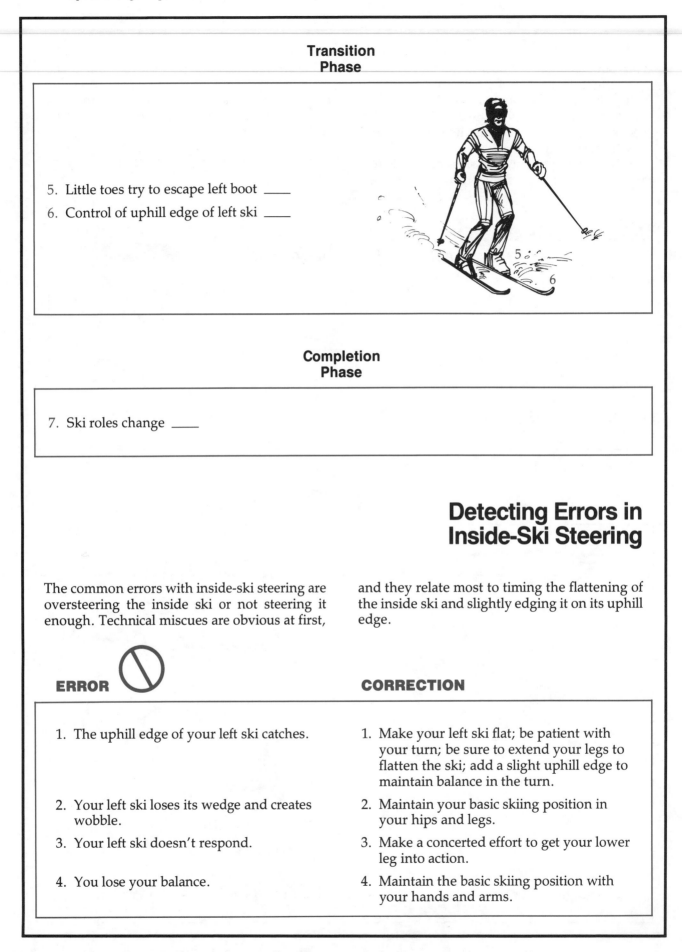

5. Little toes try to escape left boot ____
6. Control of uphill edge of left ski ____

## Completion Phase

7. Ski roles change ____

# Detecting Errors in Inside-Ski Steering

The common errors with inside-ski steering are oversteering the inside ski or not steering it enough. Technical miscues are obvious at first, and they relate most to timing the flattening of the inside ski and slightly edging it on its uphill edge.

**ERROR** 🚫

**CORRECTION**

1. The uphill edge of your left ski catches.

2. Your left ski loses its wedge and creates wobble.

3. Your left ski doesn't respond.

4. You lose your balance.

1. Make your left ski flat; be patient with your turn; be sure to extend your legs to flatten the ski; add a slight uphill edge to maintain balance in the turn.

2. Maintain your basic skiing position in your hips and legs.

3. Make a concerted effort to get your lower leg into action.

4. Maintain the basic skiing position with your hands and arms.

## HOW TO SIDESLIP

Sideslipping tests several other on-the-snow skills: your ability to move in balance; full-footedness; edging, riding a flat ski, boot steering, basic skiing position of hands and arms; countering the upper body. Learning to combine these skills leads to more coordinated skiing and is particularly important to the transition from beginning to intermediate skier. In fact, many of the technical flaws in upper level skiing can be traced back to an inadequate development of sideslipping and balance skills during beginning and intermediate skiing.

Sideslipping is a skill in its own right (see Figure 7.3), because it tests your ability to gradually release the edging of both skis and, through subtle foot, ankle, and lower leg movements, to control the lateral, down-the-slope movement of your skis.

The more familiar you become with the biomechanics of sideslipping, the easier it will become to incorporate the active use of the inside ski in your skiing, because controlling the uphill edge of your inside ski is one of the crucial elements of inside-ski dynamics. Sideslipping proficiency will help you develop a tactile feel for this edge control. Farther ahead in your skiing, sideslipping is a useful skill for learning beginning parallel skiing.

The essence of sideslipping is the tipping of your ankles and lower legs beneath a balanced and calm upper body. In sideslipping, it's important that you remain countered (i.e., your upper body, chest, arms, and shoulders are facing down the fall line while your legs and lower pelvis are facing across the fall line). This countered position is important to parallel skiing as well, and can be perfected while sideslipping.

As you tip your ankles down the hill, the edges of your skis are released, and the skis slip sideways. You can control the speed of this slipping by the degree of edge release you allow. The more you slope-flatten your skis (i.e., make them perpendicular to the slope), the faster you sideslip. You can direct the sideslipping of skis fore and aft by the flexing of your lower legs in either direction while sideslipping.

## Figure 7.3   Keys to Success: *The Basic Sideslip*

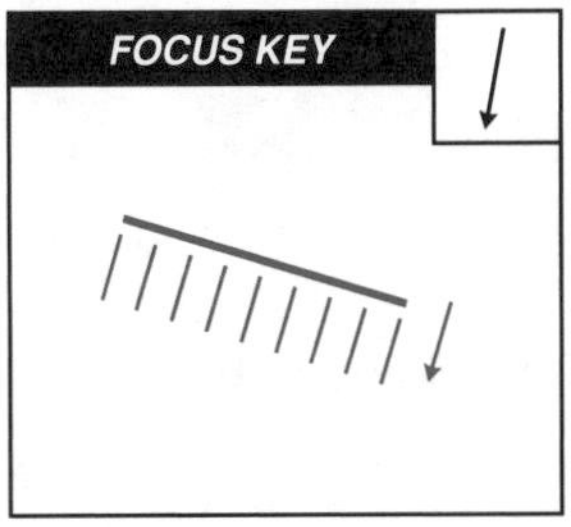

FOCUS KEY

**Preparation Phase**

1. Sidestepping stance (facing across the fall line), skis inches apart ____

2. Ankles tipped slightly uphill ____

3. Knees flexed to hold edge ____

4. Countered body position ____

5. Hands and arms in basic skiing position ____

## Execution Phase

6. Tip boots downhill ____
7. Decrease edge angle ____
8. Extend legs for speed ____

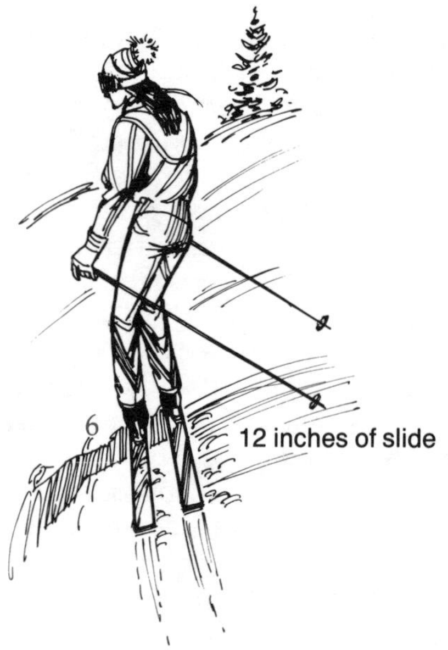

12 inches of slide

**a**

## Transition Phase

9. Slope-flatten skis ____
10. Slip as fast as hill allows ____
11. Slow descent by edging ____

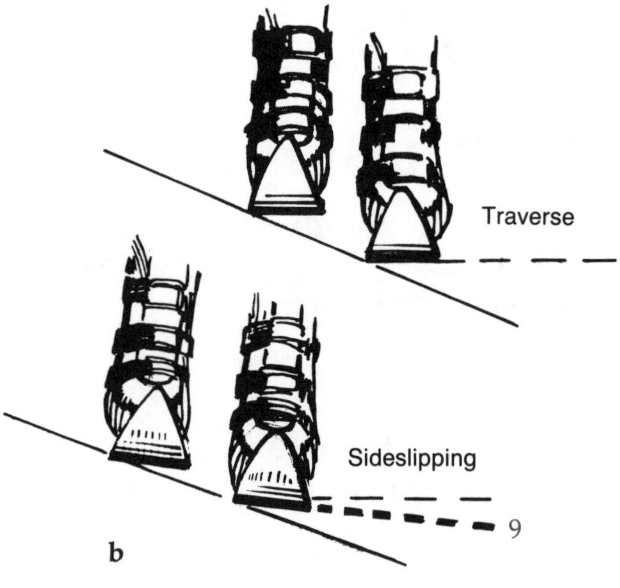

Traverse

Sideslipping

**b**

**Completion
Phase**

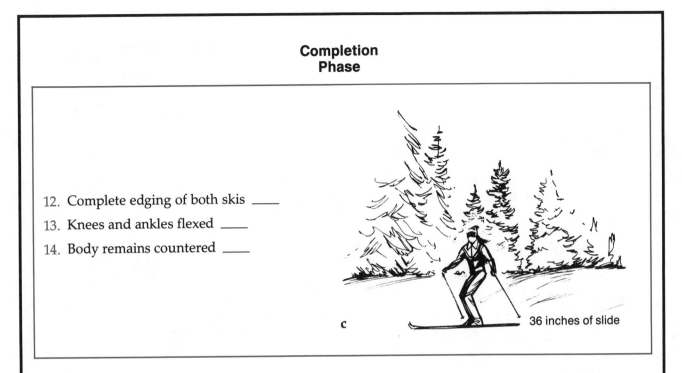

12. Complete edging of both skis _____
13. Knees and ankles flexed _____
14. Body remains countered _____

c                                                          36 inches of slide

# Detecting Errors in Basic Sideslip

Most errors result from a lack of coordination between the edging and the flattening of skis. As well, muscle tightness and a lack of use of both flexion and extension create problems. Maintaining a strong countered upper body and good skiing stance with arms and hands are essentials of sideslipping in control.

**ERROR**                                                 **CORRECTION**

1. Your downhill ski gets stuck.

2. Your skis slip crookedly.

3. Your uphill ski catches.

4. Your skis heave and stop.

5. Your skis slip and stop, slip and stop.

1. You must roll the boot downhill.

2. Maintain a countered position.

3. Release the edge by extending your leg.

4. Distribute your body weight as evenly as possible; relax your knees and ankles.

5. Be patient with your boots; don't overdo the edging.

# Inside-Ski Steering and Sideslipping Drills

## 1. Quick Circle

Stand on the flats with skis on. Draw an imaginary circle around you on the snow. Gripping poles for balance in the maneuvering position, stay within the imaginary circle and make two complete circles to the right and two complete circles to the left. Observe yourself: Which ski always moves first?

When performing the drill be sure to take small steps, of approximately the same size for the inside and the outside ski; step far enough laterally to make room for your other ski to follow; keep your hands high and poles widely spaced; and extend your legs when you step.

**Success Goals** = 2 complete circles to the right, then to the left, staying within the imaginary circle and stepping in a relaxed manner without tripping over your skis or poles

**Your Scores** =

a. (#) _____ circles completed to the right without tripping

b. (#) _____ circles completed to the left without tripping

## 2. Steer Down a Slight Hill

Stand on a slight hill (e.g., your practice hill) in traverse position with your right ski downhill and your left uphill, and step your right ski down the hill as if to start to make a circle. After you've stepped down, your skis will want to go down the hill. As soon as you feel the tug of gravity, assume a basic skiing position in a wedge, look down the hill, project your hip down the hill, and steer your left ski down the hill and turn.

When performing the drill be sure to steer your right ski as well as your left. Even though you begin the turn with your right ski (the inside ski for a right turn), be sure you continue to steer it along with the left ski (outside ski). You must extend your left leg when you begin steering your outside ski, and you must keep your hands and arms in position.

**Success Goals** = Make a complete half-circle turn to each side

**Your Scores** =

a. (#) _____ successes to right

b. (#) _____ successes to left

## 3. Inside-Shoulder Lever

Using beginner terrain, take two chair-lift rides and runs during which you make a series of linked wedge turns. Imagine your shoulders are welded to your knees and boots: right shoulder to right knee and boot, left to left. When making your turns, be aware that as soon as your shoulders turn to the right or left, they are initiating a turn to that side, and the knee and boot of that side must move too.

Take a step to the left. Which shoulder moves that way first? The left. Try this on skis, and maintain your basic skiing position.

When performing this drill be sure to turn your shoulders slowly, and not swing them past your knees to influence the turn; and be sure to steer both skis correctly, even as the shoulder turn appears to assist the skis's turning.

**Success Goal** = 2 chair-lift rides and runs linking 4 or more turns, with smoothness and control during each run

**Your Score** = (#) _____ times 4 or more turns were linked without hesitation

## 4. Knees on a Rubber Band

Imagine your inside knee is hooked to a large rubber band each time you turn, and that this band is anchored to the top of the hill. Make a series of linked wedge turns down the hill. Each time you turn across the fall line, your uphill (inside) knee will be pulled up the hill by the band. Exaggerate the movement of your knee up the hill as you make each turn. Your outside ski is steered as usual, as is the boot of your inside (uphill) ski. The only modification to your normal style is the uphill knee movement after you've crossed the fall line.

When performing this drill be sure to flatten the uphill ski as it's steered up the hill; maintain a strong basic skiing position with hands and arms; and make sure the outside ski keeps pace.

**Success Goal** = Observe that your turns seem to have more roundness as you cross the fall line

**Your Score** = (#) _____ (on scale of 5)

5 (substantial roundness)

4 (above-average roundness)

3 (average roundness)

2 (little roundness)

1 (no roundness)

## 5. Sideslip Right, Sideslip Left

Using a basic sideslip on beginner terrain, slip to the right (your right side) then to the left. Begin by trying to slip a distance of 6 inches, then 12, then a yard. Sideslip right for 6, 12, and 36 inches, then make a left turn and sideslip left for 6, 12, and 36 inches. Follow this progression for the entire drill.

If the terrain seems too flat, or balance is a bit off, you can use an assisted sideslip to the right and left. In this form of sideslip, you flex your knees and ankles to get a little closer to the snow so you can push with your poles. In this position there's more resistance, and travel is slower and may be more abrupt. Use the assisted sideslip (use your pole tips uphill to push you down the hill) for the required distances. As with turning, you may find you sideslip better to one side than the other, assisted or not.

**Success Goals** = Sideslipping laterally on the snow under control for a distance of (a) 6, (b) 12, and (c) 36 inches during each turn

**Your Scores** =

    a. (#) _____ inches covered to the right

       6 inches (good)

       12 inches (very good)

       36 inches (excellent)

    b. (#) _____ inches covered to the left

       6 inches (good)

       12 inches (very good)

       36 inches (excellent)

## 6. Directed Sideslip

Start in a basic sideslip. Your new task is to control this sideslip diagonally as well as laterally. This drill should be attempted only after perfecting the basic sideslip of 36 inches. Start by sideslipping laterally for several inches, and then attempt to sideslip diagonally forward to an imaginary target you've sighted on the snow. To sideslip forward is actually to skid (sideslip with steering—see Step 9).

To sideslip diagonally forward, press your lower legs fore, as you flex your ankles and knees in the diagonal direction you want to slip, and continue sideslipping as usual, at all times directing your boots/feet where you want to go.

Come to a stop by fully engaging your edges with a tipping of your boots and knees into the hill. If you like, use your poles for balance.

Next, attempt to slip backward. Start by sideslipping laterally for several inches, and then sideslip backward, press your lower legs against the back and downhilll side of your boots, and continue sideslipping as usual to another imaginary target you've sighted on the snow. At all times, direct your boots/feet where you want to go.

**Success Goals** = 5 correct transitions from a lateral sideslip to a directed sideslip diagonally forward or backward, with control of the forward and backward movement

**Your Scores** =

    a. (#) _____ times you reached your imaginary target to the right with control

    b. (#) _____ times you reached your imaginary target to the left with control

## 7. Sideslip to Stop . . . Stop . . . Stop

On more advanced beginner or low-intermediate terrain on which you feel comfortable and from which you can exit without needing to ski beyond your ability, do a basic sideslip for 5 to 10 feet, and come to a stop in sideslip position. Release your edges without using your poles in the snow for support, and slip a similar distance to a stop. Do this once more. Again, the key element in stopping and starting up again in a sideslip is flexing the ankles and knees to stop, and extending the legs to flatten the skis and resume sideslipping. This is an acquired skill, and it takes time and practice to learn it.

**Success Goal** = To control the lateral descent down more advanced beginner and low-intermediate terrain while alternating sideslipping and stopping

**Your Score** = (#) _____ of successful stops and starts in succession

# Inside-Ski Steering and Sideslipping
# Keys to Success Checklists

Ask a friend to observe you deliberately using your inside ski to steer while turning. Have your friend observe you at the beginning of a turn, while in the fall line, and completing a turn. The areas of most concern are your smoothly getting into and out of turns, maintaining balance while steering your inside ski, and fine-tuning the association between inside and outside skis—all while maintaining a basic skiing position. Your friend can use the checklist in Figure 7.2 to evaluate your performance and provide corrective feedback.

With respect to sideslipping skills, ask your friend to command you to sideslip laterally, forward or backward, or to sideslip and stop on her or his command. Your friend can use the checklist in Figure 7.3 and the illustration in Drill 5 to evaluate your performance and provide corrective feedback. Areas of particular concern to sideslipping are staying countered, standing tall during most of the slipping, using flexion to control edge angle and stopping, and relying on the edge-control action of your boots and lower legs.

# *Step 8* **Skiing the Fall Line**

I call an aggressive attitude about skiing the fall line the "second stanza" in learning to ski. There's a saying I like to use with students at any level of skiing development: "Fight the fall line, and you diminish the freedom of skiing; fear the fall line, and you obscure the feeling of skiing; flow with the fall line, and you become liberated!"

Recall, the fall line is the path of least resistance down the slope, and further, that at any point on the slope the fall line may change. Skiing the fall line is important because it allows you to use your balance and skills in harmony with the forces of nature (e.g., gravity, momentum, leverage).

At all times on the hill, be aware of the fall line, and try as much as possible to ski in it (see Figure 8.1), whether it's a path down a narrow trail, a course you chart across a wide-open expanse of terrain, or down the side of a mogul. As soon as you enter intermediate terrain, you'll have the opportunity to ski on moguls.

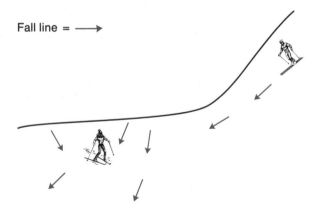

Fall line = ⟶

**Figure 8.1** Sample fall lines (paths of least resistance).

Moguls are mounds of snow created by countless skiers turning in the same place over and over again, packing and brushing away loose snow. The snow over which they don't ski is left to mound up, and moguls are formed, offering skiers another challenge (see Figure

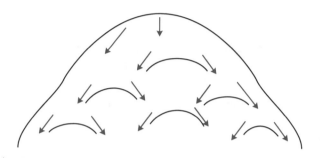

**Figure 8.2** Moguls are found within the fall line of a ski run.

8.2). Moguls may be as small as a beach ball and as large as a sports car.

In this step, you'll learn how and why to use different sizes of wedge to ski a variety of fall lines, thus opening more of the mountain to your enjoyment. You'll also learn about choosing an appropriate turning rhythm when skiing the fall line, and how to effectively use the turning skill of angulation to control the shape of your turns and your speed of descent. And you'll learn about three precisely shaped turns—long, medium, and short radius—and when each should be used in your skiing.

## WHY USE DIFFERENT SIZES OF WEDGE TO SKI THE FALL LINE?

From your experiences with stopping, you know that the wider the wedge, the slower you glide. On the other extreme, the narrower the wedge, the faster you glide. Because fall line is the fastest line of descent down a hill, speed control is important. Varying the size of your wedge when you're a beginner is one of your most reliable tools for controlling speed in the fall line. As you develop confidence in all beginner terrain and can turn, your wedge size and turn shapes are used to control your speed when skiing the fall line.

To discover the size of wedge most suitable to your level of skiing proficiency, you must experiment with different wedge sizes while skiing the fall line. In doing so, however, you must be careful to select terrain that's both appropriate to your skiing ability and suitable for experimenting with turn shapes. Crowded, narrow ski trails, for example, would not be good for experimenting with wedge sizes. Wide-open, uncrowded trails, however, would be ideal.

## WHY YOUR CHOICE OF TERRAIN IS IMPORTANT

When the terrain is too steep (or conditions too demanding), survival instincts replace skiing skills. You don't learn to ski better on steep or demanding terrain; you learn to mount a better defense against the mountain. For all drills and free skiing, select terrain that's suitable to your level of skill development.

More is definitely not better when developing the basic complement of skiing skills presented thus far. Too advanced terrain can make a reasonably good intermediate skier look like a beginner; too fast a leap to intermediate terrain can make a good beginner forget how to grip the poles. Ski easier terrain very well, and your skiing development will progress more rapidly than if you go out to conquer difficult slopes.

## WHY YOU SHOULD USE TURN RHYTHM

Turn rhythm is symmetry, and the more symmetry in your skiing, the more balance is apparent in your ski technique. Each enhances the other. Basically, symmetry means that if you travel 20 feet down the fall line during a right turn, the left turn that follows should also take you 20 feet down the fall line.

The behind-the-scenes essence of symmetry, however, is a new concept you have to learn: weight transfer. Put simply, even though you're steering both skis, physics (i.e., your need to resist gravity pulling you down the hill) makes you put more weight and pressure on the outside, or downhill, ski when you turn. Similarly, when you want to turn again, you have to release this weight pressure on the outside ski and move it to the new outside ski (the old inside ski). The transition between the transfer of weight is the extension and flattening of your skis. In creating symmetry, you must create a rhythmic weight transfer, turn to turn (see Figure 8.3).

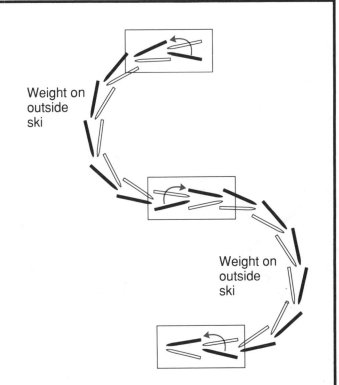

Weight on outside ski

Weight on outside ski

**Figure 8.3** A rhythmic weight transfer occurs during linked turns.

Thus, symmetry helps to create turn rhythm: a commitment to matching right and left turns down the mountain as you ski to an inner cadence. Thus, if it takes you 10 seconds to travel 20 feet in one direction, it should take you 10 seconds to travel 20 feet in the other direction.

The value of turn rhythm is further amplified when turning is your primary speed-control skill, whether or not wedge size is involved. If turns are important to temper your speed of descent, their regularity is of utmost importance. Learning to ski with rhythm helps to ensure this option.

## WHY YOU SHOULD SHAPE YOUR TURNS

A smooth and round turn creates less deviance in form, less abruptness of motion, and less variance in acceleration and deceleration during turning. Smooth turns result from continuous steering of both skis throughout the turn, and smooth, round turns occur when skiers aren't afraid of the fall line. Remember, the fall line means speed, yet smooth, rounded turns mean speed control!

Skiers reluctant to ski the fall line often opt for abrupt, ragged, zigzag turns, because these turns expose them to the speed of the fall line for only a brief moment. Ironically, ragged turns often lead to lack of speed control, problems in balance, and falling. Spend time rounding out the shape of your turns, and you'll develop smoothness in your skiing (see Figure 8.4, a and b).

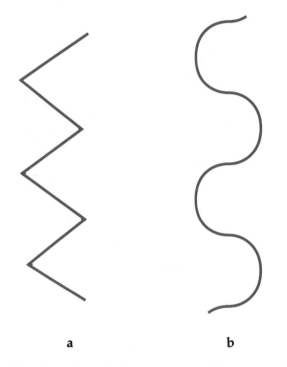

**a**          **b**

**Figure 8.4** Ragged, abrupt turns result in poor speed control (a). Smooth, rounded turns result in good speed control (b).

The shape of turn most used by a skier indicates a great deal about her or his level of skill development. Most new skiers develop a functionally shaped turn (i.e., a turn that is easy for them to make in most situations they encounter, because it employs the best of their basic skills). The problem with a functionally shaped turn is that it is the same turn in all situations.

In more advanced skiing a functionally shaped turn can test a skier's upper level skills by taking the turn into a variety of challenging terrain, but for new skiers, a functionally shaped turn is less predictable under fire, and particularly troublesome when unexpected situations are encountered.

## WHY YOU SHOULD DEVELOP PRECISE TURN SHAPES

A prime goal for early skiing is to develop a full complement of turn shapes when still skiing in

a wedge. The three most important and precise turn shapes are short radius, medium radius, and long radius. Some skiers refer to these as slalom, giant slalom, and super-G turns, because of their likeness in shape to the turns used in these racing disciplines. A turn's radius is the distance traveled between the end of one turn and the end of the next turn (see Figure 8.5, a-c).

The short-radius turn moves you into and then out of the fall line in a very short time. For you, the short-radius turn is most useful when the terrain seems steep or at other times when for whatever reason you want to more dramatically slow down your speed.

The medium-radius turn is the turn shape used by many skiers to best strut their stuff as their intermediate skiing improves. You travel faster in a medium-radius turn than in a short-radius turn, for example, and if you choose, you can use the medium-radius turn to help you pick up speed (yet remain in control) when you feel you're moving too slowly.

The long-radius turn is best used by new skiers for skiing on slightly pitched terrain. As you develop more confidence, you may use the long-radius turn on broad, smoothly surfaced

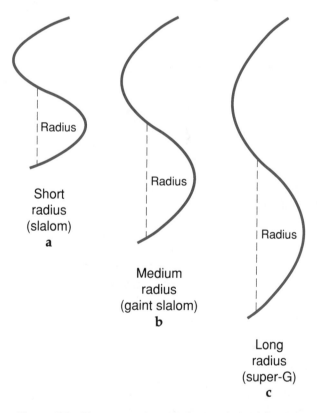

**Figure 8.5** Three turn shapes: short radius (slalom) (a), medium radius (giant slalom) (b), and long radius (super-G)(c).

intermediate trails, where it's safe to ski faster when it's less crowded and you know you can ski under control. Generally, in the long-radius turn your skis stay in the fall line more of the time; you're headed down the hill more than across the hill, but in control and with shapely turns.

## WHY YOU SHOULD USE ANGULATION

Precise turn shapes require that you do not slip too far sideways when turning. When you start traveling faster and begin using all of the three main turn shapes, you need better edge control of your skis, particularly your outside ski. And the better you control the edging of the inside ski (assuming you have outside ski control), the more finesse you have in your skiing. The turning skill of angulation will give you that support.

*Angulation* is a broad term that refers to both the product and the process of making adjustments in stance and position on the skis to affect balance on your skis when traveling at faster speeds or in more demanding terrain, and the actual control of your skis while turning.

Angulation technically occurs when you control the edging and steering of your skis by moving a body part to cause a bending or planned disruption in the horizontal plane of your spine, moving it into the hill (or uphill), or toward the inside arc of the turn. Leaning downhill over your skis is not angulation. The more dramatic the angulation and edging on your skis, the more noticeable the affect on speed control. The more steering and angulation are combined, the greater the potential for precision in your skiing.

### Parallel Stance

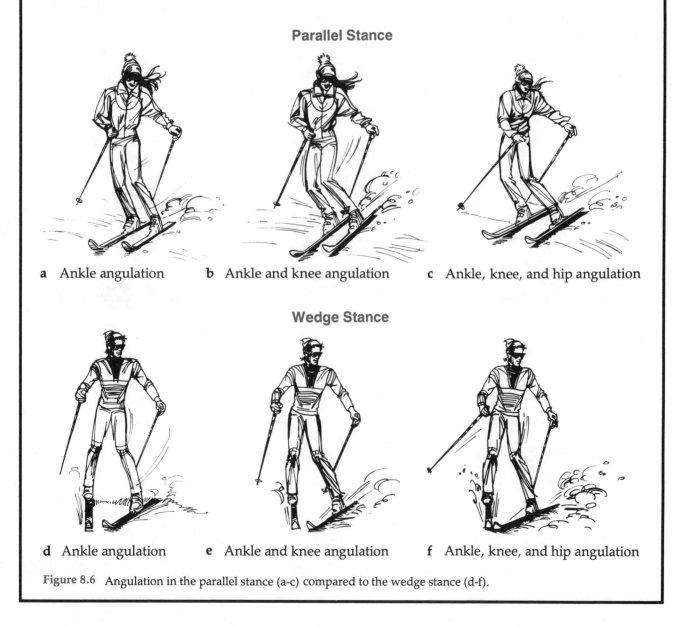

a  Ankle angulation          b  Ankle and knee angulation          c  Ankle, knee, and hip angulation

### Wedge Stance

d  Ankle angulation          e  Ankle and knee angulation          f  Ankle, knee, and hip angulation

Figure 8.6  Angulation in the parallel stance (a-c) compared to the wedge stance (d-f).

Angulation is used most dramatically in parallel skiing, but it plays a role in all of skiing. The chief forms of angulation you will use are ankle, knee, and hip, as illustrated in Figure 8.6, a-f, which compares the angulation used in the parallel stance versus in the wedge stance. Ankle angulation causes a subtle underfoot edging of your skis. Knee angulation causes a quick and dramatic edging of the skis. Hip angulation causes a strong edging along the entire length of the ski. As your skiing skills improve, you'll discover how to blend different degrees of ankle, knee, and hip angulation in your turns, and how to do this blend in different combinations for different turn shapes.

## HOW TO EXECUTE A SHORT-RADIUS TURN

Making the short-radius turn requires quick reflexes and active steering of your skis. Good balance and sound edging and sideslipping skills are useful to linking rhythmic short-radius turns. Along with a mental and physical commitment to make each turn without hesitation, it's critical to use early initiation and a clean weight transfer with extension to begin these turns (see Figure 8.7).

Always be looking down the fall line in an early initiated position, with your chest, shoulders, and abdominal region facing downhill as your legs and skis are facing across the hill while turning. As soon as you extend your legs to turn, make an immediate transfer of weight to your new outside ski. As soon as you feel that the weight is on the new outside ski, steer into the turn and begin to edge your skis with knee angulation and flexion of the lower legs. Complete the edging with ankle angulation.

At this point you're very actively steering your inside ski to lead the outside ski across the fall line. If the inside ski is too passive, the outside ski won't get around as fast as it needs to to execute the short-radius turn. After you cross the fall line in control, your skis will be well edged; stand up to flatten your skis and begin the turning process again to the other side. In the short-radius turn, everything happens quite fast.

## Figure 8.7 *Keys to Success: Short-Radius Turn*

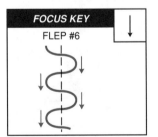

**Preparation Phase**

1. Early initiation; countered upper body ____

2. Extend ____

## Execution
## Phase

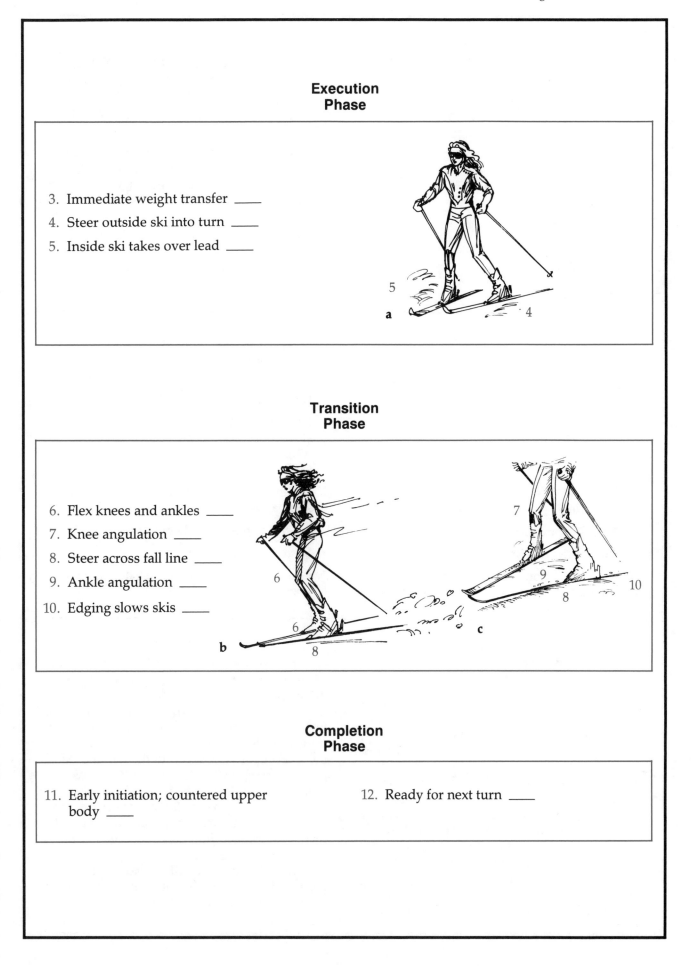

3. Immediate weight transfer ____
4. Steer outside ski into turn ____
5. Inside ski takes over lead ____

## Transition
## Phase

6. Flex knees and ankles ____
7. Knee angulation ____
8. Steer across fall line ____
9. Ankle angulation ____
10. Edging slows skis ____

## Completion
## Phase

11. Early initiation; countered upper
    body ____

12. Ready for next turn ____

# Detecting Errors in Short-Radius Turn

The principal errors occur in timing: too slow a weight transfer, lazy inside-ski steering, and late use of flexion and edge angle to control speed across fall line.

**ERROR** 🚫                    **CORRECTION**

| ERROR | CORRECTION |
|---|---|
| 1. Your turn mechanics are slow and weak. | 1. Work on steering your skis and looking ahead into your next turn. |
| 2. You start well, but your skis don't turn. | 2. Completely transfer your weight at the turn's beginning. |
| 3. Your skis slip sideways. | 3. Use flexion and edge angle to control your skis; continue steering them across the hill; monitor your edging with your inside ski. |
| 4. You have difficulty starting the second or third turn. | 4. Create a cadence; extend your legs as soon as you've crossed the fall line. |
| 5. Your skis are difficult to steer. | 5. Extend at the turn's beginning; don't flex. |
| 6. Your turns feel too rushed. | 6. *Slow down everything.* |
| 7. Your turns don't seem to have any zip to them. | 7. Use a steeper hill and more extension and flexion. |

## HOW TO EXECUTE A MEDIUM-RADIUS TURN

The medium-radius turn requires patience with the steering of your skis, confidence in your basic skiing position, and perhaps a more artistic and subtle use of early initiation, countered upper body, extension, weight transfer, and edge angle (see Figure 8.8). For most new skiers who are ready to begin to explore beginning intermediate terrain, one or another version of the medium-radius turn is the turn of choice.

Early initiation is more drawn out; you have time to think about what you're about to do. Your upper body faces more diagonally down the fall line, and the arc of your turn is longer than in the short-radius turn. It's like the differ-ence between turning a bicycle into a walkway (short-radius turn) and turning a bicycle into a driveway (medium-radius turn).

After extending to turn, you ride on flat skis for several seconds before concluding your transfer of weight and beginning a more grad-ual steering of your skis into the fall line. Most particularly, your inside ski leads the way once you get your skis into the fall line and are steer-ing the arc of the turn. It aids steering as well as keeps you balanced and inside the arc of the turn. The primary function of the outside ski is to provide edging to prevent you from slipping sideways, but in the medium-radius turn, edg-ing is aided more by hip and ankle angulation than by knee and ankle angulation.

*Figure 8.8   Keys to Success:*
*Medium-Radius Turn*

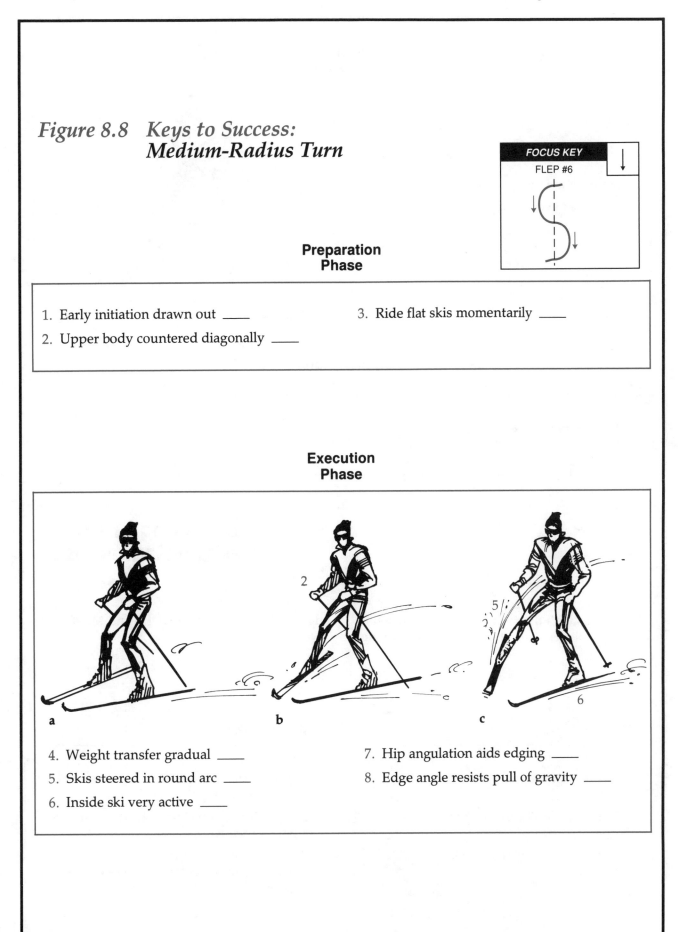

**FOCUS KEY**

FLEP #6

**Preparation
Phase**

1. Early initiation drawn out ____

2. Upper body countered diagonally ____

3. Ride flat skis momentarily ____

**Execution
Phase**

a

b

c

4. Weight transfer gradual ____

5. Skis steered in round arc ____

6. Inside ski very active ____

7. Hip angulation aids edging ____

8. Edge angle resists pull of gravity ____

## Transition Phase

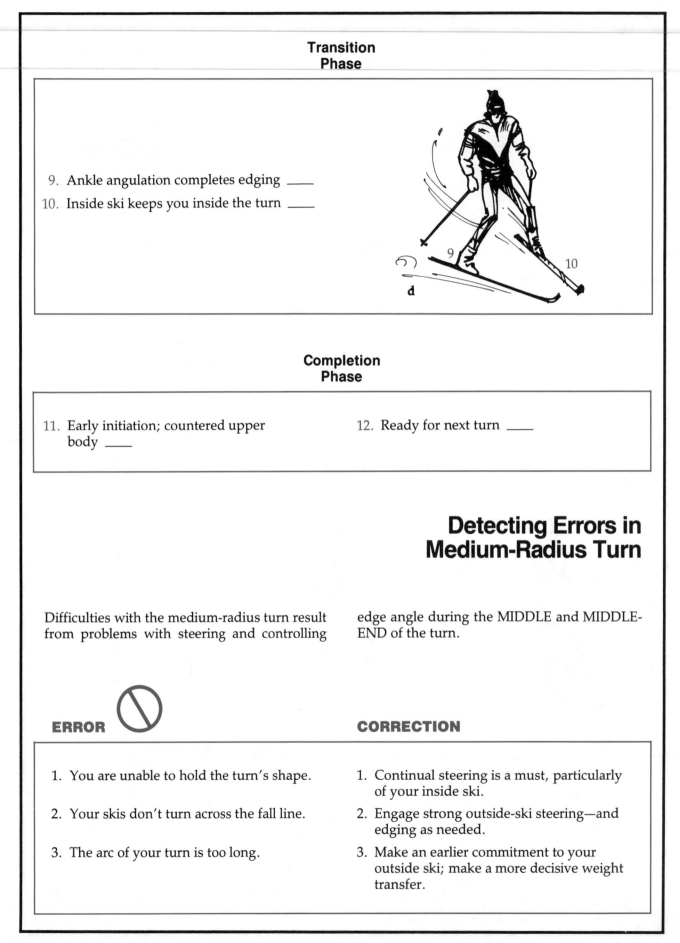

9. Ankle angulation completes edging ____
10. Inside ski keeps you inside the turn ____

## Completion Phase

11. Early initiation; countered upper body ____

12. Ready for next turn ____

# Detecting Errors in Medium-Radius Turn

Difficulties with the medium-radius turn result from problems with steering and controlling edge angle during the MIDDLE and MIDDLE-END of the turn.

**ERROR**

**CORRECTION**

1. You are unable to hold the turn's shape.

1. Continual steering is a must, particularly of your inside ski.

2. Your skis don't turn across the fall line.

2. Engage strong outside-ski steering—and edging as needed.

3. The arc of your turn is too long.

3. Make an earlier commitment to your outside ski; make a more decisive weight transfer.

## HOW TO EXECUTE A LONG-RADIUS TURN

The long-radius turn requires extreme patience with steering, as well as steady hands and arms. The use of early initiation and a countered upper body are limited, and extension and weight transfer are more subtle and drawn out. You ski on slightly edged, almost flattened, skis much of the time between turns. Your basic skiing position is very upright, and speeds are fastest in this turn (see Figure 8.9).

Your vision is expansive, and thus little is hurried in the long-radius turn. Early initiation is more casual. Extension is more subtle because you're already in a fairly upright stance. Weight transfer happens more gradually than abruptly, and the steering of both skis is largely with the feet. Ankle angulation accomplishes much of the edging that's needed, and the arc of the turn is long. It's like turning your bicycle around the corner of a large intersection, versus the driveway and walkway analogy.

*Figure 8.9   Keys to Success: Long-Radius Turn*

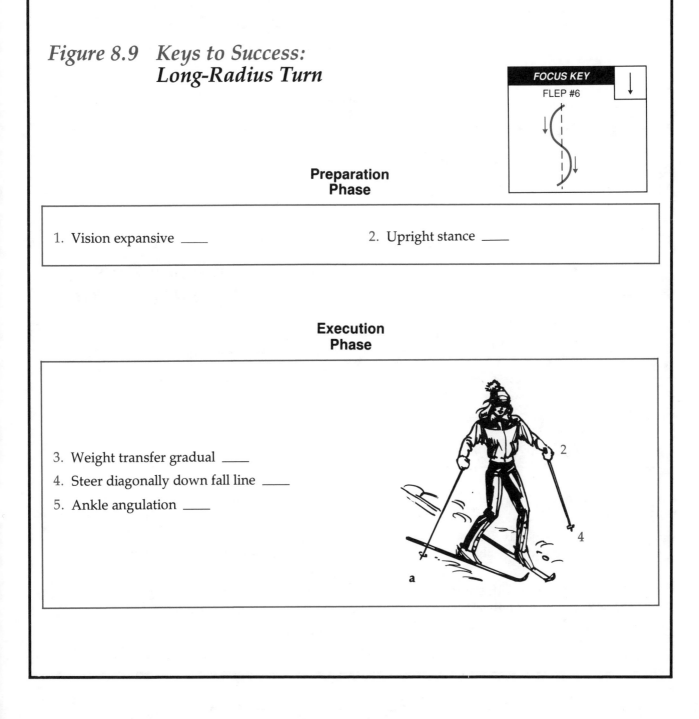

**FOCUS KEY**

FLEP #6

**Preparation Phase**

1. Vision expansive _____

2. Upright stance _____

**Execution Phase**

3. Weight transfer gradual _____

4. Steer diagonally down fall line _____

5. Ankle angulation _____

**Transition
Phase**

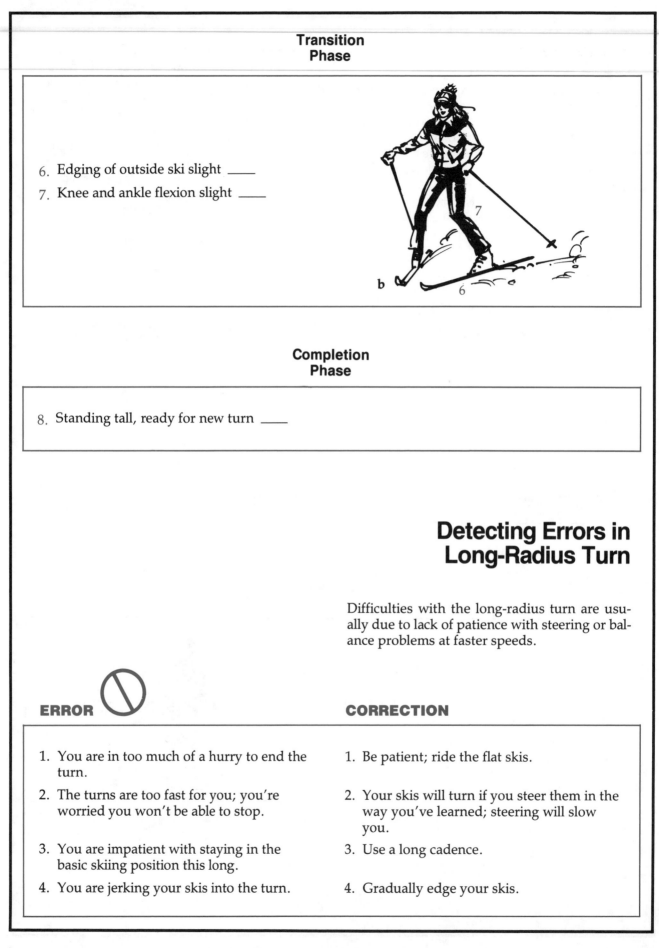

6. Edging of outside ski slight ____
7. Knee and ankle flexion slight ____

**Completion
Phase**

8. Standing tall, ready for new turn ____

# Detecting Errors in Long-Radius Turn

Difficulties with the long-radius turn are usually due to lack of patience with steering or balance problems at faster speeds.

**ERROR**

**CORRECTION**

1. You are in too much of a hurry to end the turn.

1. Be patient; ride the flat skis.

2. The turns are too fast for you; you're worried you won't be able to stop.

2. Your skis will turn if you steer them in the way you've learned; steering will slow you.

3. You are impatient with staying in the basic skiing position this long.

3. Use a long cadence.

4. You are jerking your skis into the turn.

4. Gradually edge your skis.

# Skiing the Fall Line Drills

## 1. Four Wedge Sizes

Assume there are four sizes of wedge, #1 to #4 (see Figures a and b). Begin in a basic skiing stance on a level patch of snow. Extend your legs, project your hips, and make a #4 wedge and return your skis to a parallel position. This lateral steering of your skis should be most natural, and you shouldn't need to use your poles in the snow for balance. Following this procedure, make four #4 wedges in succession.

To complete the drill, follow the same procedure and make #3-, #2-, and #1-size wedges, each time making four in succession. If you need to, place the tips of your poles in the snow for balance. This drill will help you discover which wedge size feels most automatic to you, as well as test your stationary steering and balance.

**Success Goals** = 4 successive wedge sizes coming to parallel between each, without the assistance of poles for balance, and using the following wedge-size order: #4; #3; #2; and #1

**Your Scores** =

a. (#) _____ successive times making #4 wedge

b. (#) _____ successive times making #3 wedge

c. (#) _____ successive times making #2 wedge

d. (#) _____ successive times making #1 wedge

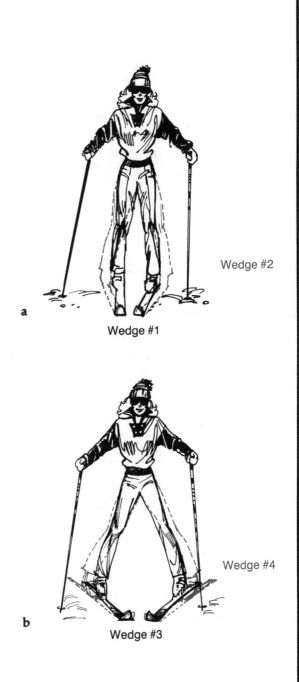

Wedge #2

a

Wedge #1

Wedge #4

b

Wedge #3

## 2. Dynamic Wedge Sizes

For this three-part drill, ask a friend to observe you make each wedge size so he or she knows what each looks like. Do parts a and b completely to prepare for the drill's task in part c.

a. Your friend calls out any number of wedge size, and you are to "hop" into it (literally lifting your body and skis in the air prior to landing in the appropriate wedge size). Have each wedge size called out twice in whatever order your friend selects. Make a mental note of which wedge size feels more natural.

b. Ask your friend to watch you ski a series of six turns and observe which wedge size you used during your turns. Was this the same size that felt most natural to you? If not, ask your friend to manually position your skis in the size of wedge in which you skied. Look down at it, and make a series of six more turns during which you make a conscious effort to stay in this wedge size. Does this wedge feel more natural than the wedge of the same size that you made in part one of this drill?

c. If the wedge size you skied in was the size in which you felt most natural, try making three or four turns in a wedge size that's one count smaller. Let's say a #3 wedge was your most natural wedge. Try three or four turns in a #2 wedge. If you feel in control, ski all the way down, and go back up the lift and make another top-to-bottom run down the hill in the smaller wedge.

You can return to this drill at any time in your skiing and try to ski with as small a wedge size as you can; the smaller your wedge size, the easier it will be to add versatility to your skiing and to become a parallel skier, because your feet and lower legs will be more accustomed to being closer together while you ski, and thus more prepared for the transition between the sequential steering of skis into a wedge turn and the simultaneous steering of skis into a parallel turn.

*Drill advisory*: Although some skiers warrant a two-size jump, I don't advise moving two wedge sizes smaller at one time unless I actually see the skier ski.

**Success Goals** = Discover your most natural wedge size and ski a series of 3 or 4 turns in the wedge size that's one count smaller

**Your Scores** =

    a. (#) _____ turns made in size smaller wedge

    b. (#) _____ wedge size of choice (subjective)

    c. (#) _____ wedge size within reach (subjective)

## 3. Edging, Angulation, and Controlled Skidding Practice

Your angle of traverse affects your speed more than the pitch of the slope, and accordingly, your degree of edging and the ankle, knee, or hip angulation you need to maintain it will vary depending on how fast or slow you wish to ski. Moreover, your degree of edging and angulation will affect the preciseness with which you make differently shaped turns. In turns, much of your skidding is controlled by how much or how little you use angulation, and which form you use. Still, the general rule is that at all times while edging, angulating, or skidding, you should steer both skis through the turn.

Start in FLEP #2 on relatively steep intermediate terrain. Ski diagonally across the slope, and play with creating different degrees of edging and controlled skidding. First, concentrate on ankle angulation by tipping only your ankles into the hill. Do a traverse twice to each side, trying to alter course slightly uphill by variably increasing ankle angulation. Second, traverse the hill first using ankle, then knee, angulation, this time trying to markedly alter the uphill direction of your traverse.

After playing with the control you can effect with ankle and knee angulation, experiment with trying to pick up more speed from FLEP #5, and bend your hip into the hill as you turn, at the same time as you elongate your outside leg. Do this twice to each side; don't try to be graceful, but do drop your hip into the hill as much as you can (review Figure 8.6).

**Success Goals** = 2 traverses with (a) ankle, (b) ankle and knee, and (c) hip angulation, with control

**Your Scores =**

   a.  (#) _____ traverses with ankle angulation

   b.  (#) _____ traverses with ankle and knee angulation

   c.  (#) _____ traverses with hip angulation

## 4. Jump Start Your Turns

On more advanced beginner or low-intermediate terrain, start in FLEP #3 in a comfortable wedge, and as you extend your legs, "hop" onto your outside ski and point it down the fall line. Begin the turn with your inside ski in contact with the snow, but not as firmly etched in the snow as the outside ski. Steer your skis through the turn and come to a stop. Do the same to the other side. Repeat this procedure five times to each side.

**Success Goals** = 5 smooth turns to the right and 5 to the left after dramatically transferring your weight to the new outside ski while in the fall line

**Your Scores =**

   a.  (#) _____ smooth turns to the right

   b.  (#) _____ smooth turns to the left

## 5. Small Wedge–Larger Wedge Turning

On low-intermediate terrain, start in FLEP #4 and travel 10 to 15 feet in a size #2 wedge. When you're ready to turn, begin early initiation by looking into the next turn. Counter your upper body, and extend legs as you simultaneously steer your skis into a size #3 wedge and immediately transfer your weight to the outside ski. Complete the turn as usual. When you start across the fall line, try to steer your skis back into a #2 wedge. If you want to increase the challenge without changing wedge size, increase the FLEP number. Do this to both sides five times.

This drill can be done beginning in any size of wedge, opening to the next highest size wedge. It's critical at all times that you steer both skis into and through the turn as soon as you make the wedge larger. At the most advanced stage of this drill, you can begin in a parallel traverse in a high FLEP #, open to a #1 wedge, and begin the turn.

**Success Goals** = 5 smooth turns on low-intermediate terrain, having added some skidding of your skis to begin the turn, first to the right, then to the left

**Your Scores =**

   a.  (#) _____ smooth turns to the right

   b.  (#) _____ smooth turns to the left

## 6. Cadence Drill

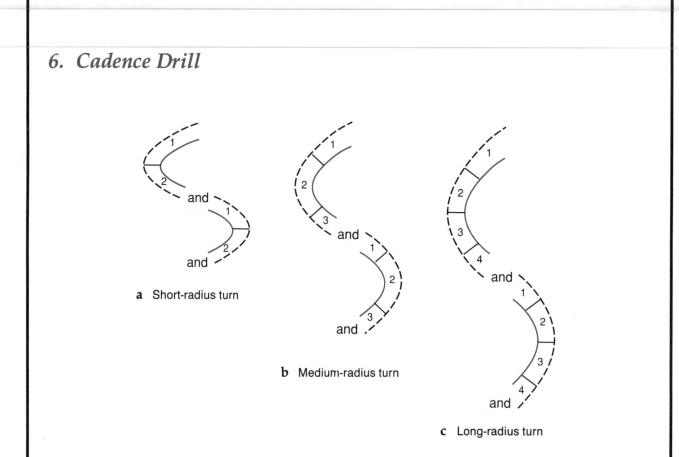

**a** Short-radius turn

**b** Medium-radius turn

**c** Long-radius turn

To develop a feel for how rhythm in your turning works in helping you ski the fall line, it's helpful to increase the pitch of the terrain. If your turning skills are basically sound, and you can link turns of short and medium radius in wedge size #1 or #2, go to intermediate terrain.

a. Start in FLEP #5, pick up a little speed, and try a short-radius turn by counting 1-2 *and* 1-2 *and*. . . . When you count, actually pace it as if you were counting ''1 for my ski-ing, 2 for my ski-ing, *and* 1 for my ski-ing, 2 for my ski-ing *and*. . . .'' Repeat these aloud to yourself right now, and get the feel of the cadence. Try to make a series of 4, then 8, then 12, such turns.

b. Start in FLEP #3 and make a medium-radius turn by counting 1-2-3 *and* 1-2-3 *and*, using the same ''for my ski-ing'' pacing. Try to make a series of 4, then 8, then 12, such turns.

c. Stay on the same intermediate terrain, but select a wide-open stretch of slope that is slightly less steep. Start in FLEP #6 and make a long-radius turn by counting 1-2-3-4 *and* 1-2-3-4 *and*, using the same ''for my ski-ing'' pacing. Try to make a series of six of these turns.

**Success Goals** = Remain at a steady speed while making a series of (a) 4, 8, then 12 short-radius turns, (b) 4, 8, then 12 medium-radius turns, and (c) 6 long-radius turns

**Your Scores** =

a. (#) _____ short-radius turns made at steady speed

b. (#) _____ medium-radius turns made at steady speed

c. (#) _____ long-radius turns made at steady speed

## 7. Radius Drills

After you are proficient at making short-, medium-, and long-radius turns, you are ready to intermix radii in the same run. On intermediate terrain, start in FLEP #6, pick up some speed, and make four short-radius turns, four medium-radius turns, and two long-radius turns in succession.

Next, reverse this and start with two long-radius turns, followed by four medium-radius turns and four short-radius turns. Evaluate how the use of different radii gives you opportunities for speed control. Transitions from long- to short-radius turns are not appropriate to your present level of skiing. Short to long radius, however, should present no problem in technique and would be helpful in developing versatility in the fall line of beginning and low-intermediate terrain. In your free skiing you can experiment with random transitions in turn radii.

**Success Goals** = The ability to move fluidly in and out of different radii turns while skiing at a steady pace

**Your Scores** = Rate your level of satisfaction with transitions between different radii turns: 1 to 5, with 1 = very satisfied; 5 = very dissatisfied

a.  _____  transition short to medium radius

b.  _____  transition medium to long radius

c.  _____  transition long to medium radius

d.  _____  transition medium to short radius

# Skiing the Fall Line
# Keys to Success Checklists

Your selection of wedge size is really a personal matter, and whichever wedge size you prefer, perform your turns as best you can. The observer's role is to watch and evaluate your turning, not to evaluate the size of your wedge (unless this is your preference). If you choose, ask your friend to observe you skiing in various wedge sizes (your choice) with various turn radii on a variety of terrains. As your skills become more ingrained, wedge size will decrease without a thought.

What your observer should be looking for is turn shape and turning rhythm in your skiing.

Wedge sizes may change without thought; they may even appear sloppy at times, but your efforts should be at turn shape and rhythm. Of course, better form makes it easier to shape your turns and maintain cadence. Have your friend observe you skiing the fall line on a variety of terrains, using all three turn shapes. Your friend can use checklists in Figures 8.7, 8.8, and 8.9 to observe technique and offer corrective feedback. Your friend should watch for balance skills and the smooth steering of your skis in different wedge sizes.

# *Step 9* Skid Now, Parallel Later

Recall from the last step that skidding is skis slipping diagonally, and under control, on the snow. With skidding, your skis' slipping is directed by the steering action of your feet and lower legs exerted on the skis through your boots. Skidding is a desirable skill to master on your way to parallel skiing. Still, skidding during turns might not be intentional, but instead a survival-instinct reaction that is more representative of sloppy skiing. Your use of skidding depends on you, the skier, and how you want to ski.

In this step you'll learn why it's important to use controlled skidding in your skiing, and what happens when you do not. For the first time you'll learn to divide a turn into four major stages: BEGINNING, MIDDLE, MIDDLE-END, and END. You'll learn about how the turning skill of edge change boosts steering, eases the transition between turns, and sets the stage for parallel skiing. Finally, you'll learn how to make a skidded wedge turn, and you'll be introduced to the mechanics of making the BEGINNING of a skidded parallel turn.

## WHY IT'S IMPORTANT TO USE CONTROLLED SKIDDING

For the new skier, learning to use controlled skidding is a fundamental skill for developing confidence and control on the slopes. In the long run, sound, controlled skidding skills pave the way for the acquisition of a broad base of upper level skiing skills that will be instrumental in steep and difficult terrain, as well as in mogul skiing and for finesse games (e.g., turning on the outside and inside edges of a single ski in a variety of terrain, including the bumps). Most importantly, and with respect to immediate and reachable skiing goals, controlled skidding is a valuable transition to beginning parallel turning.

One of several outcomes are possible when skiers don't take the time in their skiing development to learn controlled skidding. For most recreational skiers who don't learn to use controlled skidding, turning and speed control are unpredictable when the terrain exceeds their comfort zone. Basic skidding skills can be used

to help a skier out of most unexpected terrain challenges, save special deep snow, old snow, and snow with a breakable crust.

A fair number of "unschooled" recreational skiers mistake random braking for controlled skidding when they turn. Instead of patiently guiding their skidding skis through a turn, they enter the turn in a hurry and slide the tails of their edged skis laterally, brushing away the snow and creating a braking effect.

A general way to identify whether skidding is controlled or intentional braking is to look at the shape of the turn. Controlled skidded turns can have a rounded, almost artistic shape, whereas braking turns are more ragged and unpredictable.

## FOUR STAGES OF A TURN

Turns can be broken down in a variety of ways to explain when certain skills are better applied than others during the arc of the turn. Until now, a distinct understanding of turn stages was unnecessary because rudimentary skills were being learned and coupled to produce a variety of functional turning shapes and strategies for skiing the fall line. From this point forward, the stages of the turn will take on new importance because each will signal times in the turn where specific skills need to be applied to produce controlled skidding in both wedge and parallel turns.

Here are the four stages (see Figure 9.1) I use to explain the turn:

1. **BEGINNING**—the time when early initiation, countered upper body, extension, weight transfer, hip and upper body projection, inside ski steering, and outside ski steering happen in succession.
2. **MIDDLE**—the time when you challenge the fall line and decide how you are going to ski it, and thus react accordingly with appropriate steering and edge angle, controlled skidding, or flattened skis.
3. **MIDDLE-END**—the time where you follow through with what's necessary to continue the turning decision reached in the MIDDLE of the turn. Very often this

is an active steering of both skis, more precise edging, skidding and angulation (see the next section), the appropriate use of flexion, and a further refinement of skidding (and at more advanced levels of skiing, more precise carving) of both skis.

4. **END**—the time where skidding ends, edges are engaged appropriate to the terrain, the steering of skis momentarily ceases, and the body begins to assume a posture of early initiation and counteredness for the next turn.

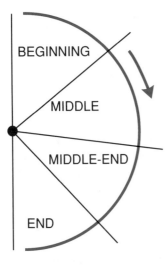

Figure 9.1 Four stages of the turn.

## WHEN TO SKID YOUR SKIS

Actually, your skis can be skidded at any time in the process of turning. When you are learning to skid skis while making wedge turns, it's best to practice skidding skis at the very BEGINNING and MIDDLE-END-to-END of turns. At turn's BEGINNING you may skid one or both skis; at turn's MIDDLE-END and END, you skid only the inside ski to "match" the outside or downhill ski.

As you become proficient with skidding and "matching" your skis, you will want to try to "match" your skis in the MIDDLE of the turn—right in the fall line—and then skid them in parallel position across the fall line into the MIDDLE-END of the turn and through the END of the turn. After you've acquired this

turning skill, you'll be ready to begin your turns with skis "matched" and be on your way to making the BEGINNING stage of a skidded parallel turn.

## HOW TO EXECUTE A SKIDDED WEDGE TURN

Begin in FLEP #4 and traverse a low-intermediate slope in a basic skiing position, skis parallel. After picking up a little speed, begin early initiation and counter your upper body down the hill. As you extend your legs to begin the turn, form a small-size wedge and go immediately into steering your skis down the hill. Thus, as you skid apart your skis to form a wedge, you simultaneously steer them into a turn. This is one form of a skidded wedge turn in the BEGINNING stage of the turn.

As you go through the motions to turn in whatever shape or radius you choose, hold your skis in their wedged position, but allow them to skid closer together if they're inclined to do so. Very often, just adding some speed and a little sidesloping to the ski trails will make your skis skid more naturally and smoothly. At any time during the turn, it's appropriate to skid (i.e., steer) your skis back into parallel association.

One method of doing so is to edge the outside ski so it's stable but gliding easily through the turn, and when you're ready, to sideslip the inside ski next to the outside ski. This is to match the skis together, and again, matching can take place at any stage during a skidded wedge turn. In a skidded parallel turn, matched skis BEGIN and END the turn (see Figure 9.2).

Another skillful method of matching inside and outside skis is to slope-flatten the inside ski and match it to the outside ski by steering the inside ski laterally on its uphill edge. When the inside ski is off of its downhill edge and on its uphill edge, it cannot get caught up in the snow when an attempt is made to match it to the outside ski. Two biomechanical aids to steering the inside ski on its uphill edge are thinking of skiing with your boots together (though they won't really be together), and driving the inside knee uphill or to the inside of the turn as you steer to a match. Recall Drill 4 in Step 7.

## *Figure 9.2   Keys to Success:*
## *A Skidded Wedge Turn*

**FOCUS KEY**

FLEP #4

**Preparation
Phase**

1. Parallel traverse, FLEP #4 _____

2. Early initiation; countered upper
   body _____

**Execution
Phase**

3. Extend and flatten skis; brush out both
   tails _____

4. Make #2- to #3-size wedge _____

5. Hip influence in direction of turn _____

6. Steer both skis down fall line _____

7. Keep looking into turn _____

8. At MIDDLE, hold skis in wedge _____

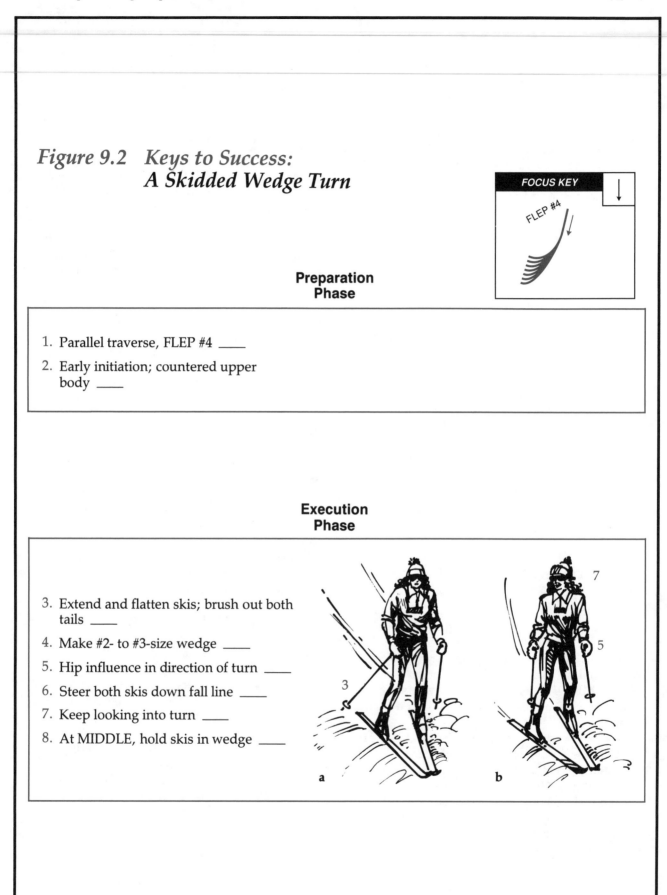

**Transition
Phase**

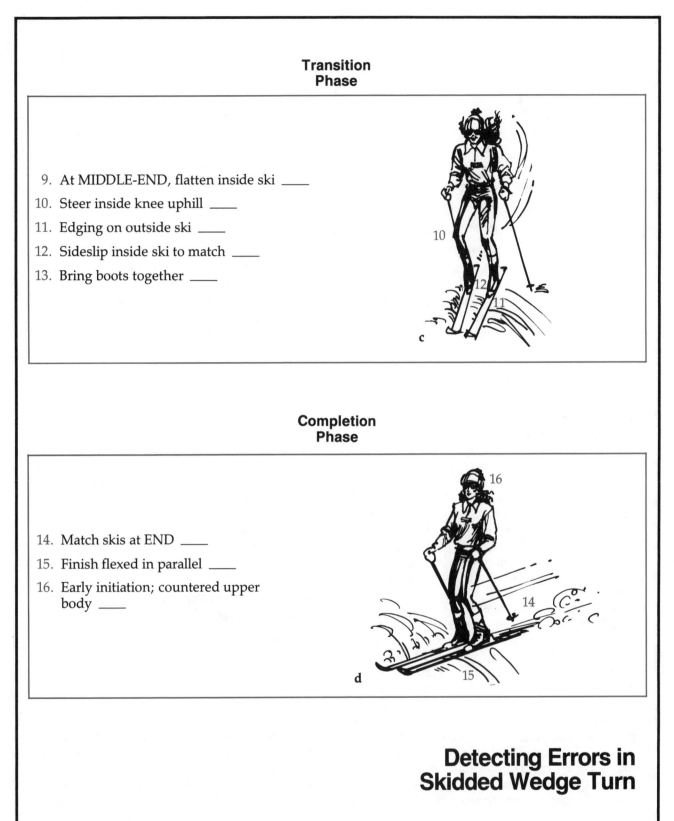

9.  At MIDDLE-END, flatten inside ski ＿＿

10. Steer inside knee uphill ＿＿

11. Edging on outside ski ＿＿

12. Sideslip inside ski to match ＿＿

13. Bring boots together ＿＿

**Completion
Phase**

14. Match skis at END ＿＿

15. Finish flexed in parallel ＿＿

16. Early initiation; countered upper body ＿＿

# Detecting Errors in Skidded Wedge Turn

The problems most evident when skiers first attempt controlled skidded turns relate to steering difficulties, balance, timing, and flattening the inside ski to aid its steering.

**ERROR** 🚫                              **CORRECTION**

1. Only the inside ski is brushed out.

2. Your wedge is slow to form.

3. Your skis don't turn down the fall line.

4. Your inside ski gets caught when you try to match.

5. You lose balance when you try to sideslip your inside ski to match.

1. Steer both skis apart; flatten both skis.

2. Extend both legs first.

3. Look into the turn; project your hips; actively steer your inside ski.

4. Flatten your inside ski first, with knee directed uphill; use edge angle on your outside ski to stabilize your skiing stance.

5. Maintain basic skiing stance, especially your hands and arms; use edge angle as needed; think of controlling your uphill boot.

## ADDING EDGE CHANGE TO YOUR TURNS

Edge change is an important turning skill to add to your turns when your skidded turns begin to approach parallel skiing. Without thinking about it, you have employed edge change from the very first day you were on skis and you tipped your skis edge to edge. Since that time, you have actually employed edge change with every moment of weight transfer to begin a turn.

With respect to more dynamic turning, specifically a skidded wedge turn and a skidded parallel turn, edge change plays a more commanding role. In the dynamic skidded wedge turn, after your inside (uphill) ski changes from its outside to inside edge to BEGIN the turn and become the new outside ski, it remains on its inside edge through every phase of the turn. In the same turn, your outside ski, which becomes your new inside ski at turn's beginning, remains on its inside edge until the MIDDLE-END of the turn, where it changes to its outside edge, where it remains through the END of the turn.

In the skidded parallel turn, the edges of both skis change at the turn's BEGINNING and remain changed through every phase of the turn. The hallmark of a parallel turn is the simultaneous edge change of corresponding edges (i.e., the right or left edges of both skis to the left or right edges, respectively, of both skis), along with the skis' being steered alongside but not pasted together through the turn. Until your skidding skills are more developed and control is second nature, smooth parallel skiing is a distant goal. Nevertheless, after you've learned basic skidding skills, along with other turning skills, it is advantageous to experiment with making BEGINNINGS to skidded parallel turns.

## HOW TO EXECUTE THE BEGINNING OF A SKIDDED PARALLEL TURN

There are several critical elements to making the BEGINNING of a skidded parallel turn: simultaneous edge change; proper weight distribution to outside and inside skis; active steering of both skis, particularly the inside ski; and most especially the projection of your hips and upper body down the fall line and into the turn. All the elements of turning are at play, but more than ever before, your extension at the outset sets the tone for the skills that must follow, and your projection makes it all work.

Extend tall and get your body weight off your inside ski, but keep it in contact with the snow. I like to say, let it caress the snow as you go to work on the outside ski. Actually, though, the inside ski never really rests in this turn; it's just that you've taken the burden of it steering with weight applied to influence its movement.

At the moment when you transfer the main thrust of your weight to your new outside ski, you must also simultaneously change edges (see Figure 9.3) and very decisively project your upper body and hips into the fall line as you actively steer your skis into the fall line. At this point in your skiing you must begin to exaggerate hip influence when beginning turns. To set yourself up biomechanically for the moment of projection, it helps to maintain a countered upper body and to look well ahead and to the direction you wish to turn to. You must remember that your feet are doing all the work with your skis in the BEGINNING of a skidded parallel turn, and all your other actions just make the work of your feet more fluid.

## Figure 9.3   Keys to Success: BEGINNING of a Skidded Parallel Turn

FOCUS KEY

FLEP #4

**Preparation Phase**

1. Parallel glide, FLEP #4 ____

2. Early initiation; countered upper body ____

**Execution Phase**

3. Extend and flatten your skis ____

4. Weight transfer to outside ski; simultaneous edge change ____

5. Project hips and upper body ____

6. Exaggerate hip influence ____

7. Look into turn ____

**Transition
Phase**

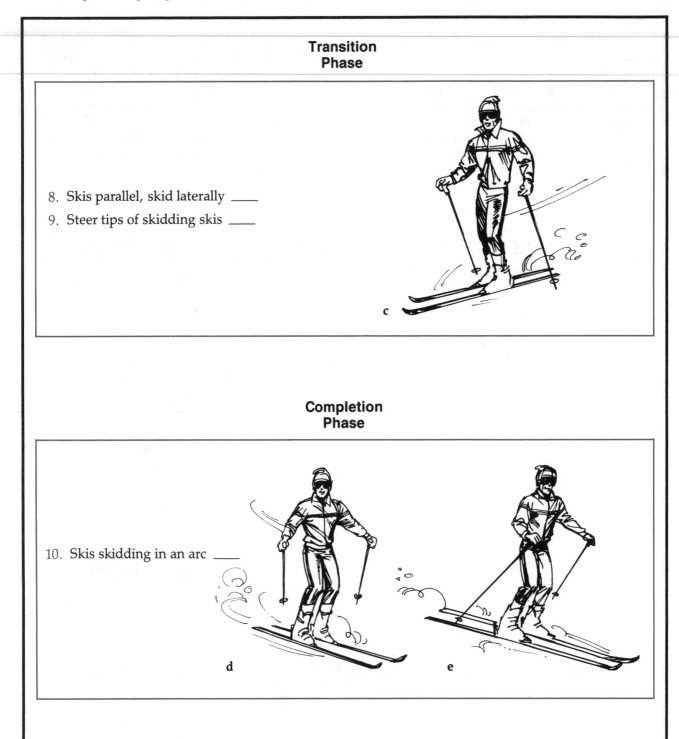

8. Skis parallel, skid laterally ____
9. Steer tips of skidding skis ____

c

**Completion
Phase**

10. Skis skidding in an arc ____

d          e

# Detecting Errors in
# Skidded Parallel BEGINNING

The skidded parallel BEGINNING is a sophisticated step in skill development, and it's almost as if it has to be a leap in performance that happens all of a sudden. Common errors relate to immature steering skills, reluctance to break away from the stability of the wedge, and difficulty in controlling the skidding of your skis.

| ERROR ⊘ | CORRECTION |
|---|---|
| 1. Your edges are not changing together. | 1. Focus on moving your boots simultaneously, particularly the inside boot at the time of weight transfer. |
| 2. One or both of your skis are getting caught up. | 2. Extend very tall and flatten skis. |
| 3. Your skis are not controlled. | 3. Don't use angulation excessively; both skis must work together. |
| 4. Your skis are slow to get into a turn down the fall line. | 4. Project your hips; you need a commitment to turn and very active inside-ski steering. |

# Skidding and Parallel Turning Drills

## 1. Skidding Wedge Exercises

a. Starting in FLEP #4, in a #3 wedge on low-intermediate terrain, make a series of rather static (i.e., more or less stiff-legged) wedge turns to control your speed; use the turn shape appropriate to the terrain. After four to six turns, decrease the wedge size to #2 or #1 to pick up more speed, and make four more turns. At the BEGINNING of these turns, exaggerate the extension and projection of your upper body after weight transfer and let your skis skid into the MIDDLE of the turn as you flex to control steering through the MIDDLE-END and END of the turn (see Figures 9.1 and 9.2).

b. Starting in FLEP #5 on low-intermediate terrain in a #3 wedge, try making a series of short-radius turns that are triggered by a dramatic weight transfer to your outside ski at turn's BEGINNING. Exaggerate the extension and weight transfer, and let the inside ski sort of float along as it's steered through the turns. Get used to steering a skidding outside ski.

c. Starting in FLEP #4 on intermediate terrain, begin making wedge turns in a #3 wedge. After you've made four to six turns and picked up a little speed, begin trying to steer your skis into a #2 or #1 wedge at any time before the END of the turn.

In all of these exercises, be sure to work on turning to both sides.

**Success Goals** = Achieve the sensation of controlled skidding during wedge turns (a) into the MIDDLE of the turn, (b) at turn's BEGINNING, and (c) at any time before the END of the turn

**Your Scores** =

   a. (#) ____ successes to the right

      (#) ____ successes to the left

   b. (#) ____ successes to the right

      (#) ____ successes to the left

   c. (#) ____ wedge used in BEGINNING

      (#) ____ wedge used in MIDDLE

      (#) ____ wedge used in MIDDLE-END

## 2. *Experiment With Speed*

It's well known in ski-instruction circles that simply increasing the speed at which you travel in a wedge, given the application of sound turning skills, will result in various forms of spontaneous skidding. This spontaneous skidding may occur in both skis, sequentially (i.e., one following the other) or simultaneously (which is requisite for beginning parallel skiing).

   In a #2 or #1 wedge, begin in FLEP #5 or #6 on intermediate terrain and ski 15 to 20 feet before beginning your turn. At first, concentrate on making only one turn to each side. After extending to begin your turn, try to keep your skis lightly on the snow as you turn. Experiment with one turn to each side by increasing the speed you pick up going into the turn.

   Elaborate on the above, and try to link turns in which you ski lightly and skid your skis through the turn.

**Success Goals** = Achieve the sensation of controlled skidding while turning both (a) right, and (b) left, with an increase in speed

**Your Scores** =

   a. (#) ____ successes to the right

   b. (#) ____ successes to the left

## 3. *Converging Wedge Turn*

Begin in a parallel traverse at FLEP #3 on low-intermediate terrain. When you're ready to turn, extend tall, steer your inside (uphill) ski into a half-wedge position, transfer your weight to this new outside ski (now pointed into the turn), and begin turning downhill by leading the way with your new inside ski (which you have flattened and are steering down the fall line). Do one turn to each side several times until you are proficient, then link a series of six converging turns.

   The critical points to making this turn a workable and emergency turn in early skiing are three: (1) good extension, (2) clean and direct weight transfer, and (3) inside-ski steering to lead the way for outside-ski steering.

**Success Goals** = Proficiently make a converging skidded wedge turn to each side, and then, link a series of 6 converging turns

**Your Scores =**

    a. (#) _____ proficient converging turns to the right

    b. (#) _____ proficient converging turns to the left

    c. (#) _____ of linked converging turns

## 4. Matching Skis in Medium-Radius Turns

You're ready to experiment with your skidding and steering skills by a controlled matching of your skis at different times during the turn. Complete proficiency with this drill signals your readiness for parallel skiing. On low-intermediate terrain, start in FLEP #3, in a #2 or #3 wedge.

    a. Match your skis at MIDDLE-END. This is how: Make a converging wedge turn to begin, and hold the wedge through the turn until you complete the radius of the turn. As soon as you complete the radius, begin steering your inside (uphill) ski to match the downhill ski. Remember flat ski mechanics. The essential element is patience; gradually steer the inside ski to a match with the downhill ski. Remember the slow-motion drills in which you first made a wedge.

    After this pattern is learned one turn at a time, link a series of turns in which you match the skis no sooner than MIDDLE-END in each turn.

    b. Match your skis at MIDDLE. This is how: Begin the turn as usual. Your outside ski will be edged in the snow as it turns down the hill, and as soon as it's in the fall line, flatten your inside ski and steer it to match your outside ski. At this point in the turn, the flattening is done principally through your boot, influenced by the tipping of your knee to the inside of the turn. Continue to steer both skis, now skidding, through the turn.

    c. Match your skis at BEGINNING. This is how: Approach the turn in a #1 or #2 wedge, and as you extend tall to begin the turn, get your upper body facing downhill into the turn. Make your converging of the outside ski short and brief, counting a quick 1-2 to yourself. "1" is your outside ski steering out; "2" is your inside ski matching. Leave your inside ski flat when you steer the outside ski, and it will be ready to be matched in an instant. A bit more speed and a higher FLEP number help accomplish this early match.

**Success Goals** = Achieve the controlled matching of skis in specific phases of a medium-radius turn: (a) at MIDDLE-END (ME), (b) at MIDDLE (M), and (c) at BEGINNING (B)

**Your Scores =**

    a. (#) _____ successes matching skis to the left at ME

       (#) _____ successes matching skis to the right at ME

    b. (#) _____ successes matching skis to the left at M

       (#) _____ successes matching skis to the right at M

    c. (#) _____ successes matching skis to the left at B

       (#) _____ successes matching skis to the right at B

## 5. *Parallel Traverse, Skidded Parallel Beginning*

Starting in FLEP #5 on intermediate terrain, traverse diagonally to pick up speed. After traveling 20 to 30 feet, exaggerate your extension, flatten your skis, make a quick weight transfer and edge change, and try to steer the tips of your skis downhill as you skid the middle of your skis (under your boot) laterally. Do this to both sides, making long medium-radius turns, one at a time, until it works for you. This is an important step to parallel skiing, as it teaches you to simultaneously and patiently steer your skis into a turn.

**Success Goals** = Correctly execute the BEGINNING of a skidded parallel turn to (a) the right, and (b) the left

**Your Scores** =

   a. (#) _____ successes to the right at B

   b. (#) _____ successes to the left at B

## 6. *Boot-Knee Swivel Turns*

This is not a method of turning, but a method of learning to simultaneously steer your boots and lower legs. Start with skis parallel, in FLEP #4 on low-intermediate terrain. Stand with knees and ankles flexed more than usual, and traverse to pick up a comfortable speed (you want to move as fast as is comfortable). After achieving this comfortable speed, extend tall and simultaneously swivel (i.e., steer) both boots and twist your knees and project your hips and upper body to the side you want to turn to: When traversing left, swivel right; when traversing right, swivel left. After the swivel, let your skis sideslip laterally to a stop. Do this to both sides several times.

If you can't accomplish this at first, this doesn't mean it won't work. This is one of the more difficult early parallel drills to do well, because you must overcome your reliance on sequentially edged skis where one ski plays off the balance created by the other. If you have trouble with the drill, take off your skis and swivel your boots in the snow. What swivels with your boots? Your knees. Now accentuate the movement of both knees and boots as you swivel, and swivel using flexion in between extension to the right and extension to the left.

Challenge your skiing at this point, remembering three points:

- Edges that are flattened when skis are in traverse position will "seek the fall line," or sideslip down the hill, because gravity pulls your mass down the hill. Flat skis offer little resistance to the tug of gravity.
- Although there are other ways to flatten the skis and release the pressure on their edges, at this point in your skiing, extension is the most appropriate method of flattening both skis to enable you to swivel or steer them simultaneously.
- Well-positioned hands and arms and an upright body are critical to successful steering drills.

**Success Goals** = Correctly make a directional change (a) to the right, and (b) to the left, by simultaneously steering your skis, and then sideslipping to a stop within 5 feet

**Your Scores** =

   a. (#) _____ successful directional changes to the right

   b. (#) _____ successful directional changes to the left

## 7. Parallel Traverse, Takeoff, and Turn

Starting in a traverse on what for you is moderate to challenging terrain, flex a bit more than normal at the knees and ankles (e.g., the way you're flexed at the end of your turns). Stand in early initiation with a countered upper body poised to go into a turn downhill. To execute this phase of the drill, do one thing: Project your head, shoulders, hands, knees, and hips downhill. Do nothing else, just project, and your skis should begin diagonally sideslipping down the hill, together in parallel. Use your earlier skills to direct this sideslip.

Practice this "takeoff" at least 10 times to each side, and concentrate on early projection of a countered body with skis parallel.

After taking off, continue to steer both boots and make a turn with an arc. You can make it a very-long-radius turn by steering very gradually, or more of a medium-radius turn if your steering is well-developed. The inside ski is steered to keep it out of the way of the outside ski as it leads the outside ski through the turn. The outside ski is steered to the degree of edge needed to resist the forces of gravity that want to pull you laterally down the hill. As both skis are steered, both skis are skidding.

**Success Goals** = 10 takeoffs in parallel to begin your turns, and direct your skis across the fall line in parallel position (a) to the right, and (b) to the left

**Your Scores** =

a. (#) _____ takeoffs and skids to the right

b. (#) _____ takeoffs and skids to the left

# Skidding
# Keys to Success Checklists

Ask a friend to watch you make a skidded wedge turn on easy, then more challenging, terrain. Your friend can evaluate your performance and offer corrective advice by using the checklist items in Figure 9.2. What you must consider when skidding in a wedge is good independent control of your skis, yet steering your skis in unison. Whenever controlled skidding is used, balance also becomes a prime concern: Check your hand and arm position.

Ask a friend to watch you attempt the BEGINNING of a skidded parallel turn on intermediate terrain. Your friend can evaluate your performance and offer corrective advice by using the checklist items in Figure 9.3. Overall, the essential skill to accomplish before moving on in your skiing is turning in balance while skidding and simultaneously steering your skis.

Your ability to make a simultaneous edge change along with a distinct weight transfer, and your ability to extend and project your body into the turn, are critical to BEGINNING a skidded parallel turn, and later, to completing a skidded parallel turn BEGINNING through END.

# *Step 10*   Making Parallel Turns

The process of making linked parallel turns (i.e., turns in which both skis are steered simultaneously into and through each turn) is what many call parallel skiing. Within parallel skiing there are different levels of performance. In this step you'll learn to identify the different levels of parallel skiing, and you will learn about the importance of the turning skills of timing and anticipation to making parallel turns. You'll learn how to make a preturn, and how linking parallel turns is a means of controlling speed and adding versatility to your skiing. Finally, you will learn how to combine all of your turning skills and make beginning parallel turns.

## FOUR DIFFERENT LEVELS OF PARALLEL SKIING

There are four levels of parallel skiing, each distinguished from the other by the nature of the parallel turn: beginning, intermediate, advanced, and expert. In what I call beginning parallel skiing, the parallel turn occurs with both skis remaining on the snow at all times during the turn. Steering is aided by controlled skidding. In more intermediate parallel skiing, skis still remain on the snow, but their steering is aided by better edging and basic angulation skills to accompany a more selective use of controlled skidding (e.g., skidding at different times in different turns, or skidding at only the beginning or end of turns).

In advanced parallel skiing, the outside ski remains on the snow, though the inside ski may be lifted off the snow even as it is simultaneously steered with the outside ski. This practice is an aid to creating greater carving of the outside ski. As well, both incidental and planned angulation are used in advanced parallel skiing to manipulate edging and the amount of pressure placed on the skis to resist the tug of gravity, and thus affect ski performance and turn shape.

In expert parallel skiing, skis (one or both) remain on the snow or are steered entirely in the air—it depends on the conditions and situation. In expert parallel, all skills are used as needed, in all conditions and terrain. More dynamic associations occur between the inside and outside skis; inside-ski steering is more athletic at times, and more pronounced. Angulation may be extreme at times, and very subtle in less demanding conditions. Expert parallel is "automatic," and it is summating, containing all that preceded it, including beginning parallel.

## WHY TIMING AND ANTICIPATION ARE IMPORTANT TO PARALLEL TURNS

In effect, you want to train yourself to view the END of your turns as "the event" that signals you to release the energy you've built up in anticipation of the next turn. In Step 11, we'll work with pole use. Interestingly, a pole swing (in preparation for a pole touch or pole plant) in a medium-radius turn actually signals the END of one turn and the anticipation for, and BEGINNING of, the next.

The reason timing is so important is that you want to ensure that the body and skis move naturally through the transition between turns. Imagine walking alongside skis being steered through a turn. Just as you do not break stride or speed of foot strike when walking at pace, you do not stop the orderly flow of your body between ski movements.

The key to a smooth transition between the slower speed achieved while in the END stage of one turn, and the increased speed you often need and experience when steering into the next turn, is not extension, weight transfer, or simultaneous edge change (though these are necessary prerequisites for the parallel turn), but anticipation. The turning skill *anticipation* is the combination of supercharged early initiation and a countered upper body. Anticipation is a qualitative skill you've been slowly developing all along. It commits your mind, eyes, shoulders, abdominal region, and hip into the new turn before you actually extend, flatten your skis, transfer your weight, and change edges (see Figure 10.1).

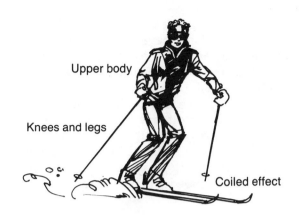

**Figure 10.1**   Anticipation precedes a turn.

The power of using anticipation in making parallel turns is biomechanical. The upper body looks down the fall line while the lower body skis across the fall line. The net result is a twisted body. When legs flex at the END of a turn, this twisted effect between upper and lower body concentrates energy. It's like a coil that's twisted and then pushed down. When you extend your legs to begin your new turn, at the same time keeping your upper body directed into the new turn, it is as if you release the coil. This action prompts your legs to follow the lead of the upper body. The key to this effect is strong and toned abdominal muscles, particularly the internal and external obliques (see Figure 10.2, a and b).

A corollary to the uncoiling effect that is as much a function of timing as anything else is the projection of your hips and upper body into the turn. When making parallel turns, in particular, this projection is a method of boosting the release of the energy you've built up by using an anticipated stance. Using stored energy this way actually propels you into the turn.

You can time the release of stored energy by projecting your hip and upper body as soon as you transfer your weight and make a simultaneous edge change. Think of this hip projection as exaggerated hip influence. At the same time you exaggerate hip influence, begin to actively steer your skis into the turn. At this point your torso actually crosses over the imaginary path your skis would have traveled if they had continued across the hill.

**Figure 10.2**   A ''coil'' image is important in concentrating energy when the skier's upper body looks down the fall line while the lower body skis across the fall line (a) and releasing energy when the skier's legs extend (b), which turns the flattened skis in the direction of the upper body.

## WHY A PRETURN IS IMPORTANT

A preturn is a skiing maneuver where you steer parallel skis slightly uphill, just before you're ready to extend and flatten your skis to begin a turn. Preturns are entirely optional in parallel skiing, but are best used as stabilizing aids when the terrain seems too steep or you appear to be carrying too much speed into each turn, thus fouling your ability to make precise turns.

As an adjunct to anticipation, a preturn gives you a moment of pause in your "coiled" position during which your energy can be mounted even as your speed has been curtailed. Moreover, a preturn makes it easier for your torso to cross over during projection into the new turn.

Properly used, a preturn can neutralize the pitch of any terrain, and thus increase your confidence by reducing your fear or ambivalence at the time of turning. The momentary slowing provided by preturns helps skiers overcome those scary moments every skier goes through at one time or another when she or he must turn down a hill with more pitch than ever before.

Preturns have a role in parallel skiing at all levels, and relatively speaking, there is "steep" terrain for every level of skiing, although what terrain is "steep" is not necessarily the same for all skiers (e.g., intermediate skiers may feel intimidated by expert terrain, but expert skiers may not give intermediate terrain a second thought). Learn to make preturns now, and making parallel turns on a variety of intermediate terrain will be easier.

It's possible that learning a preturn at this point in your skiing development may reveal a weakness in your ability to steer your lower legs uphill to one side or the other. If so, this is the time to correct it, or it may haunt you for years to come. It may be that from day one on skis, you've had a difficult time steering in one direction or the other, but it was not until you needed to make parallel turns that it became unmanageable. If so, pay special attention to this underdeveloped skill when practicing your preturns.

## HOW TO EXECUTE A PRETURN

As you END one turn and are in a flexed, anticipated position, steer your skis slightly up the hill. Your preturn will cover a distance of 18 to 28 inches wherein your edged skis will displace a little snow as they skid uphill. This steering of your skis is accomplished almost entirely by quickly and forcefully turning, or sometimes actually pushing, your feet uphill as you drive your knees and lower legs uphill. As you do so, be sure to form platforms beneath your skis to prevent you from slipping downhill (see Figure 10.3).

Once you reach this point of pause, the preturn is complete, and you are ready to turn or to stop. Your fear of the terrain is gone, and you're ready to take charge. That is it—a short maneuver that yields tremendous benefit and power if done correctly. Even expert skiers use preturns on very steep terrain.

## Figure 10.3   Keys to Success: Preturn

**Preparation Phase**

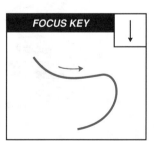

1. Flexed, anticipated position ____

**Execution
Phase**

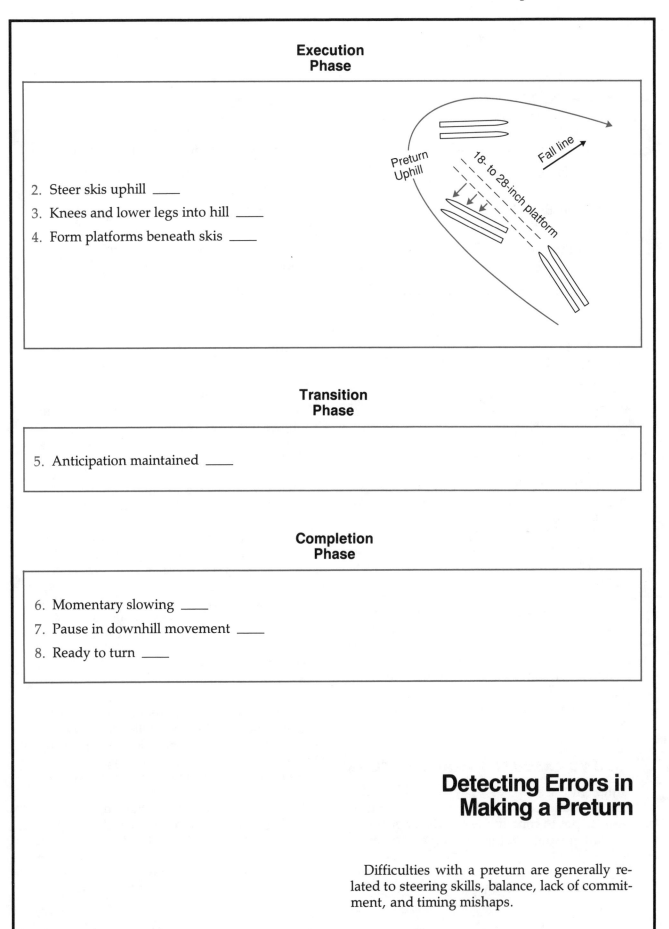

Preturn
Uphill

18- to 28-inch platform

Fall line

2. Steer skis uphill ____

3. Knees and lower legs into hill ____

4. Form platforms beneath skis ____

**Transition
Phase**

5. Anticipation maintained ____

**Completion
Phase**

6. Momentary slowing ____

7. Pause in downhill movement ____

8. Ready to turn ____

# Detecting Errors in Making a Preturn

Difficulties with a preturn are generally related to steering skills, balance, lack of commitment, and timing mishaps.

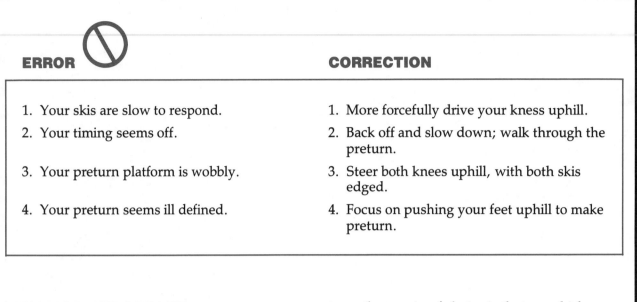

| ERROR | CORRECTION |
|---|---|
| 1. Your skis are slow to respond. | 1. More forcefully drive your kness uphill. |
| 2. Your timing seems off. | 2. Back off and slow down; walk through the preturn. |
| 3. Your preturn platform is wobbly. | 3. Steer both knees uphill, with both skis edged. |
| 4. Your preturn seems ill defined. | 4. Focus on pushing your feet uphill to make preturn. |

## WHY IS IT IMPORTANT TO LINK PARALLEL TURNS?

Parallel turns offer the ultimate in control and grace on the mountain, but without linkage, it is difficult to predict control, and random turning soon ensues. Moreover, linked turns early on in parallel skiing pave the way for a vast exploration of the mountain and conditions.

It is often said that unless you're committed to ENDING one turn in a controlled fashion, you're not committed to BEGINNING a new turn. Linked turns equal speed control! The ill result of a lack of commitment is ragged, unreliable turns that are parallel at times and wedged at times.

By learning to make linked parallel turns, you obviate trial-and-error experimentation with speed control strategies, and raise the likelihood that you'll be able to ski relaxed while feeling more confident. Emotional ambivalence about descending a hill is devastating to one's skiing. ''Turn now or die'' skiing sabotages the best of parallel skills and the most ambitious of skiers.

## HOW TO EXECUTE A PARALLEL TURN

Although the shape of a parallel turn dictates the application of skills, the most appropriate turn shapes to concentrate on when perfecting beginning parallel turns are long and medium radius. Steeper, more challenging terrain that requires short-radius turns is fine for adventure time, but for perfecting your beginning parallel turn, the terrain of choice is that on which you ski in long- and medium-radius turns. If you try to learn a parallel short-radius turn too early in your skill development, you may create more abruptness and frustration than finesse and confidence in your skiing.

Look at the four stages of a parallel turn, and how turning skills are applied at each stage of the turn (see Figure 10.4). In the BEGINNING of the turn, there's a definite commitment to turning. Your body is fully anticipated, with skis parallel, and you're ready to extend up, transfer your weight, and change edges in one flowing movement. To complete the BEGINNING stage of the parallel turn, you uncoil your fully anticipated body and project your hips and upper body into the turn, and at the same time you begin actively and simultaneously steering both skis into the turn.

In the MIDDLE stage of the parallel turn, you remain tall on your skis, but begin to regulate the speed and shape of the turn by the length of time your skis are flat in the fall line. When you stand tall, and your skis are flat in the MIDDLE of a medium-radius parallel turn, your skis will skid laterally. If you add steering to the MIDDLE of the turn, the skidding skis will be edged appropriately so they will turn on an arc while skidding.

In the MIDDLE-END of the turn, steering and slight edging are not enough to complete the arc of the turn across the fall line, and a certain degree of flexion in knees and ankles is needed, along with appropriate angulation. These skills will fine-tune the turn by decreasing or increasing skidding as needed. Very active steering, particularly of the inside ski, is essential, to remain parallel as you turn across the fall line. Hand and arm position is crucial for overall balance and keeping your body aligned for the turn. This is also the time in the turn when you want to begin to anticipate the next turn.

In the END of the parallel turn, you fine-tune a host of skills. Edging is concluded with finely tuned ankle angulation. Steering remains continuous, but a preturn fine-tunes the final moments of steering by providing a transition to weight transfer and edge change. Without a preturn, the steering is fine-tuned right up to the point of weight transfer. Full anticipation signals the finish of the turn, as you are poised and biomechanically ready to enter your new turn.

## Figure 10.4   Keys to Success: Four Stages of a Parallel Turn (Medium Radius)

FOCUS KEY

FLEP #3   FLEP #5

Medium radius

Long radius

**BEGINNING Stage**

1. Fully anticipated ____

2. Extend; flatten skis ____

3. Transfer weight; simultaneous edge change ____

4. Uncoil; project upper body ____

5. Steer skis into turn ____

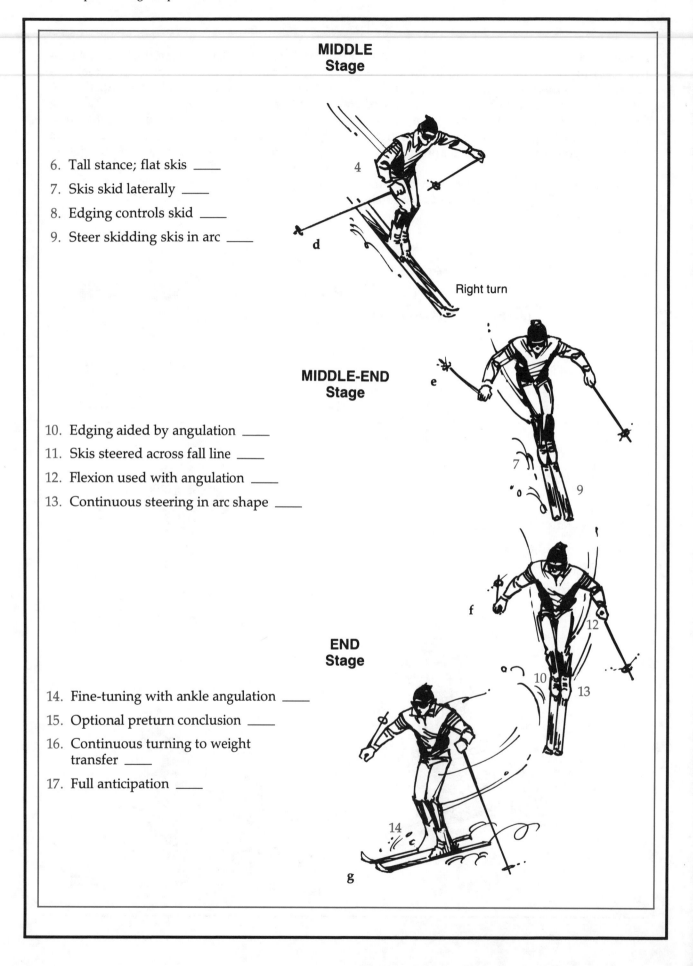

**MIDDLE
Stage**

6. Tall stance; flat skis ____
7. Skis skid laterally ____
8. Edging controls skid ____
9. Steer skidding skis in arc ____

Right turn

**MIDDLE-END
Stage**

10. Edging aided by angulation ____
11. Skis steered across fall line ____
12. Flexion used with angulation ____
13. Continuous steering in arc shape ____

**END
Stage**

14. Fine-tuning with ankle angulation ____
15. Optional preturn conclusion ____
16. Continuous turning to weight transfer ____
17. Full anticipation ____

# Detecting Errors in Parallel Turn

The main challenges to making parallel turns are making an early weight transfer and simultaneous edge change with skis parallel, continuously steering both skis with skis parallel, and subtle edging skills during the MIDDLE and MIDDLE-END of the turn.

**ERROR** ⊘

**CORRECTION**

| ERROR | CORRECTION |
|---|---|
| 1. Your anticipation is partial. | 1. Check your hands, shoulders, head, abdominal region, and hips. |
| 2. Your weight transfer is awkward. | 2. Extend more fully and make skis flat. |
| 3. Your weight transfer is slow; your onset of steering is slow. | 3. Be committed to a new turn when finishing your prior turn; uncoil and cross over. |
| 4. You are unable to control skid. | 4. Make the edge angles on both skis the same; evenly distribute your weight to the skis. |
| 5. You are unable to steer your skis in an arc across the fall line. | 5. Reduce the amount of flexion and angulation in the fall line; decisively steer your skis across the fall line, then add flexion and angulation. |

# Parallel Turning Drills

## 1. Parallel Beginning of a Turn

On low-intermediate terrain, look for a place where the hill slopes away on an angle for a short way. If you cannot, that's fine; the drill can still be done. But first, start in FLEP #2 and traverse to the left for 15 feet. Now sidestep up the hill with your left ski while you are still moving. Remember, when you do this, the right ski must have a platform beneath it, or you will slip laterally. Balancing momentarily on the uphill edge of your left ski, step your right ski up the hill to match your left, again,

while moving in a controlled traverse. Repeat this step-and-match action every 15 feet (see Figure a). Do it three times to each side.

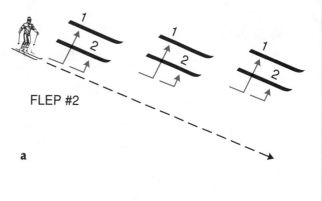

FLEP #2

a

Now, go to that hill that slopes away. If possible, approach the hill in a FLEP #2 traverse to the left. As above, take one, then two, steps up with your left ski and match your right ski while traversing. When you get to the part that slopes away, take your third step but don't match. Instead, step up and as soon as your left' ski touches the slope, begin steering it down the fall line of the slope. As soon as you begin steering the left ski, match the right ski by skidding it next to the left as you actively steer both skis down the slope that falls away (see Figures b and c). Try this to both sides five times.

b

c

**Success Goals** = 5 successful skidded parallel BEGINNINGS to a turn (a) to the right, and (b) to the left

**Your Scores** =

a.  (#) _____ successful of 5 BEGINNINGS to the right

b.  (#) _____ successful of 5 BEGINNINGS to the left

    5 of 5 (excellent)

    4 of 5 (very good)

    3 or less (need more practice)

## 2. *Preturn Formation*

Starting in FLEP #2, traverse across intermediate terrain, and at a selected point, ski to a preturn platform and come to a stop. Change direction, and do the drill to the other side. Next, increase to FLEP #3 and repeat the drill. Continue through FLEP #5, making different kinds of preturn platforms after each traverse.

**Success Goals** = Create various balanced preturns in response to different speeds and angles of descent

**Your Scores** =

| | Balanced Preturns in FLEP # | |
|---|---|---|
| | To Left | To Right |
| a. | | |
| b. | | |
| c. | | |
| d. | | |

## 3. *Preturn Exit*

Repeat the previous drill, but add the element of crossover to the end of each preturn. At the instant the preturn is completed, exaggerate a crossover and turn the skis downhill. Skid to a complete stop after each crossover.

**Success Goals** = Smooth transitions from a preturn to skis entering the fall line for a turn, then skid to a stop, repeating on both sides

**Your Scores** =

|  | Crossovers From FLEP # | |
|---|---|---|
|  | To Left | To Right |
| a. | | |
| b. | | |
| c. | | |
| d. | | |

## 4. *Keep Your Boots Parallel*

Go out on a moderately challenging slope and make a series of medium-radius turns where you "insist" on skiing with your boots parallel. Don't think about your skis being parallel; just ski with boots parallel—focus on keeping your heels close together, but not touching. Don't leave the slope until you get your boots in parallel. After you make a turn, get your boots parallel. When you glide, get your boots parallel. Each time your boots are parallel, remember your takeoffs from Step 9, Drill 7, and try to couple that sensation with the crossover effect.

Thinking of skiing with boots parallel, try to progress through all four phases of the medium-radius parallel turn, in pyramiding fashion. Start by just doing the BEGINNING (B) of a turn, then stop. Then do a BEGINNING and MIDDLE (M) of a turn, then stop. Next, do a BEGIN-NING, MIDDLE, and MIDDLE-END (M-E), then stop. And finally, do a completed turn, and stop (END or E). Next, work your way back down the pyramid to doing only a BEGINNING to a stop. Do to both sides.

**Success Goals** = Completion of the pyramid with boots parallel to each side

**Your Scores** = Mark success with an "X"

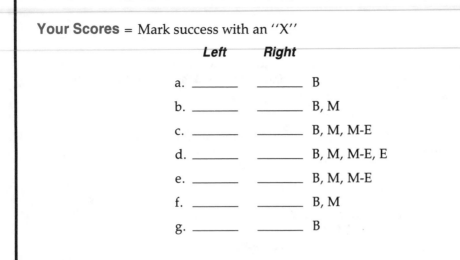

|  | Left | Right |  |
|---|---|---|---|
| a. | _____ | _____ | B |
| b. | _____ | _____ | B, M |
| c. | _____ | _____ | B, M, M-E |
| d. | _____ | _____ | B, M, M-E, E |
| e. | _____ | _____ | B, M, M-E |
| f. | _____ | _____ | B, M |
| g. | _____ | _____ | B |

## 5. Medium-Radius Garlands on the Slope

On another traverse in FLEP #3, ski across the slope and tip your ankles downhill to slope-flatten your skis. While your skis are skidding, extend tall and steer your skis, in parallel, into the fall line as if to begin a medium-radius turn, but *don't* turn. Instead, steer your skis back out of the fall line and back into the diagonal course of your traverse. Repeat this across the hill in both directions, several times. The steering of your skis out of the fall line tests your ability to control your skidding by adding appropriate degrees of edging.

This exercise orientation is called a "garland progression" and can be applied to the development of many skiing skills where you want to use the relative pitch of the fall line, yet do not want (or need) to complete turns each time you commit to the fall line. One goal of this garland drill is to keep your skis parallel as much of the time as possible. This exercise is particularly helpful for learning to steer your skis with both boots at the same time.

*Note*: If you find yourself on terrain that appears too steep, yet on which you must ski to get down the mountain, you can use a garland maneuver or sideslipping to get through the difficult portion of the run. With the garland you pick up speed as soon as you get in the fall line, but you neutralize and decrease the speed as soon as you turn out of the fall line.

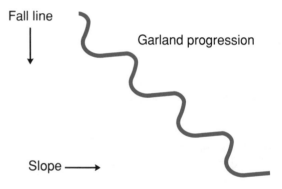

Fall line

Garland progression

Slope →

**Success Goals** = Create garland half-turns to both sides across intermediate terrain

**Your Scores** =

a. (#) ____ of garland half-turns in series to the right

b. (#) ____ of garland half-turns in series to the left

## 6. *Making Dynamic Platforms*

As you know, platforms are formed by the interaction of the bases of your skis and the snow they have displaced under your skis. Beginning parallel platforms are an important part of your development as a sound parallel skier, and well worth the effort.

Stand on a moderately steep hill, with both skis edged across the fall line. At first, use your poles for balance and bounce up and down without leaving the snow. Remove your poles from the snow, but have them in hand, and hop up off the snow and make another platform as you land. Do this repeatedly as you hop from platform to platform down the slope.

Simultaneously edging your skis to form a platform requires balance and a certain degree of courage, because unlike a sequentially formed platform, where you can use one ski for balance at all times, with a simultaneously formed platform you risk losing balance if you don't edge both skis with the correct angles and degree of pressure. The need to simultaneously edge your skis to ensure balance is particularly important as parallel skiing gets more demanding and more fun!

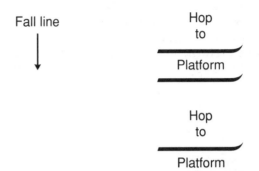

**Success Goals** = 5 hops from one platform to another in sequence (a) to the right, and (b) to the left

**Your Scores** =

a. (#) ____ of platforms formed in sequence to the right

b. (#) ____ of platforms formed in sequence to the left

   5 of 5 (excellent)

   4 of 5 (very good)

   3 of 5 (good)

   2 or fewer (need balance work)

# Parallel Turns
# Keys to Success Checklists

Ask a friend to observe you making beginning parallel turns. Checklist items in Figures 10.3 and 10.4 can be used to evaluate your performance and to offer corrective feedback. Your observer should pay particular attention to whether your skis remain parallel throughout the turn, and should notice whether you are using a preturn, and recognize terrain on which it might be appropriate to do so if you are not.

The degree of skidding you do does not matter, as long as your skis remain parallel and you steer them throughout the turns.

If your parallel turns are smooth, ask your friend to observe you linking a series of four to eight turns. Your observer's focus should be on the transition between turns. As necessary, review the checklist items in Figure 6.8.

## Step 11   Using Your Ski Poles

Admittedly, a lot of skiers' first introduction to ski poles is having them sized when they purchase or rent them. Beyond the maneuverability usages of ski poles, a good many skiers do little else with their poles, and lacking instruction or guidance on using their poles, they more or less carry them around with them when skiing, waiting to get to the lift line to use them. Or worse, they use them in ways that interfere with their skiing development and safety.

There are different opinions about when to introduce pole use as an integral part of one's skiing. Early in my teaching I was hounded to teach skiers to use poles right away in their skiing. When skiers were introduced to the poles too early in their skiing, I found many either relied too much on their poles (i.e., leaned on them and pushed off with them) or became very confused about incorporating them into their learning when they were struggling with biomechanically memorizing the most basic turning skills. Some new skiers actually get worse when poles are added to their skiing too early in their development.

In recent years, and today, my preference is to wait until skiers possess basic skidded parallel skills before introducing the pole swing, pole touch, and pole plant to their skiing. In this way, I believe, pole use makes what they know already even more useful. Introducing pole use at this point in their skiing makes them better skiers.

This step will briefly review the generic uses of ski poles and familiarize you with the three principal functional uses of ski poles in parallel and more advanced skiing. As well, you will learn how dysfunctional pole use can interfere with your development of skiing skills and actually risk injury. You will learn how to make a reliable pole swing, pole touch, and pole plant, and why learning to use ski poles is a gradual process for the beginning parallel skier.

### WHY SKI POLES HAVE A GENERIC VALUE TO ALL SKIERS

There are a number of uses of ski poles that at one time or another are accessed by skiers of all ability levels: maneuvering on the flats, getting into and out of lift lines, cleaning snow off boots, getting up after falling, towing children around behind you, waving to friends, picking up litter, inscribing messages on sidehills, pushing yourself out of tree wells, and more generally, giving you a tactile sense of the snow conditions.

### Three Functional Uses of Poles

The three principal functional uses of poles are using them to create a pole swing, to make a pole touch, and to make a pole plant.

1. The *pole swing*, once learned, dictates the shape and frequency of your turns down any slope. The pole swing, when coupled with a pole touch, promotes rhythm in your skiing, which is particularly important when you use turning to control speed. Why? Because in beginning parallel skiing the pole swing occurs at only one time in the turn: just as you are ENDING the turn.

As you swing the downhill pole forward, your body begins to assume full anticipation and is prepared to move fluidly into extension and early weight transfer when your pole touches the snow. The rest of the turn proceeds as learned. Sometimes the pole swing and what accompanies it are referred to as preparation for the turn. In the way I conceive of it, the pole swing BEGINS the new turn.

When you are preparing to turn left, swing your left pole; when you are preparing to turn right, swing your right pole. Once learned, the swinging of the poles signals full anticipation. Although the pole is always touched on the downhill side of your skis, the most appropriate place to touch the pole in the snow will vary depending on terrain, speed, and shape of turn (see Figure 11.1, a-c).

2. The *pole touch* is also called a "pole tap," because the action of the pole touch is really to tap the snow with the tip of the pole. When the pole tip touches the snow, you know it's time to get into the turn mechanics: extend off the touched pole and transfer weight to your new

**a**                    **b**                    **c**

**Figure 11.1**  Pole touch. For short-radius turns touch slightly in front of your boots as you reach downhill with your poll (a); for medium-radius turns touch midway up the front of your ski (b); and for long-radius turns touch near the tip of your ski (c).

outside ski. In addition to its timing value, the pole touch gives you feedback about the position of your skis relative to your upper body when you're getting ready to turn.

Moreover, a pole touch reminds you of the snow's texture, the pitch of the hill you're turning down (or up), and the speed at which you're traveling. All of this information is transmitted to you through your hands and your senses of proprioception (i.e., your sense of position within the space within reach).

As sensory information about the snow is conducted to your hands, ski poles can carry input that prompts your body to send neuromuscular messages to your skiing muscles and joints to alter edging, angulation, flexion, or the timing of weight transfer, for example.

3. Unlike the pole touch, the *pole plant* is actually a distinct and powerful placement of the tip of your downhill pole in the snow below you, and it is used specifically when skiing the fall line of challenging and demanding terrain (e.g., steep terrain, mogully terrain). An effective pole plant will momentarily slow your body's mass so it won't cross over the path of your skis before you're ready to turn them.

Thus, a pole plant allows you to get balanced—and fully anticipated—for your next turn (see Figure 11.2a). When you add a preturn to the pole plant, you create a highly stable stance from which to extend, transfer your weight, project, and steer into the fall line to BEGIN a new turn (see Figure 11.2b)—extending off the preturn.

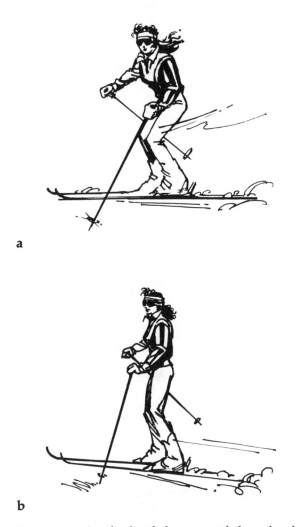

**a**

**b**

**Figure 11.2**  A pole plant helps you get balanced and fully anticipated whether preparing for your next turn (a) or extending off the preturn (b).

### When Pole Use is Dysfunctional

Briefly, the following ski-pole-related actions are bound to get you in trouble with yourself or other skiers on the mountain.

1. Swinging your ski poles side to side like helicopter blades, turn to turn, may cause erratic skiing or strike another skier.
2. Dragging the tips of your poles next to your skis for the ''rooster tail'' effect, hands glued to the sides of your mid-thighs or hips, may cause you to ''trip'' over your poles.
3. Using a pole plant as a braking mechanism midway through a turn may lead to an abrupt, arm-wrenching fall.
4. Skiing with the tip of one or both poles out in front of you as if probing for a place to be touched or planted in the snow may lead to another skier getting speared, or your pole dropping unexpectedly to the snow and causing a kick-back spearing of yourself.

## WHY LEARNING TO USE SKI POLES IS A PROCESS THAT REQUIRES PATIENCE

Although a pole swing and pole touching or planting are biomechanical activities that follow a logical course and seemingly straightforward application, in practice they rarely seem so forthright when skiers try them. Sure, some skiers watch another skier demonstrate how to use their poles, and they copy very well—at first. The goal of ski-pole use in skiing is long-term adherence to using poles, to making pole use an automatic part of skiing. This takes time, plenty of time, on skis.

The problems associated with establishing functional pole use as part of your skiing are often subtle, and like other timing skills, they are resolved through disciplined practice over many repetitions. Even the firmness with which you grasp the grip, or the design of the grip itself, may be at issue in your learning: a common predicament with molded grips is their fitting too tightly for a good pole swing. You can generally avoid fitting problems by using grips with straps.

Overall, probably the biggest stumbling block to learning pole use is the very thing you're aiming to achieve: timing. What you're doing with your arms and hands must be timed with what you're doing with your feet and legs, shoulders, and head—and all at the same time you're coursing down a slope among other skiers. Beginning parallel skiers need more than a season to ''groove'' their parallel turns; ''automatic'' parallel turning, where there's no thought about what to do to make smooth, rounded turns, takes years to develop for most skiers.

Expecting pole use to instantly click into place is rarely a realistic assessment of this skiing skill, especially when you learn later that pole use itself takes on many more subtleties as skiing skill-level rises. If pole use doesn't come immediately, don't conclude it's a hopeless goal for you. Please, allow time to develop pole use in your skiing, and if as you learn the functional uses of ski poles you learn also to avoid the dysfunctional uses, you'll be way ahead of the game.

Remember, the degree of slipping of your skis on the snow, the nature of the snow, terrain choice, other skiers on the slopes, lack of practice time, actual skiing speed, wind velocity, outdoor temperature, clothing bulk, gloves, weight of ski poles—all of these may affect your learning to use ski poles. If pole use doesn't come after repeated practice, back off a bit. Take some time to free ski and have fun. Watch ski instructors and other form-conscious skiers use their poles, and go back out and work more casually with your poles. If poles come to you right away, great! Now perfect their use.

## HOW TO USE SKI POLES

Ski poles are a certain length for skiers so that when they are standing upright, their poles will be able to swing forward without catching in the snow, and be touched or planted accordingly so a turn can proceed as planned. Too long a pole will catch up the skier every time; too short a pole will lead to a stooped-over skiing stance.

The intention for the pole swing is to set up the pole touch or plant. The swing itself has no functional use in skiing beyond its being a timing device for when it's time to get ready to make your new turn. Very often, the direction or arc of the pole swing will predict the shape of turn to follow, so it is an important technique to learn well.

When the pole swing is toward the tip of your skis, this usually predicts a pole touch for a long-radius turn. When the pole swing is angled toward the downhill side of the forebody of your ski, it usually predicts a pole touch for a medium-radius turn. When the pole swing is directed well down the hill somewhere between your boots and the forebody of the ski, it usually predicts a pole plant for a short-radius turn.

The only pole you swing is the downhill pole. The other pole remains in a basic skiing position at all times during the turn until its turn comes to be swung. As your pole touches you begin to turn.

Biomechanically, you swing a pole by flipping your wrist forward, tempering the swing of your pole with your forearm. Grasp the pole securely with your thumb, palm, and index and middle fingers, and relax your little and ring fingers as you let the grip of the pole swing through your hand. At all times, try to keep your pole-swinging hand level with your midsection. If you maintain this focus, you'll know instinctively when to flex to accommodate your pole touch and your pole plant.

As a rule, the farther you reach away from your skis, the more you must be flexed to keep your grip at waist level. If you must reach far down the hill, you probably need to be flexed to hold an edge on your skis. For example, if you reach your pole down steeper terrain, you'll have to flex to maintain the waist-level focus, yet on steeper terrain you need the flexion. Conversely, on shallow terrain, a pole touched alongside the forebody of the ski will not require much flexion to maintain a midsection height with your grip.

When your pole touches the snow, your grip should be secure. When your pole is planted in the snow, your grip must be very secure, with your wrist cocked back a bit and locked to make it a stronger joint. When your pole is either touched or planted, it is a signal to begin to execute the turn appropriate to the pole use. Thus, the first step to successful pole use is making the swinging and touching and planting of the pole part of your anticipation for each new turn (see Figure 11.3).

*Figure 11.3  Keys to Success:
Using Ski Poles
(For Medium- and
Short-Radius Turns)*

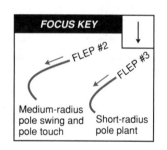

**Preparation
Phase**

1. Basic skiing stance, parallel \_\_\_\_

## Execution
## Phase

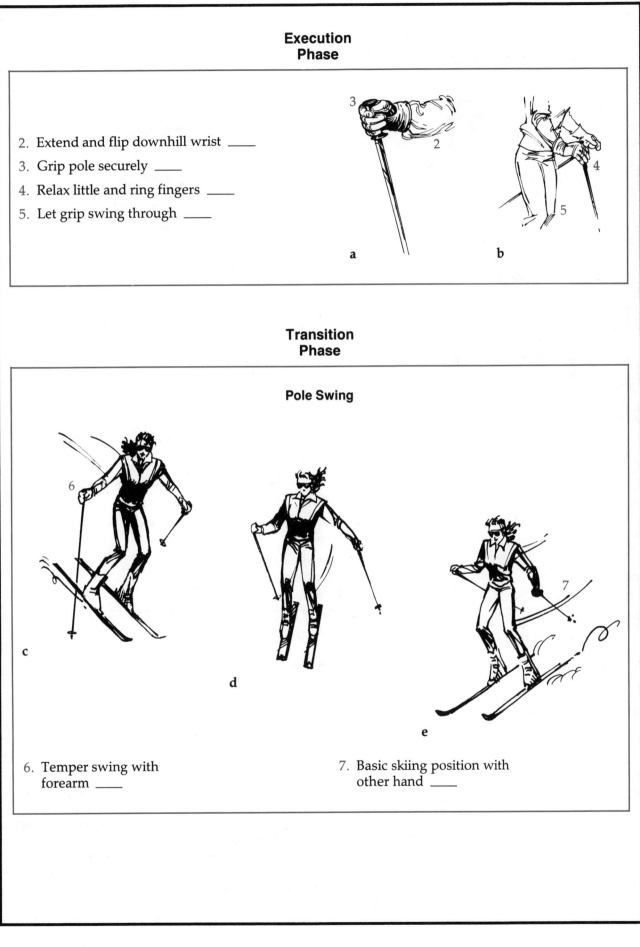

2. Extend and flip downhill wrist ____
3. Grip pole securely ____
4. Relax little and ring fingers ____
5. Let grip swing through ____

a

b

## Transition
## Phase

### Pole Swing

c

d

e

6. Temper swing with
   forearm ____

7. Basic skiing position with
   other hand ____

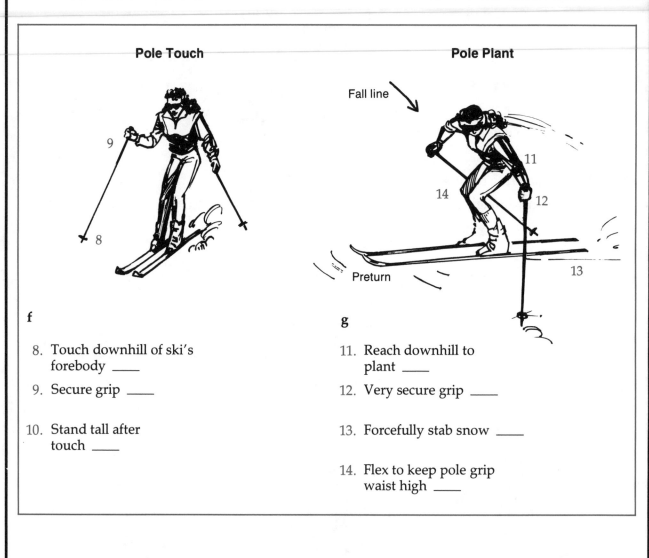

**Pole Touch**

**Pole Plant**

Fall line

9

8

11

14

12

13

Preturn

**f**

**g**

8. Touch downhill of ski's forebody ___

9. Secure grip ___

10. Stand tall after touch ___

11. Reach downhill to plant ___

12. Very secure grip ___

13. Forcefully stab snow ___

14. Flex to keep pole grip waist high ___

## Completion Phase

15. Execute appropriate turns ___

# Detecting Errors in Pole Use

Timing is critical in effective pole use. In addition, pole-swing errors are largely grip errors, while pole-touch errors often involve steering problems, and pole-plant errors are usually related to weak grip strength, poor placement of poles, and lack of complementary edging and angulation skills.

**ERROR**                                              **CORRECTION**

### Pole Swing

1. Your pole tip catches in the snow during its swing forward.

2. Your pole doesn't swing freely.

3. Your stationary arm (with the uphill pole) relaxes and drops to the side.

4. You flex too soon after the forward swing of the pole.

5. You pause at the forward swing point.

6. Your downhill arm drops to the side after the forward swing.

7. Your downhill arm swings from the shoulder.

1. Extend very tall; keep hand and arm in basic skiing position.

2. Relax the grasp of your little and ring fingers.

3. Resist relaxing the tension in gripping the uphill pole.

4. Reach out to lengthen at the time of the forward swing.

5. Maintain continuous motion and make snow contact.

6. Your return to basic skiing position is critical to the subsequent turn.

7. Swing your pole by flipping your wrist.

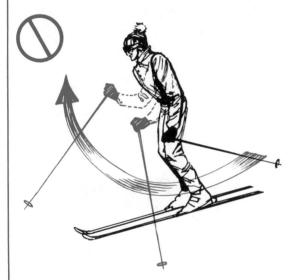

### Pole Touch

1. Pole touch occurs after your turn begins.

2. Your turn is too square and abrupt.

3. Your turn is jerky; your pole touch pulls your body out of position.

4. Your pole tip gets caught in the snow during the touch.

1. Speed up your pole swing; work on the timing of your swing.

2. Touch your pole in the way that is appropriate to the turn shape.

3. Don't exaggerate the pole swing so the pole swings too high in front.

4. You are applying too much force to the touch; tap the snow!

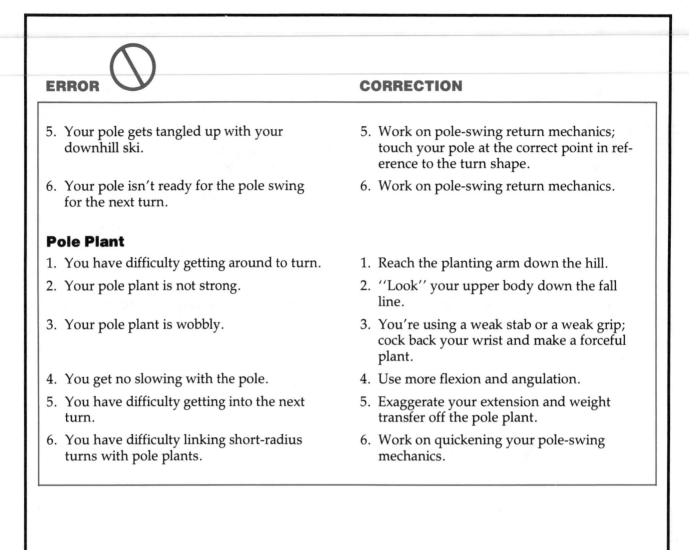

| ERROR | CORRECTION |
|---|---|
| 5. Your pole gets tangled up with your downhill ski. | 5. Work on pole-swing return mechanics; touch your pole at the correct point in reference to the turn shape. |
| 6. Your pole isn't ready for the pole swing for the next turn. | 6. Work on pole-swing return mechanics. |

**Pole Plant**

| | |
|---|---|
| 1. You have difficulty getting around to turn. | 1. Reach the planting arm down the hill. |
| 2. Your pole plant is not strong. | 2. ''Look'' your upper body down the fall line. |
| 3. Your pole plant is wobbly. | 3. You're using a weak stab or a weak grip; cock back your wrist and make a forceful plant. |
| 4. You get no slowing with the pole. | 4. Use more flexion and angulation. |
| 5. You have difficulty getting into the next turn. | 5. Exaggerate your extension and weight transfer off the pole plant. |
| 6. You have difficulty linking short-radius turns with pole plants. | 6. Work on quickening your pole-swing mechanics. |

# Pole-Use Drills

## 1. Static Coordinated Pole Swing

Position your hands and arms as you would while skiing in a basic skiing position. Standing on a flat part of the slope, swing one pole forward and one back while keeping your hands and arms in a basic skiing position. Swing the pole forward by flipping your wrist and releasing your little finger as the pole grip swings past. At the same time, bend the other wrist downward, releasing the index finger as the grip drops away.

As soon as you establish the pole-swing rhythm, add a flexion/extension rhythm where you're extended each time the poles cross paths by your boots, and flexed when one pole is reached forward and the other back. Now test yourself.

**Success Goal** = 10 consecutively coordinated pole swings in rhythm with the lower body's flexing and extending

**Your Score** = (#) _____ consecutively coordinated pole swings with correct flexion and extension rhythm

9 or 10 (excellent)

6 to 8 (good)

5 of 10 (average)

4 or less (need more work)

## 2. *Dynamic Downhill Pole Swing*

Start on easy intermediate terrain in a traverse. Begin swinging your downhill pole, but don't touch the snow with it. Start your traverse, continuing to swing only the downhill pole while the uphill pole is held in a basic skiing position. Traverse to each side several times, using the humming of a tune for rhythm. After you have the coordinated swinging rhythm, add the same rhythm of flexion and extension as in the previous drill. Now test yourself, but on only the downhill pole swing, looking downhill each time you swing as if to prepare yourself to turn.

**Success Goals** = Complete traverses to each side in rhythm, coordinating pole swing and flexion/extension

**Your Scores** =

a. (#) _____ traverses to the right

b. (#) _____ traverses to the left

## 3. *Pole Swing in the Fall Line*

After developing some semblance of feel and rhythm in the pole swing, you're ready to try something entirely new. Start in FLEP #6 on a slope with a very slight pitch. Ski parallel or ski in a comfortable wedge as follows:

a. Ski straight down the run for 50 feet, rhythmically and slowly swinging your poles—one forward, one back—without letting the tips touch the snow.

b. Ski another 50 feet, continuing to rhythmically swing your poles, but now letting the tip of the forward swinging pole lightly touch the snow.

When doing this action in parallel, concentrate on flexing your knees and ankles as if you're making pole plants each time the pole touches the snow; your knees and ankles will be slightly flexed, resembling the edging at the end of a turn.

When doing this action in a wedge, concentrate on flexing the knee and ankle on the side of your pole touch. However, now your pole touching the snow will be your signal to extend out of the flexed position on that side of your body, and immediately transfer your weight to the other ski, where you'll repeat the same procedure.

As you're doing this from side to side, you establish a rhythm of "down and up" motion to accompany the pole touch, and each time you swing a pole forward, remember to give a look that way with your head and shoulders.

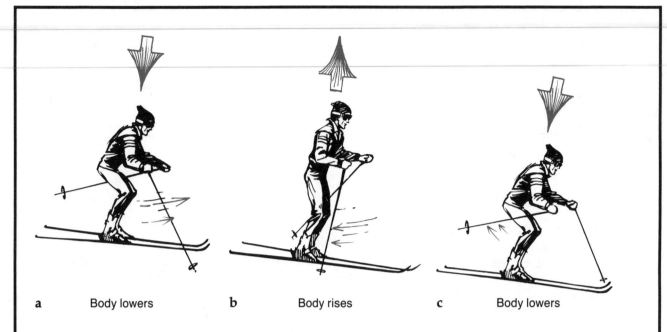

**a**      Body lowers      **b**      Body rises      **c**      Body lowers

**Success Goals** = Link a series of 12 pole swings and touches (6 to each side), coordinating pole swing and flexion/extension

**Your Scores** =

a. (#) _____ of pole swings linked

b. (#) _____ of attempts to be this successful

## 4. Pole Touch in Linked Wedge Turns

On intermediate terrain, employ the method of pole swing and flexion/extension from the previous drill, but lengthen the distance between swings and make slow-speed, short-radius wedge turns.

**Success Goals** = Link a series of 10 wedge turns, coordinating pole touch and flexion/extension

**Your Scores** =

a. (#) _____ of linked wedge turns

b. (#) _____ of attempts to be this successful

## 5. Pole Touch in Linked Parallel Turns

Return to parallel skiing, and start in FLEP #6 on a slope on which you can travel at a comfortable speed, but one that is fast enough for making fluid parallel turns. Do Drill 4, but with skidded parallel turns of medium to long radius. You'll notice an increase in speed, as well as the need to always look ahead into your next turn. Incidental to the exercise and speed, you may feel an increase in pole deflection with each pole touch. This drill affords a great opportunity to discover the optimal speed for your turning and pole swing and touch. Go out afterward and try it in your free skiing.

**Success Goals** = Link a series of 10 skidded parallel turns, coordinating pole touch and flexion/extension

**Your Scores** =

a. (#) ____ of linked skidded parallel turns

b. (#) ____ of attempts to be this successful

## 6. *Pole-Touch Garlands*

A great drill to coordinate the action of the pole touch triggering extension into the new turn is to make a series of garlands across comfortable intermediate terrain. Begin in FLEP #6, and after picking up a little speed, turn out of the fall line. As soon as you turn out of the fall line, you'll be slightly flexed. As you initiate a downhill pole swing, you will begin to rise and extend. When the tip of your pole touches the snow, you should be fully extended and ready to turn down the fall line. Turn, but travel only 5 to 10 feet and turn out of the fall line again. Repeat the process across the slope, three times to each side. Use either skidded, wedge, or parallel turns.

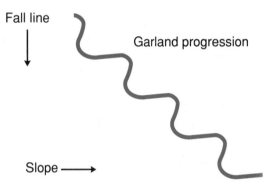

**Success Goals** = 3 completed series of 4 pole-touch garlands (a) to the right, and (b) to the left

**Your Scores** =

a. (#) ____ completed series of 4 pole-touch garlands to the right

b. (#) ____ completed series of 4 pole-touch garlands to the left

## 7. *Pole-Plant Follow Me*

Pair up with a friend and let her or him lead the way. Follow 15 to 20 feet behind. Your friend's assignment: Make as many and as varied pole plants on intermediate terrain as she or he can. Your assignment: Match as many of your friend's pole plants as you can, trying to stab the snow in the same place as your friend.

**Success Goals** = To enjoy the drill and subjectively test your quickness to respond to and to correctly position yourself for your friend's pole plants

**Your Scores** =

a. ____ Did you enjoy yourself? (yes or no)

b. How would you rate your performance?

____ Excellent

____ Good

____ Fair

____ Poor

## 8. Pole Plant in Moguls

Time for a little adventure, if you haven't already enjoyed some. Look for a patch of developing or small moguls on easy intermediate terrain. They may be difficult to find, so look to the bottom sections of more demanding intermediate runs. Ski up to a mogul, plant your downhill pole right on its top, and try to turn around it by skidding your skis around its front side. Try again and again, one mogul at a time. Next, try to do this to a series of four to eight moguls.

**Success Goals** = To enjoy the drill and subjectively assess both your comfort zone in moguls and your ability to make short-radius turns in this condition

**Your Scores** =

a. ____ Did you enjoy yourself? (yes or no)

b. (#) ____ of turns linked in the moguls

c. How would you rate your performance?

____ Excellent

____ Good

____ Fair

____ Poor

# Ski-Pole Use
# Keys to Success Checklist

Ask a friend to observe each phase of your pole use. During your pole swing, pay particular attention to the action of your wrists and the position of your "resting" pole. During your pole touch, pay particular attention to its use as a trigger mechanism for turning. Is it rhythmic, on time, too late, or even too early? During your pole plant, pay particular attention to its slowing affect on your turning. Are you flexing enough, fully extending to get into your next turn? Is your upper body "looking" into the next turn? Checklist items in Figure 11.3 can be used to evaluate your performance and offer corrective feedback.

# Step 12   Adapting to Varying Terrain and Snow

Enough is just never enough, is it? Here you are a beginning parallel skier, and I'd be less than honest if I didn't throw you a few more curves that, coincidentally, have little to do with turn shape. In this discussion of how varying terrain and snow impact your skiing, I will present no drills or Keys to Success. Both are beyond the scope of this book. I will, however, offer some observations about different terrains and kinds of snow, and a tip or two about how you can adapt to each, given your present level of skill development.

## SNOWMAKING SNOW

When the weather is cold enough (freezing and below), water is pumped through elaborate networks of hoses with specially designed high-pressure valves that emit a spectacular mist that, upon exposure to the cold air, forms what may be characterized as a granular, heavy "flake" that is very skiable after it's been packed and machine groomed.

Snowmaking snow is best skied when it's cold. As soon as the air warms near or above freezing, these crystals start breaking down, making it more challenging and demanding to ski. A destructive force to snowmaking snow that has accumulated for several days, or been spread thick by grooming, is excessive skier traffic. The end result is the snow mounding up and thickening.

### Adaptation Tips

- If snowmaking is the snow of the day, ski it only if it stays cold.
- If skier traffic is heavy, ski early and avoid the mounds of thick snow.

## SKIER-PACKED SNOW

After a new storm has dropped new snow, there will be trails on the mountain that are left ungroomed. The powder snow will be skied through by thousands of skiers and, in the process, packed down. The surface may be uneven and bumpy, and depending on how much snow fell, the bumps may be insignificant rolls or large moguls. This is called skier-packed powder (or skier-packed snow) after a storm.

Another form of skier-packed snow is trails that had been groomed one day, skied over, and left for skiers to ski as is on the subsequent day.

### Adaptation Tips

- Don't ski this passively, but don't try to overpower the bumps and ridges.
- Make decisive turns, matching your skis early in the turn.
- Keep skidding to a minimum.
- Ski the fall line as much as possible.

## MOGULLY SNOW

Speaking of bumpy, moguls are formed after thousands and thousands of turns have been made in relatively the same place in new and softly packed snow. Moguls are the bain of many skiers, because they appear as obstacles between them and the other end of the run. Mogul fields are decreasing in number, but some of those left to mature appear as monsters reserved for the gallant to slay.

Moguls come in all shapes and sizes, and their look scares the "jeebies" out of the "heebies" in many inexperienced skiers. The more intermediate the hill, the more raggedly shaped the moguls. Moguls can be soft when formed from new snow; hard, when they've been left to mature and the weather has warmed up a bit (then cooled down at night); and very slushy and soft, when the weather is warm during the ski day (45 to 55+ degrees Fahrenheit).

### Adaptation Tips

- The main focus of your skiing in moguls should be to link turns.
- Shorter radius turns allow for more speed control and a greater comfort zone. Think very quick feet!

- Some mogul fields on intermediate trails can be skied with linked medium-radius turns.
- The important tactic with moguls: Get a mental and visual picture of where you want to go, and follow through.
- Make the moguls conform to your turns, and don't afford them the status of obstacles against which you are engaged in battle.
- Use a solid pole plant to prevent your upper body from crossing over too soon in the bumps.
- Keep looking ahead of you, and try to keep your upper body fully anticipated.

## FLUFFY POWDER

This is new snow that sometimes looks and fluffs like white feathers. You can actually blow it off your skis or clothing. It's next to impossible to form snowballs with this fluffy snow, because the water content is so low. It can be any depth, but once it has fallen you must try skiing it. Everyone can ski 3 to 5 inches of this fluff on any slope with which they are familiar. Deeper amounts are also very skiable for even the inexperienced.

### Adaptation Tips

- If you get the chance to try turning in fluff, don't pass it up.
- Turn as you would normally turn, but concentrate on a slower than normal rhythm, full anticipation, good extension, and the feel of "light" feet as you steer your skis.

## HEAVY WET SNOW

Just the opposite of fluff, heavy wet snow looks and acts like feathers drenched in oil. You can't blow it off your skis and clothing with an air compressor, and the snowballs you could make with this snow could put a hole in a brick wall if thrown with enough force. Some think: Not fun stuff. In the Sierra Nevada Mountains of California and Nevada, this snow is half-affectionately called Sierra Cement. Nevertheless, it does offer another skiing challenge that's worth it if you have basic parallel skills and the snow is not too deep.

Many skiers refuse to ski this kind of snow. Frankly, I think they're missing out on a fantastic opportunity to test their skills and learn about their level of adaptability to varied snow conditions.

### Adaptation Tips

- If the snow's heavy and wet and only 3 to 6 inches deep, go out and give it a try.
- If the snow's much deeper than 6 inches, and you lack powder experience, you risk injury.
- The most important adaptation you need to make in your skiing is plenty of extension and very active lower leg and foot retraction and steering. When you retract your legs, you bend them at the knees and pull them toward your chest, like you'd do when hopping laterally over an obstacle with your feet together.
- An active anticipation and projection of your upper body into the new turn may aid steering in heavy wet snow.

## DEEP POWDER

Deep powder is snow you should not be skiing. It is simply the remains of a new storm that, for new skiers, measure anywhere from 18 inches to 2 feet plus. For more experienced skiers who still lack a certain degree of confidence with parallel skills, 2 to 3 feet is deep. Even very good skiers may find anything over 3-1/2 to 4 feet too deep unless the terrain is steep.

### Adaptation Tip

- Stay out of deep powder until this book is ancient history to you.

## SPRING SLUSH

Spring slush is wet stuff, but it's fun snow to ski because it is very forgiving of your technical snafus. Skis skid well in slush that's not too deep or wet, and slush bumps (moguls) are a seasonal joy for a good many mogul mashers. Because slush is later season snow that's melted in the sun's rays, skiing slush is both technical and social. There are ways to ski it best, indeed, but the fun of being out with skiers in shorts and bathing suits is unlike other experiences on skis.

Slush snow is so named because it is literally like slush: granular, wet, loosely configured. It can appear sticky and slow, but that's the nature of this condition.

### Adaptation Tips

- Definitely ski spring slush, but make adaptations in your skiing.
- Let your inside (uphill) ski ride lightly atop the snow, and do most of the contact work with the snow with your downhill ski. Actively steer your inside ski at all times in slush, but keep it lightly on the snow.
- Don't use a lot of edge angle in slush.
- Try to make your turns as much as possible in the fall line with very little traverse between turns.

## CORN SNOW

Corn snow is slush snow that's firmed up and frozen overnight, and that in the morning is like millions of ball-bearing-size snowballs riding atop the frozen slush base. Cold nights and warm days are a prerequisite for corn snow, but it's a fond sight for many avid "cornhuskers."

### Adaptation Tips

- Get out early and ski it if you can.
- Steeper, more challenging slopes offer the best corn snow skiing, because pitch aids travel through corn snow over a frozen slush base.
- Corn snow is good for only a limited time before the corn turns to slush, and the slush gets wetter and more slushy.
- Get out early and follow the sun as it warms different areas on the mountain.

## POORLY LIT SNOW

You'll get to situations where everything seems to blend together—the snow, the trees, the rocks, the skiers. It's frightening, because the light can change so suddenly and you're totally unprepared. In this case you've got to ski out, but how? You can't see a thing. Similarly, when it's snowing heavily, or when it's snowing and windy, visibility is severely restricted.

### Adaptation Tips

- If your skills are suspect and you know lighting or visibility will be poor, it's best to stay off the more challenging and well-traveled slopes.
- Listen to the messages you receive from your feet, hands, and ears, and reduce your speed. With too fast a speed in these conditions, you may actually tend to lean back and away from where you want to be.
- Use any trees, large rocks, ski towers, buildings, and the like that may be near the run as objects of contrast against the snowy white flat light. Increase the contrast, and you increase your "visibility" in poorly lit snow.
- Look ahead to any sense of horizon that may be there, and stay in perspective.
- Ski standing centered over your skis, and ski tall so you can adjust either way to unseen terrain.
- Open your stance a bit, and ski with skis a bit wider apart.

## "SNOW CRUNCHIES"

The grooming machines were out last night, and they raked over a number of runs while they were still slushy. The result: When the snow firmed up, it did so as small to large chunks of snow and ice. When these are skied, the going is rough and tumble, and were you to tumble among "snow crunchies," you might wish you were at home watching TV. The clumps seem to be out to deflect the tips of your skis, and they are difficult to ski until they soften and can be skied like slush and skier-packed snow.

When the snow gets quite firm and no new snow has fallen for some time, some resorts will "till" and groom certain trails. The tilled snow can also produce snow crunchies of a sort, and tilled snow can also act like snowmaking snow in its breakdown. Just be aware, and ski with care!

### Adaptation Tip

- Snow crunchies may never actually be fun to ski, but there is some satisfaction when skiing them just before they turn to slush.

# The Alpine Experience

Indeed, there are a vast number of different snow conditions and situations in which you may at one time or another find yourself. Many will simply be new chapters in your book of alpine adventures; others will be true challenges to your level of skill development; some will seem unnerving. An examination of the Appendix, ''Controlling the Fears Between Your Ears,'' might be appropriate on more than one occasion. Refer to it again and again, and remember that the most important reason for being out on the mountain may not be to succeed at the sport, but to succeed at enjoying the many alpine experiences skiing offers you. Enjoy the snow, the vistas, the other skiers, the thrill of accomplishment, the conquest of fear, the pride in learning—and most importantly, if you'll permit me a bias, enjoy your moment alone with the mountain.

# Rating Your Total Progress

Alpine or downhill skiing, like Nordic or cross-country skiing and snowboarding, is a wonderfully exhilarating experience in which you, given the proper equipment and know-how, cojoin with nature at specific times of the year to satisfy your hunger for on-snow adventure. Each skier's experience of these variables is unique unto him- or herself, and for me this is both the lure and the magic of skiing.

Through this introductory book to alpine skiing, you've been exposed to all of the essentials, and more, necessary to guide you from novice to beginning parallel skier. Your success with the steps and drills herein will prepare you for a lifetime of commerce with any mountain you choose to ski. Moreover, your success can also be the success of your friends and family as you share your fundamental knowledge and experiences with them.

Learning to ski is not an overnight, 1-week-a-year process. Your skiing will continue to develop for as long as you ski and find challenge in the mountain and wish to fine-tune your style and expertise. To be sure, skiing proficiency is tested at every level of performance, and development as a parallel skier is variable for each skier.

Some may "get it" after several days on the snow; others may take a period of years, if skiing visits are more vacation oriented and sporadic than regular and sport-development oriented. Regardless of your pace, breathe easy: What you do learn biomechanically, your body actually never forgets.

The following self-rating inventory is provided so you can evaluate your overall progress to this point. Be kind to yourself, but be candid and as objective as you can. You might even want to do this evaluation with a friend with whom you ski.

## PHYSICAL SKILLS

There are a host of specific skiing skills that are both developmental and progressive in nature. One often builds on another, and then several work together to produce various desired effects. How would you rate yourself on the following skills?

|  | Very good | Good | Okay | Poor |
|---|---|---|---|---|
| **Balance** | | | | |
| Sidestep up a hill | ___ | ___ | ___ | ___ |
| Sidestep down a hill | ___ | ___ | ___ | ___ |
| Herringbone up a hill | ___ | ___ | ___ | ___ |
| Walk a complete circle on the flats with skis on | ___ | ___ | ___ | ___ |
| **Gliding Skills** | | | | |
| Straight run, skis parallel | ___ | ___ | ___ | ___ |
| Straight run, skis in wedge | ___ | ___ | ___ | ___ |
| Straight run moving skis in and out of wedge | ___ | ___ | ___ | ___ |
| Right to left traverse | ___ | ___ | ___ | ___ |
| Left to right traverse | ___ | ___ | ___ | ___ |
| **Stopping Skills** | | | | |
| Ease to a stop | ___ | ___ | ___ | ___ |
| Stop out of the fall line | ___ | ___ | ___ | ___ |

| | Very good | Good | Okay | Poor |
|---|---|---|---|---|
| Stop on demand | _____ | _____ | _____ | _____ |
| Stop in the fall line | _____ | _____ | _____ | _____ |
| Hop to platform to the right | _____ | _____ | _____ | _____ |
| Hop to platform to the left | _____ | _____ | _____ | _____ |
| **Wedge Turning Skills** | | | | |
| Turn to the right | _____ | _____ | _____ | _____ |
| Turn to the left | _____ | _____ | _____ | _____ |
| Skidded turn to the right | _____ | _____ | _____ | _____ |
| Skidded turn to the left | _____ | _____ | _____ | _____ |
| 2 to 4 linked turns | _____ | _____ | _____ | _____ |
| 5 to 10 linked turns | _____ | _____ | _____ | _____ |
| #1 wedge turns | _____ | _____ | _____ | _____ |
| #2 wedge turns | _____ | _____ | _____ | _____ |
| #3 wedge turns | _____ | _____ | _____ | _____ |
| Short-radius turn | _____ | _____ | _____ | _____ |
| Medium-radius turn | _____ | _____ | _____ | _____ |
| Long-radius turn | _____ | _____ | _____ | _____ |
| **Skidding Skills** | | | | |
| Controlled sideslip to the left | _____ | _____ | _____ | _____ |
| Controlled sideslip to the right | _____ | _____ | _____ | _____ |
| Directional sideslip to the left | _____ | _____ | _____ | _____ |
| Directional sideslip to the right | _____ | _____ | _____ | _____ |
| Skidding to BEGIN turn | _____ | _____ | _____ | _____ |
| Skidding to control speed in MIDDLE of turn | _____ | _____ | _____ | _____ |
| Skidding at MIDDLE-END of turn | _____ | _____ | _____ | _____ |
| **Skidded Parallel Turning Skills** | | | | |
| Preturn to the right | _____ | _____ | _____ | _____ |
| Preturn to the left | _____ | _____ | _____ | _____ |
| Turn to the right | _____ | _____ | _____ | _____ |
| Turn to the left | _____ | _____ | _____ | _____ |
| 2 to 4 linked turns | _____ | _____ | _____ | _____ |
| 5 to 10 linked turns | _____ | _____ | _____ | _____ |
| Short-radius turn | _____ | _____ | _____ | _____ |
| Medium-radius turn | _____ | _____ | _____ | _____ |
| Long-radius turn | _____ | _____ | _____ | _____ |

|  | Very good | Good | Okay | Poor |
|---|---|---|---|---|
| Parallel with skis 4 to 6 inches apart | —— | —— | —— | —— |
| Parallel with skis 7 to 12 inches apart | —— | —— | —— | —— |

**Turning Versatility**

| | | | | |
|---|---|---|---|---|
| Change from short- to medium-radius turn | —— | —— | —— | —— |
| Change from medium- to long-radius turn | —— | —— | —— | —— |
| Change from medium- to short-radius turn | —— | —— | —— | —— |
| Change from long- to medium-radius turn | —— | —— | —— | —— |

**Ski-Pole Use Skills**

| | | | | |
|---|---|---|---|---|
| Maneuverability while climbing | —— | —— | —— | —— |
| Generic uses of ski poles | —— | —— | —— | —— |
| Rhythmic pole swing | —— | —— | —— | —— |
| Rhythmic pole touch | —— | —— | —— | —— |
| Pole plant | —— | —— | —— | —— |
| Rhythmic pole plant | —— | —— | —— | —— |

**Turning Skills**

| | | | | |
|---|---|---|---|---|
| Early initiation | —— | —— | —— | —— |
| Countered position | —— | —— | —— | —— |
| Anticipation | —— | —— | —— | —— |
| Extension | —— | —— | —— | —— |
| Weight transfer | —— | —— | —— | —— |
| Edge change | —— | —— | —— | —— |
| Hip influence | —— | —— | —— | —— |
| Projection | —— | —— | —— | —— |
| Crossover | —— | —— | —— | —— |
| Inside-ski steering | —— | —— | —— | —— |
| Outside-ski steering | —— | —— | —— | —— |
| Edging | —— | —— | —— | —— |
| Flexion | —— | —— | —— | —— |
| Angulation | —— | —— | —— | —— |

## MOUNTAIN SAVVY

There are a number of responsibilities you have as a skier, both to yourself and to those with whom you share the mountain. Collectively, these embrace a broad scope of behaviors designed to make skiing a safe and enjoyable sport for all. How would you rate your ability to use the following when skiing?

|  | Very good | Good | Okay | Poor |
|---|---|---|---|---|
| **Falling and Getting Up Skills** | | | | |
| How to fall | ____ | ____ | ____ | ____ |
| How to get up unassisted | ____ | ____ | ____ | ____ |
| When to take one or both skis off to get up | ____ | ____ | ____ | ____ |
| How to get up with both skis on | ____ | ____ | ____ | ____ |
| **Mountain Transport Skills** | | | | |
| How to board and ride a surface tow | ____ | ____ | ____ | ____ |
| How to board and ride a chair lift | ____ | ____ | ____ | ____ |
| How to board and ride a T-bar and poma lift | ____ | ____ | ____ | ____ |
| **Skier Safety Skills** | | | | |
| Skier responsibility code | ____ | ____ | ____ | ____ |
| How to read a trail map | ____ | ____ | ____ | ____ |
| How to prevent injury | ____ | ____ | ____ | ____ |
| How to get help when in need | ____ | ____ | ____ | ____ |
| **Your Range of Skiable Terrain** | | | | |
| Beginner runs | ____ | ____ | ____ | ____ |
| Low-intermediate runs | ____ | ____ | ____ | ____ |
| Intermediate runs | ____ | ____ | ____ | ____ |
| Advanced intermediate runs | ____ | ____ | ____ | ____ |
| Advanced runs | ____ | ____ | ____ | ____ |

## OVERALL SKIING PROGRESS

Considering all the physical skills and mountain savvy listed previously, how would you rate your overall progress?

____ Very successful

____ Successful

____ Fairly successful

____ Barely successful

____ Unsuccessful

## SO WHAT DO YOU THINK?

After all you've gone through, are you ready to call yourself a skier? You're not a beginner anymore. Are you ready to assume your new mantle and the never-ending challenge to continue to explore your place on the mountain? Do you want to invest time in becoming a better skier? Are you willing to practice at least something every time you go skiing, and wanting to practice mountain safety? If you're in the affirmative on all or most of these points, you're a welcome addition to the sport of skiing.

# Controlling the Fears Between Your Ears

If fear whittles your sights such that you see only that which you fear when it's present in a situation, and nothing else, you are literally cut off from reality by your fear. While skiing, you don't ever want to be cut off from reality. Much of the fear of beginning skiers is triggered more by hearsay than by empirical knowledge—that is, this fear is triggered by the stories and opinions of others, not from actual fearsome experiences.

Regardless of origin, the factors that trigger fear when you are learning to ski must be addressed at some time in your learning. Deny these, and they may repeatedly frustrate your skiing; learn to make these fears your allies instead of enemies, and they may make it easier for you to learn to ski.

## THREE MAIN FEAR TRIGGERS

The three most common triggers of fear for beginning skiers are falling, speed, and failure. The good news—you don't have to overcome these to learn to control them. So, Rule 1: Acknowledge their existence. Rule 2: Realize their effect on your skiing.

### Falling

Falling triggers fear due to its association with at least four elements: (1) risk of injury; (2) worry about not being able to get back up; (3) threat of excessive fatigue; and (4) worry over appearances—''I really don't want to look like a beginner.''

### Risk of Injury

Although some beginning skiers do fall and get injured, you're more likely to get injured at home than when learning to ski. Falling injuries in beginning skiing usually happen to persons who attempt the sport with no physical preparation or who lack instruction about basic ski maneuvers and skills.

The best advice about reducing the risk of injury from falling is fourfold:

- Stop skiing when you are tired or fatigued.
- If you are doing drills, be sure that you understand the intention of the drill, that you understand what's expected of you, and that you're performing it on the correct terrain.
- Look, look, look before starting off on a ski run; make sure it's safe to take off.
- Learn how to fall—that is, when you know you're ready to fall, relax and don't fight the momentum of your body falling. Think of meshing with the snow rather than repelling it, and you'll fall more safely.

### Worry About Not Being Able to Get Back Up

Ski bindings can be adjusted to accommodate different height, weight, age, and skiing ability demands; ski shops and rental shops set beginners' bindings at a level where your boots will release at the slightest serious torquing. A friend's, or your own, ''best guess'' about the release setting at which to set your bindings may not meet the manufacturers' standards for appropriate skier safety. If you buy used skis and bindings, have the bindings safety-tested at a ski shop, and the bindings set according to the manufacturer's standards.

A good many falls by beginning skiers lead to boots releasing from the bindings, and with one or both skis off, it's really quite easy to get up. If one or both skis don't come off, and you feel panic about to set in because you're helplessly down, your muscles feel like gelatin, and both skis are still on, remember you can always kick off one or both skis, and stand up.

Every so often when learning to ski you have to take a moment or two to remind yourself that you don't have to be immobilized by your fears, because you have skills and abilities that can neutralize these fears. Great athletes use their minds to help them both control fears and create opportunities. Use a little self-talk encouragement about getting up after falling as you're climbing to your practice hill. Remind yourself: Good skiers know how to get up after falling; promptly getting up after falling is a sign of a good skier.

### Threat of Excessive Fatigue

Very often, the fatigue beginning skiers experience during their first few days on the slopes is due to the fact that they approach skiing as primarily a muscular endeavor. Making skiing an activity where your muscles and joints are asked to take a series of orders from your conscious (i.e., alert) mind will wear you out in no time at all.

My advice to beginners (and advanced skiers as well): Think less, feel more, and by all means don't make skiing a workout. The focus ought to be, I believe, on learning to work with the mountain, not on conquering it. Friends of mine speak of skiing as a dance with the mountain; think about dancing—you don't compete with your partner, but cooperate with him or her.

When most people miss a beat in dancing, they don't throw down their hands and tough it through, they are creative and fake it. When you fall repeatedly in skiing, don't tough it out and use a "gold medal get-up" each time, use the most energy-efficient get up technique. You're the only one who knows how tired you are when you're skiing and falling, so be kind to yourself, and if you must, kick off a ski or two, stand up slowly, take a few breaths, take in the scenery, and get back into the saddle.

Another cause of excessive fatigue may be characterized as an overzealous ego. Believing it's wimpy to kick off a ski to get up, or feeling the need to keep up with more experienced spouses, friends, or children, many beginner skiers attempt to complete every fall with a "gold medal get-up."

My advice: Outsmart your ego, and conserve energy at every opportunity; you'll have more fun on and off the slopes. Don't be afraid to take a break, or two or three breaks, during the morning or afternoon. As a private and group instructor, I use breaks with clients to rest their muscles and reorient their minds. We talk about skiing, but we don't make the "chalk talk" the only reason we break. The end result is a more spirited and confident approach to learning.

Be smart in another way about preventing excessive fatigue from falling, and realize that if you are repeatedly falling, something is wrong with one or more of your basic skills. Return to your basic maneuvers, stopping and turning, and work from the ground up. If this doesn't help, consider a private or group lesson to work on basic skills.

## Worry Over Appearance

For a moment, readjust your self-concept and accept the inevitable: Regardless of how smartly you are dressed, the state of the art of your equipment, or how well you talk skiing, as soon as you step into your bindings and start to move on your skis, everyone who can ski will know you're a beginner—everyone!

While I was in graduate school at UCLA, a professor advised a group of us in his always cryptic fashion: When on stage, act. He wasn't referring, of course, to being phony or deceptive, but to what is the mantle of an actor. Part of the mantle of a beginning skier is to look awkward and clumsy, and on occasion, to fall. This is not to suggest you look forward to falling, or enjoy your tumbles, but that you accept that you will fall.

Eventually, falling becomes an incidental part of skiing—something all skiers know as they add higher speeds and more challenging skiing conditions to their mountain experiences. For all skiers, beginners to experts, falling remains teacher and traffic cop for as long as you ski.

## Speed

"I'm going too fast . . . Whoa! . . ." These are often the words uttered just before beginning skiers tense their leg muscles, throw their hands into the air, or thrust the tips of their ski poles into the snow in front of them to try to halt their skiing.

To be sure, speed is a relative concept in beginning skiing, and for those with little or no like speed experience, any speed that exceeds walking may be frightening. The foremost worry I have for skiers afraid of speeding up, and who lack basic skills, is their tensing up on the slope and risking injury to themselves and others nearby. A close second worry is how a "fear" for relative speed impedes learning to ski.

Any new sport or activity where the speed of movement is controlled by factors beyond the immediate control of the person poses a potential for speed fear, because speed equates with loss of control, and loss of control with falling, risk of injury, or the terror of almost falling.

My teaching experience suggests that repeated episodes of "almost falling" are destructive to your skiing development from both psychological and skills-acquisition perspectives. "Almost falls" teach out-of-balance to balance skiing—they teach survival, not skill, and they actually reinforce a fear of falling that sabotages skill development. Too many "almost falls" in your skiing is an indication that basic skills are yet too undeveloped to progress further in your skiing at any level. Further, too many attempts to achieve balance by correcting out-of-balance ski technique make it difficult to relax your muscles while skiing, a necessary component of preventing fatigue and progressing in skill development.

As with falling, speed is part of skiing . . . forever. What you must concentrate on is neutralizing your fear of the loss of control, by keeping your mind focused on learning, and the merging of your spirit to continue learning (regardless of this fear) with your body's existing skills from which more evolved skills can develop. Your mind is a useful tool in reminding yourself that you have learned certain skills to get you as far as you are at present, and your spirit is a force to impassion you to keep building on these skills by pushing your body to continue trying.

Know that speed control is skill control. Ski well with the basics, and you'll never need to fear speed. Instead, like the best of skiers, you'll use speed to energize yourself and add the edge of excitement to new challenges. In this way, you will be the master of speed!

## The Issue of Failure

Failure is a tough problem to tackle, because it's usually historical in persons (i.e., they have failed at various sports or exercise endeavors in the past, and expect to fail at new sports). The fear of failing once again cannot be dissolved in a few lines of perspective. It can, nonetheless, be explained to a degree that may help persons better appreciate the strength of their fear of personal failure, as well as the areas in which it's reversible to some degree.

If you feel you are a candidate for the fear of failure interfering with your learning to ski, consider the origins of that fear. If your difficulty with learning new sports troubles you, your best ally in learning to ski will be patience.

If your fear of failure is rooted in a lack of respect for yourself, or a battered self-image, learning to ski may well challenge you to test your personal resolve. Admit to this image of yourself, and you can use skiing to bolster your self-image. You are the perfect candidate for a teaching book like this one, because you can proceed at pace—your pace. As well, you can succeed at pace, and in so doing find moments of accomplishment to boost your self-image. Because skiing is such a personal and oft-esoteric sport, there are endless opportunities for achievement and mastery.

## COMPETE WITH THE IDEAL

In skiing, the ultimate defeat is giving up on chasing the ideal (i.e., learning to ski, and then continuing to develop as a skier). A measure of defeat occurs when you allow what others think to divert you from the process of chasing the ideal. Once you let others divert you, or once you have given in to failure and no longer look forward to your next time out, you have lost spirit with the sport. Something very wonderful about skiing is that if it doesn't work the first, or second or third, time, it may work perfectly the fourth time. It's your dance, each dance, and although you may take a partner or two to the dance along with you, it's you who does the dancing for yourself, and with the mountain.

**afd pads (antifriction device)**—An important strip of plastic teflon-like material affixed to the toe piece of your binding, against which boots are free to release if need be without the buildup of friction between a boot plastic and a binding plastic or metal.

**aft**—The rear side of center; leaning back toward the tail of the ski.

**alpine skiing**—The use of skis on which there are bindings that clamp down both the toe and heel of the ski boot. A sport that combines elements of racing, powder skiing, free skiing, mogul skiing, freestyle skiing, learning to ski, family and social/recreational skiing, ski teaching, skiwear fashion, ski equipment fashion, and the ambiance of the ski resort.

**angulation**—The process of moving the ankle, lower leg, knee, hip, shoulder, or spine to create a bending or distortion of the horizontal plane of the body, causing the ski edges to variably engage the snow more decisively.

**anticipation**—Commits your mind, eyes, shoulders, abdominal region, and hips into the next turn before you actually begin turning.

**base weld**—A very hot patching material applied to the damaged bases of skis; usually reserved for deep gouges and holes near the metal edges of skis.

**basic skiing position**—A balanced positioning of your hands and arms ahead and to your sides, holding ski poles off the snow and in position to be used to aid skiing. Basic skiing position also includes a slight flex (bend) in the knees and ankles, the spine slightly rounded, and head and eyes looking ahead to the expanse of terrain. Applies to moving on skis: turning and traversing.

**basic skiing stance**—The basic skiing position applied when standing or getting prepared for drills early in beginning skiing.

**braking: controlled**—A progressive slowing of the skis to a stop. In beginning skiing, controlled braking occurs by gradually widening the wedge as more edging is applied. As beginning skiers grow more adept at skiing in a wedge, they learn to form a larger, more edged wedge very quickly, and under control, come to a stop. In a parallel stance, controlled braking occurs when gradually (or quickly) and under control, skis are edged on their corresponding edges.

**braking: random**—When one or both skis are abruptly edged to create a slowing of the skis at different times while turning or gliding. Random braking often causes awkward, out-of-balance skiing in beginning skiers.

**camber**—The prestressed arc built into skis so a skier's weight is distributed evenly over the entire length of the ski.

**corresponding edges**—The right edges of both skis are edged in the snow at the same time; the left edges are edged in the snow at the same time.

**countered stance**—The stance at the END of one turn and BEGINNING of another, when the upper body (i.e., head, eyes, hands, arms, shoulders, and abdominal region) is facing down the fall line at the same time as the lower body is facing across the fall line, and there is a twisting at the waist.

**crossover**—When at the BEGINNING of a turn the upper body leads the way for the lower body to actually cross over the path the skis were traveling to enhance the turning: for a right turn, the ski path that is crossed over is a left path.

**"Din" setting**—The degree of spring tension set in your ski binding, calibrated to your height, weight, age, and skiing ability. Can be adjusted with a screwdriver within variable ranges of setting, depending on binding.

**early initiation**—Looking your head and eyes in the direction of the next turn while you are still ENDING the previous turn.

**edge angle**—The degree of angle between the ski's edge and the snow; greater angle creates more pressure on the ski and imparts greater resistance to the pull of gravity.

**edge change**—The changing of edge engagement from one edge to the other on one or both skis, sequentially (one after the other, as in a wedge turn) or simultaneously (at the same time, as in a parallel turn).

**edge set**—The abrupt edging of the uphill edges of both skis to stop or dramatically slow progress.

**edging**—The combination of edge angle, angulation, and steering that yields control over the skidding of the skis while turning.

**extension**—Lengthening or straightening of the legs and upper body to help flatten the skis and facilitate weight transfer and steering into a turn.

**flat ski**—A ski that is not edged.

**flexion**—The bending forward and laterally of the knees and ankles to assist steering, react to pressure and resistance, and combine with angulation to affect edging.

**fore**—The front side of the middle of the ski; leaning forward to the tip of the ski.

**forward pressure**—The amount of pressure applied through the heel piece of the binding on the rear of the ski boot when locked into the binding. Critical to the proper performance of the binding.

**four turn stages**—All beginning and intermediate turns have a BEGINNING, MIDDLE, MIDDLE-END, and END. Different turning skills are applied at different times during each of these phases.

**free skiing**—Relatively unstructured skiing time that's very important to the process of motor memory learning. To accelerate the learning process, drills and specific practice exercises should be interspersed with free skiing, but should never replace it.

**full-footedness**—The positioning of the whole foot in

the bottom of the ski boot, with body weight evenly distributed along the length of the foot.

**functionally shaped turn**—The shape and speed of turn that is most automatic and natural to a beginning skier's level of skill development, and one that she or he instinctively uses to ski all terrain; usually medium in radius.

**inside ski**—The ski that's always inside the arc of the turn; the uphill ski.

**matching**—Steering the inside ski to be alongside the outside ski at some point in a turn.

**Nordic skiing**—Includes the skiing disciplines of cross-country track and skating skiing, telemark alpine skiing, backcountry skiing, open glade skiing, and winter mountaineering.

**opposing edges**—The inside edges of both skis are edged in wedge.

**outside ski**—The ski that is always on the outside of the arc of the turn; the downhill ski.

**platform**—The surface created beneath an edged ski.

**pole plant**—A forceful placement of the tip of the ski pole in the snow, used to slow (block) the progress of the upper body.

**pole swing**—The preparatory movement of the pole forward that must precede a pole plant or pole touch; often a timing device for turning in rhythm.

**pole touch**—The light or incidental touching of the tip of the pole to connect the mechanics of pole use in medium- and long-radius turns.

**preparation**—The act of anticipation along with a pole swing.

**preturn**—A brief, short directional steering of both skis and lower legs up the hill to prepare to turn them down the hill in the direction the hands and upper body are already facing.

**preturn platform**—A preturn on steeper terrain where an edge set at the time of the preturn is necessary to pause the movement of the skis before they are steered into the fall line.

**sequential steering**—The steering of skis in a wedge turn where the outside ski is steered first to engage its inside edge to begin the turning action, and the inside ski is then steered to complement the directional change of the outside ski. At upper levels of skiing, sequential steering may occur with certain kinds of parallel turns.

**sideslip**—When, in parallel position across the fall line, the skis slide sideways down the fall line, the pace and direction of travel being controlled by the edging and balance skills of the skier.

**sidestep**—When, in parallel position on level terrain or across the fall line on sloped terrain, one ski is lifted and moved laterally away from the other ski (across level terrain, up or down a slope), and then the other ski is lifted and moved next to the first ski to re-form the original parallel position.

**simultaneous steering**—When both skis are steered at the same time in parallel position, usually to begin a turn and guide skis down and across the fall line.

**skeletal bracing**—When leg, thigh, and pelvic bones are "locked" into alignment and used as control levers on the skis; relied on when muscle power or control is lacking.

**skeletally aligned**—When the alignment of foot, leg, thigh, pelvic, and spinal bones is used to provide stability and versatility with minimal muscular effort.

**skidding**—The controlled slipping of one or both skis in a specific direction; controlled steering of sideslipping skis.

**skier levels**—Used to determine the release settings on ski bindings: 1 = beginning level skiing; 2 = intermediate level skiing; 3 = advanced level skiing.

**ski retention devices**—A device attached to the ski that keeps the ski from traveling down the slope out of control after a skier falls or is otherwise separated from the ski. Older bindings had straps attached to the heel piece of the binding that were snapped around the skier's boot, thus retaining the ski close to the skier if the ski were to fall off. Modern bindings utilize spring-controlled ski brakes that dig into the snow when the boot is separated from the ski. Understandably, these are safer for the skier.

**ski sensory system**—The coordination of your nervous, musculoskeletal, and equilibrium systems to give you up-to-the-split-second updates on what it feels like to be in or out of balance while skiing, while moving fast or slow; what the texture of the snow feels like; the position of your skis on the snow; the position of your body relative to your skis and terrain; and your degree of muscular effort or relaxation while skiing.

**skis' forgiveness**—Skis' ease of maneuvering in difficult terrain (relative to each skier), even when a skier isn't in top form or using polished technique.

**steering**—The use of feet and lower legs to initiate directional changes in ski travel or position on the snow. Steering is aided by the inward rotation of the femur and the creation of angles in the ankles, knees, hips, spine, and shoulders. The refinement of steering is an ongoing goal in alpine skiing, and leads to style and grace on skis.

**traverse**—Traveling across the fall line at different angles of descent, usually done with skis in parallel association.

**upper body projection**—Done at the beginning of a turn, this is the extending of a skier's hands, arms, shoulders, head, chest, and abdominal region down the fall line and into the new turn.

**weight transfer**—Occurs at the very beginning of a turn where the emphasis of body weight, applied to the edging of one ski, is transferred to the other ski. The transition that allows weight transfer to happen in beginning skiing (and much of advanced skiing) is a flattening (or unedging) of the skis.

John Yacenda is an accomplished skier and educator. He has coached and taught many sports since 1975, including football, soccer, baseball, track and field, skiing, snowboarding, and athletic training. He is the Alpine and Technical Director for Alpine Sports in Reno, Nevada, and he teaches skiing and snowboarding to both individuals and groups. His method of alpine skiing has been taught to skiers as young as 3 and to adults over 70.

Dr. Yacenda is the author of *High Performance Skiing*, published by Leisure Press. He is also a contributing editor for *Fitness Management* and *Let's Live* magazines and writes a *Ski Tips* column for *North Tahoe Week*. In 1975, he earned his doctorate in health education and psychology from Union Graduate School in Cincinnati.

From 1971 to 1986, he taught health sciences at several California colleges and universities. Now he devotes more time to snowboarding, skiing, and writing about skiing and athletic training.

When not on the slopes, Dr. Yacenda enjoys other sports, including tennis, cycling, and water sports. He cross-trains throughout the year, and in the summer he competes with the Masters Swim Club, the Reno Family YMCA Prairie Otters, and in United States Masters Swimming sanctioned open-water competitions. Since 1985, Dr. Yacenda has conducted a ski conditioning program with 65 adult skiers at the Reno Family YMCA. The YMCA and the Sports West Athletic Club in Reno are his two homes away from home.